THE FALKLANDS
by Tony Chater

Foreword by
H R H The Duke of Edinburgh, KG, KT, OM

Published by
THE PENNA PRESS, ST ALBANS,
HERTS. AL1 4YD, ENGLAND
in association with
THE PINK SHOP,
P.O. BOX 53, STANLEY,
FALKLAND ISLANDS.

Designed by Philip J. Gillmor
Produced by
The Penna Press, St Albans, England.

© A.R. Chater 1993.
First published November 1993.
Revised and reprinted, July 1996.
ISBN 0 9504113 1 0

The rights of A.R. Chater to be identified as the Author of this work has been asserted in accordance with the Copyright, Designs and Patents Act 1988 Section 77 and 78.

All rights reserved. No part of this publication may be reproduced or transmitted in any form or by any means, electronic or mechanical, including photocopy, recording or any information storage and retrieval system, without permission in writing from the author.

For Annie, Tom and Bill.

Front Cover: New Island.

Back cover: Rockhopper Penguins.

All photographs are covered by copyright and unless otherwise stated were taken by the author.

Earliest known photograph of Stanley taken between 1873-78 by William Biggs, a master shipwright, who made his own photographic glass plates. He was the son of James Biggs, one of the original settlers who arrived at Port Louis, in the brig *Hebe*, from Portsmouth in 1842. (Reproduced by kind permission of the photographer's granddaughter Miss Madge Biggs, MBE.)

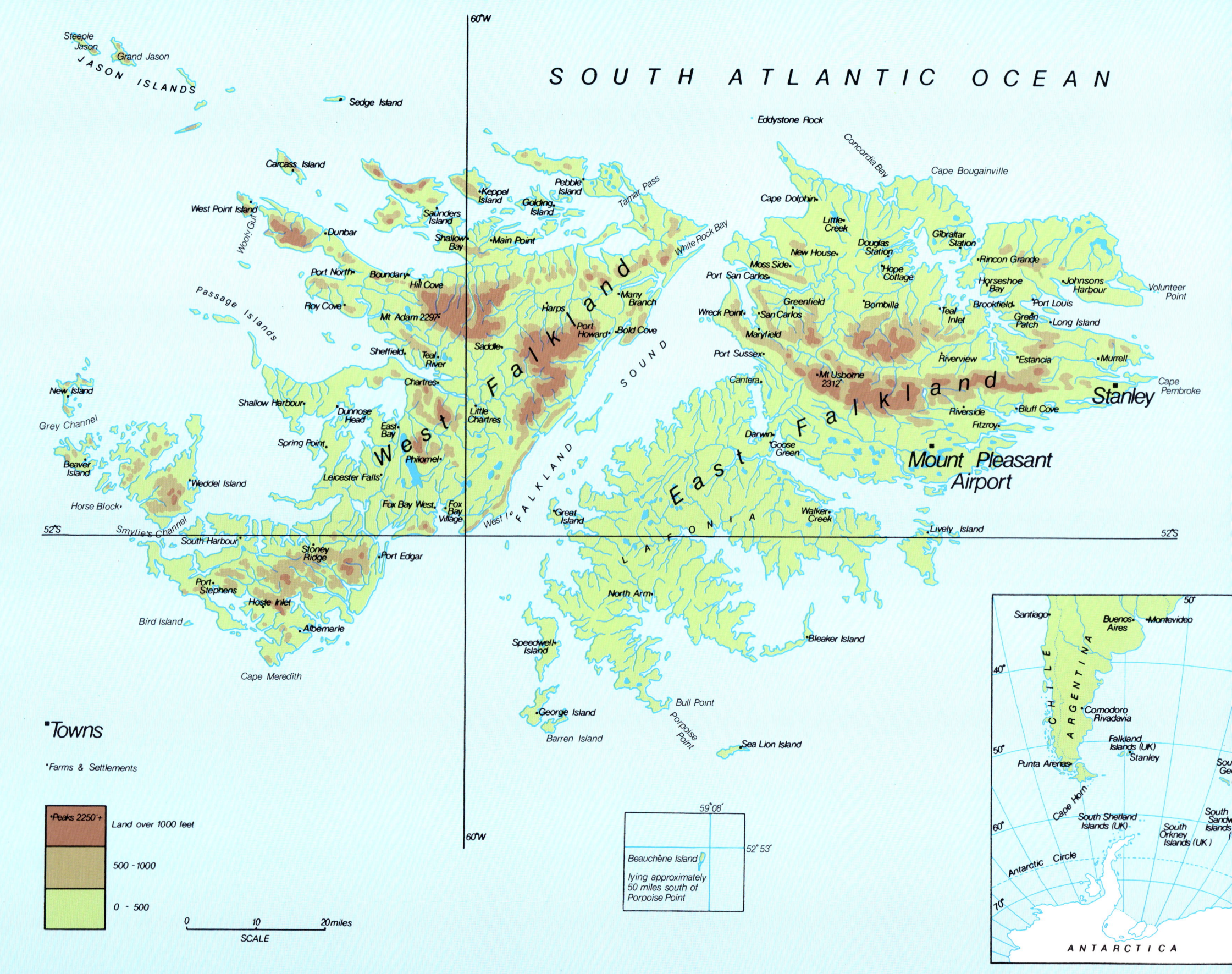

FOREWORD

HRH The Duke of Edinburgh
KG, KT, OM

SANDRINGHAM, NORFOLK

It may seem a bit odd to contemporary readers that the Falkland Islands should be a British dependency. At the furthest end of the Atlantic Ocean, with no significant natural resources, little attraction for tourists seeking the sun and not on the route to anywhere; they are a peculiarly British anomaly.

The fact is that as a major trading nation and maritime power in the days of sail, Britain collected a number of odd bits of real estate at strategic points round the world. Before the building of the Panama Canal, the route round Cape Horn was the only connection between the Atlantic and the Pacific and the Falklands are situated conveniently near the ferocious Cape that divides the two.

I was fortunate enough to visit the Islands on my way home from the 1956 Olympic Games in Melbourne. I remember them as sparsely populated, wholly dependent on sheep, a dramatic though virtually treeless landscape, but immensely rich in bird and sealife and a grave-yard for sailing ships. My next visit was 9 years after the famous war. Sheep farming had become barely economic, but income from licences to fish within its waters had brought a new prosperity.

Tony Chater has produced a vivid portrait in words and pictures of these little-known islands. I am sure that it will fascinate all those who share my interest in island communities, birds, ships and life in the seas.

Prince Philip discusses rural education with ten-year-old Matthew McMullen at Goose Green School in February 1992. (Photo Norman Clarke)

CONTENTS

MAP	4
FOREWORD by HRH The Duke of Edinburgh	5
PREFACE	8
1. LES ILES NOUVELLES	10
2. SEABIRDS	12
Rockhoppers	14
Jackass	16
Gentoos and Kings	18
Mollymauks	20
Shags and Sea Hen	22
Stinkers and Pintado	24
Nightbirds	26
3. STANLEY	28
Government House	30
The Philomel Store	32
Organic Gardening	34
Christ Church Cathedral	36
Horticultural Show	38
Sport	40
Peat	42
Architecture	44
The Dockyard	46
City Life	48
4. PREDATORS AND PASSERINES	
Turkey Vulture	50
Cassin's Peregrine Falcon	51
Carancho and Johnny Rook	52
Red-backed Buzzard	54
Songbirds	56
5. SHIPS AND SHORELINES	
The Jasons	58
Marooned	60
Whaling	62
Glengowan	64
Penelope	66
Jhelum and *Capricorn*	68
John Biscoe	70
Copious	71
Gentoo	72
Jiggers	73
Horseblock and *Foam*	74
Beefeater	74
Lady Elizabeth and *Samson*	76
Coastal Shipping	78
6. WADERS AND WILDFOWL	
Upland Goose	80
Dotterel, Plover and Snipe	82
Quark	84
Oystercatchers	86
Pampa Teal, Grey Duck and Logger Duck	88
7. CAMP AND THE CAMPERS	90
Shearing	92
Droving	94
West Point Island	96
Carcass Island	98
Inter-Island Flights	100
Fox Bay West	102
Roy Cove and Hill Cove	104
A Farmer's Life	106
Camp Sports Week	107

The *Charles Cooper* (nearest) and the *Actaeon* rest in the harbour mud in front of Christ Church Cathedral. Both vessels made port for repairs, each carrying a cargo of coal and each bound for San Francisco. Neither vessel sailed again. The 561-ton Canadian barque *Actaeon* arrived in 1853, five months out from Liverpool, having put back to Stanley after failing to round Cape Horn. She was scuttled after survey. Thirteen years later she was joined in the harbour by the 850 ton fully-rigged ship *Charles Cooper* which was described in the Colonial Shipping Register as being "leaky and in need of repairs" following a three month passage south from New York.

The Minstrel of Many Branch	108
Stone Runs	110
Winter	112
Keppel and the Indians	114
Three Old Farms	116
Radio Telephone	118

8. MARINE MAMMALS

Sea Elephant	120
Sealion	122
Albemarle	124
Old Sealers	126
Sea Leopard	128
Fur Seal	130
Peale's Porpoise	132
Long-Finned Pilot Whale	133

9. WAR

Sovereignty Dispute	134
Invasion	137
Radio Station	138
Cape Pembroke Lighthouse	140
Telephone Exchange	142
Radar Watch	143
Mike Butcher	144
Billy Poole	145
Cecil and Kitty	146
Under Occupation	148
Concentrations in Camp	150
Surrender	152
Prisoners of War	154
Aftermath	156
The Globe Store	158
Our Troops In Town	160
The Premier and the 'Commodore'	162
In Memoriam	164

10. NAMES, SOURCES and CREDITS   166

11. THE FUTURE   168

Fox Bay Village, West Falkland.

PREFACE

The Upland Goose Hotel, Stanley.

I first heard about the Islands in July 1972, answering a 'wanted ad' which sought farm labourers for the Falkland Islands Company and ended with the attractive phrase 'no experience necessary'.

Evidently my interviewer in London, a long, lean, rugged-looking Kelper called Jimmy Robertson, adjudged me suitably qualified and I was signed on to work at Fox Bay West, a sheep station on West Falkland.

By early December that year I was sitting on a suitcase in a noisy and cramped military airport building on the outskirts of the dusty Patagonian oil town of Comodoro Rivadavia. It was hot and dry and the flight to the Islands had been delayed. We waited, watching the general confusion and aimless abundance of heavily-armed conscripts. Eventually our flight departed and headed out over the South Atlantic towards the Falklands, 600 miles to the south-east. It was a clear day and from afar the outlying Jason Islands became visible, each with a cap of cloud. As we flew along the north coast the main Islands spread out below on the starboard side and after three hours we landed on Stanley's new aluminium airstrip.

After the commotion of Comodoro came the sobriety of Stanley. Inside a shed by the runway, partly surrounded by a variety of multi-coloured landrovers, the necessaries were quietly perpetrated by a customs official and a policeman. In a green jeep we rumbled and bumped over two miles of rough track through sand dunes and peat bogs to the town and I was deposited into the care of Mrs King at what was then the only hotel, the 'Upland Goose', known simply as the 'Goose'.

The following morning I awoke to cocks crowing all over town. Smoke from rekindled peat stoves rose from every chimney pot and a stray milk cow went wandering up the street. Over the years that have followed, the Falklands have become home. I have travelled widely and got to know virtually everybody in the way that one does in this tiny and remote rural community of just 2000 folk.

This book covers these past two decades, a period bisected by the brief but bloody 'Falklands War' of 1982 which features in the final chapter. Images from that period form as stark a contrast to the rest of the book as the shock of war did to the normally quiet lives of a pastoral people.

My aim is simply to present the Islands in pictures and there is no attempt to write a history or a field guide as these have already been written. However, I have accompanied the photographs throughout with a selection of short descriptions, anecdotes and archival extracts which I hope create an impressionistic collage of the moorland and seascape, wildlife and characters, which make up the Falklands.

Tony Chater
New Island, 1993

60-year-old *Cupressus Macrocapa* trees at Moody Brook, Stanley.

1 LES ISLES NOUVELLES

Grand Jason, possibly John Davis' first landfall in 1592 (next page, top).

Key to maps below (clockwise from top left)
1. Gastaldi 1548 (Earliest printed map specifically of South America)
2. Mercator 1630
3. Wytfliet 1597
4. Du Val 1688
5. Mallet 1683

Next page top to bottom
6. Frezier 1716
7. R. W. Seale 1744
8. Hawkesworth 1773

The extraordinary voyages of 16th century seafarers transformed history as newly-developed deep water sailing ships, equipped with the mariner's compass, enabled Europeans to go beyond the horizon and scour the ocean for new land, dreams and gold.

A century which began in 1492 with the Spanish-sponsored Genoese, Colombus, seeking China but stumbling across the Americas, and during which Magellan's men girdled the globe, ended with the 'official' discovery of the Falklands as mariners increasingly probed the stormy passages around Cape Horn for routes to the east.

It is possible that the Islands had been quietly known about for years by the major seapowers, as an ill-defined cluster of blobs appear, vaguely positioned near the eastern end of the Magellan Strait, on maps from 1507 onwards. They were variously labelled as 'Insule 7 delle pulzelle', 'The Maiden Islands', 'Yas de Sanson' and 'Yas de Alencam'. Amerigo Vespucci may have seen them first from the deck of a Portuguese ship as early as 1502.

But to whom did all this newly-found land belong? As 'God's Vice-regent' it fell to the Spanish Pope, Alexander VI, to decide and in 1494 he drew a line north to south down the Atlantic, 100 leagues west of the Azores. Everything to the west (which would later include the Falklands) would be Spanish, he said, and to the east, Portuguese. England disagreed, sowing the seed of the present day sovereignty dispute, and a flotilla of Elizabethan buccaneers, led by Drake, Raleigh and Cavendish, weighed anchor and set forth to explore.

It was during one such trip in 1592, to the Magellan Straits, that the little recognised but most accomplished navigator, John Davis, in his old and weather-beaten ship *Desire*, was stormblown under bare poles, from the

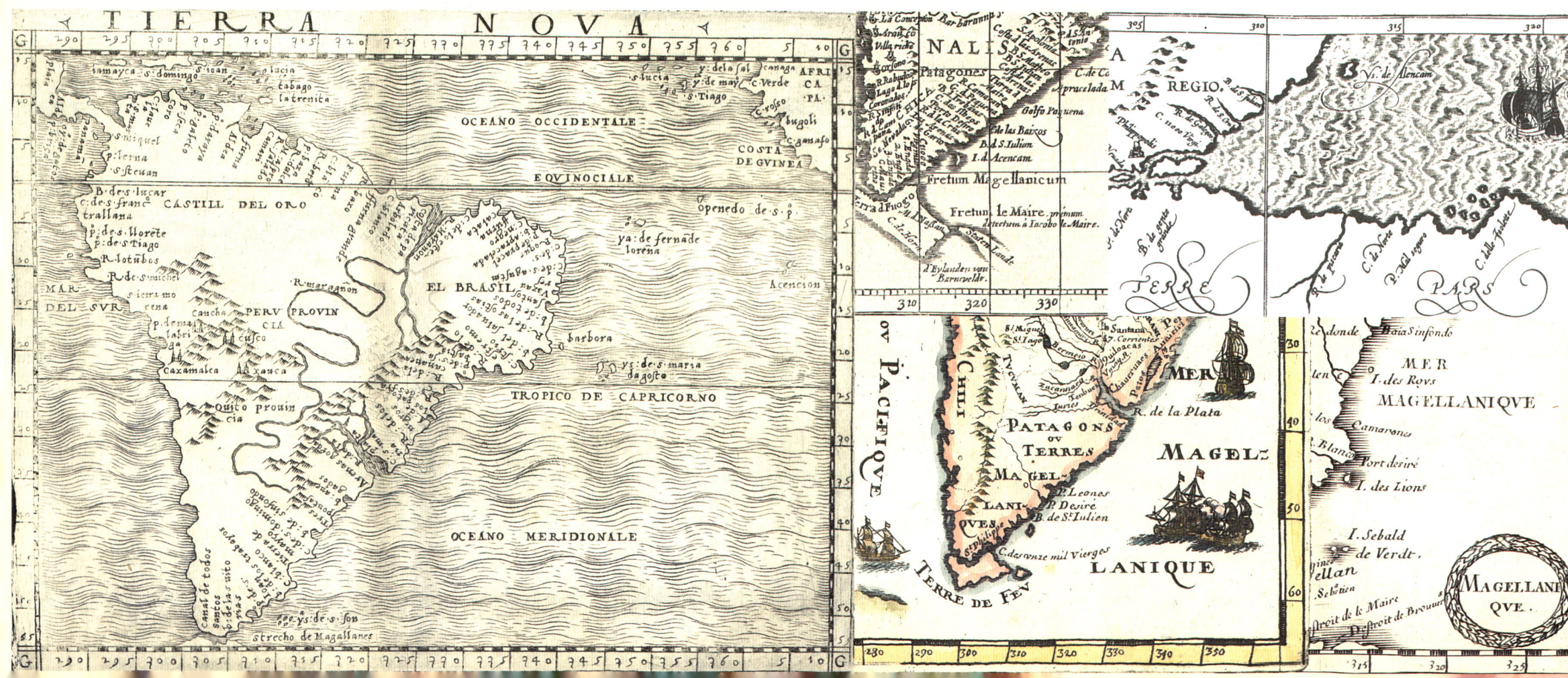

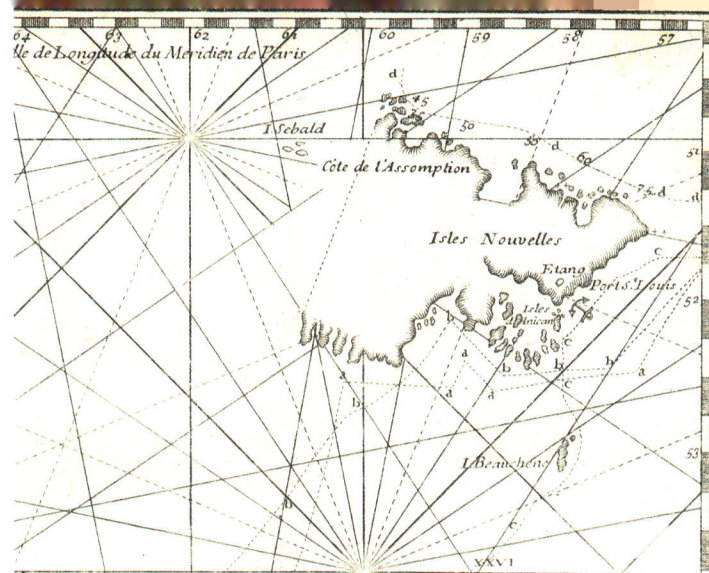

Patagonian coast out into the Atlantic and amongst these apparently unknown and unpeopled Islands. Two years later another English 'gentleman' pirate, Sir Richard Hawkins, made equally unexpected landfall, at the Jasons, while *en route* for an ill-fated spot of plunder in Peru. Shortly afterwards he wrote the earliest descriptions of the northern Falkland coastline from a Spanish dungeon. In honour of himself and of his Virgin Queen he named the Islands 'Hawkins Maydenlande'.

Belgian, Sebald de Weert, sailing past the Jasons in 1600, named these outliers the Sebaldes and 84 years later a pair of English rogues, Cowley and Dampier, aboard the *Bachelor's Delight*, also spotted them. But Cowley's editor gave a false latitude and thus invented the mythical 'Pepy's Island', named after the lecherous diarist and thereafter sought in vain by a generation of mariners.

By the early 18th century the archipelago was well known. To the English it became 'Falkland's Isle' after a viscount. The French, dreaming of girlfriends at home in St Malo, preferred 'Les Isles Malouines', hence the Hispanic 'Malvinas' and later the Americans' 'Maloons'. Others called them simply 'The New Islands' or 'Isles Nouvelles'.

But did Europeans really discover the Islands? When English privateer, John Strong, made the earliest recorded landing on West Falkland in 1690, shipmate Richard Simson pondered over the existence ashore of large foxes *"of a very antient, wild and cunning family… They cannot fly, nor likely to swim so farr as America"*.

Just how they became the only terrestrial quadrupeds in an archipelago which had been detached from the other continents since the breakup of Gondwanaland over 65 million years earlier, has never been fully understood. The Warrah, as the beast came to be known, existed in two distinct forms, one on the East and the other on West Falkland. Each was closely related to the Fuegian Fox and similar in both size and tameness.

The now extinct Yahgan Indians of Tierra de Feugo often carried hunting dogs in their canoes, probably locally domesticated species of Dusicyon (the South American foxes) or ferral crossbreds. Yahgans were known to use large dug-out canoes, up to 10 metres long, equipped with primitive sails of seal skin. At some time during the last few thousand years, they almost certainly paddled across to Staten Island, the dramatic eastern extremity of Fuegia, which lies 20 miles from the mainland, across the fearsome and strongly tidal Straits de Le Maire. They may have also been unintentionally carried out to sea by wind and currents, towards the Falklands, 200 nautical miles to the north east.

Perhaps the Yahgans arrived here, just three days' wind-assisted paddle from Staten Island, a thousand years or more before the birth of Christ? Perhaps a pregnant bitch or two came with them in the bows of a Stone Age canoe? We will never know. The only evidence was in the wolf-like Warrah, but that fell foul of sheepfarmers and was shot to extinction in the year of Little Big Horn.

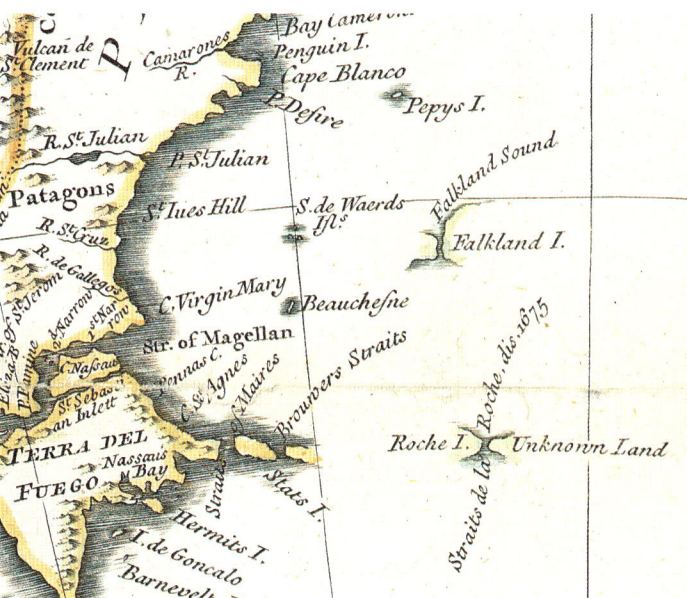

Staten Island, the Yahgans' 'Chuanisin' (Land of Plenty), lies 200 nautical miles south-west of West Falkland.

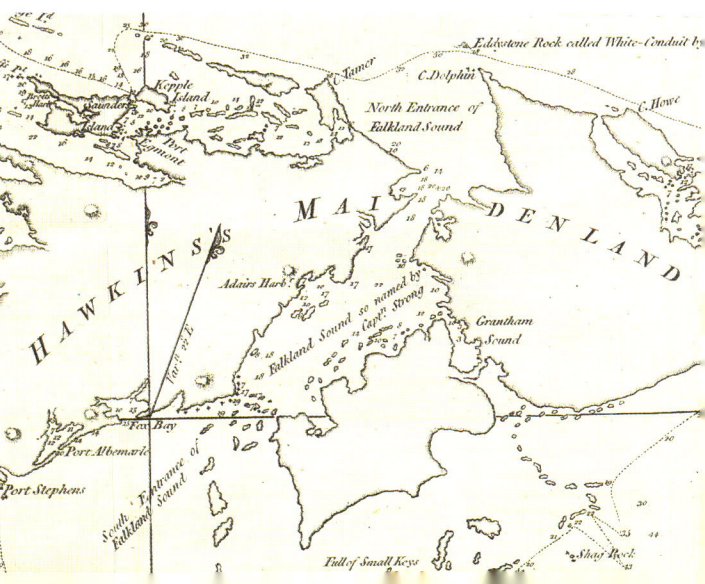

2   SEABIRDS

The vast Southern Ocean which surrounds Antarctica is home for countless millions of seabirds. Some like the petrels are largely pelagic, seldom seeing a shoreline outside the austral summer. Dainty storm petrels flutter butterfly-like above the waves under which submarine penguins hunt like tiny torpedoes. Gulls and cormorants are more coastal creatures, living largely in sight of land.

The surface waters, which extend north from the rim of the frozen continent to around 40° South, are the richest on the planet, abounding in nutrients and plankton, and can be divided into two areas. The more southerly Antarctic Zone is one of cold, heavy and comparatively fresh water which reaches to around 50° South where it meets and sinks below warmer, saltier seas along a well-defined line known as the Antarctic Convergence. From here north to the Sub-Tropical Zone at around 40° South is the area of ocean called the Sub-Antarctic. Whipped by the prevailing strong westerly winds, the 'roaring forties' and the 'furious fifties', the stormy sub-antarctic seas flow almost uninterrupted in an easterly direction around the globe, temporarily diverted only by the southern tip of South America and the South Island of New Zealand.

Amongst the myriad of seabirds which live here each mature adult requires dry land on which to breed. This is in short supply, consisting mainly of a few sparsely scattered oceanic islands. It is on these, in the summer months, that huge concentrations gather, often forming large, noisy and impressive rookeries. The largest of these sub-antarctic island groups, the Falklands, consist of over 400 islands with long and varied coastlines offering a wide choice of nest sites to suit the needs of the most discerning ocean wanderer. Surrounding seas are particularly rich in nutrients brought to the surface by the upwelling of the northward-flowing Falkland Current as it encounters first the continental shelf, then narrow inter-island channels and submerged reefs. The resultant abundance of krill, squid and fish support a wide variety of seabirds but, although most of the 70 or so South Atlantic species have been recorded here, only 23 regularly breed.

Until comparatively recently much of the coastline had been lined for millenia with a dense fringe of tussac grass growing over six feet high. This provided a habitat in which a multitude of assorted birds and seals could breed, protected to a great extent from avian predators and the elements. This all changed when, with the arrival of man in his verminous sailing ships some 300 years ago, came rats.

These two remarkably adaptive predators have had a devastating effect on some avian communities, notably amongst the burrowing petrels. Much of the tussac has been destroyed by man's fire and his grazing stock. Rats have spread throughout the archipelago like an invading army, with disastrous, irreversible results on the smaller and defenceless ground-nesting species in this treeless land. In spite of this the Falklands remain host to some globally significant seabird populations, in particular the Black-browed Albatross, Gentoo and Rockhopper Penguins and the Thin-billed Prion.

BEAUCHÊNE ISLAND

28 nautical miles south of Sea Lion lies the remotest of over 400 Falkland islands. It was spotted from the *Phelypeaux* at 7.0am on 19th January 1701 by Monsieur Jacques Gouin de Beauchesne who christened it, as people so often do, after himself.

Beauchêne is a remarkable island. It holds the colony's oldest and deepest peat deposits, annually hosts over a million seabirds and is clothed by a luxuriant and uniquely monospecific forest of tussac grass. Hairs recovered from the peat profile, which in one place reach a depth of thirteen metres, reveal the presence of fur seal for 11,000 years. But in the last quarter of the 18th Century the 'furries' were detected, then decimated by sealers. Now there are none. A fifth of the world's breeding Black-browed Albatross nest on this one 420 acre island, together with 70,000 pairs of Rockhopper Penguins. The tussac fringe teems with burrowing petrels, while boulders and slabs are undermined by fairy prions, unknown elsewhere in the archipelago.

Early evening. Rockhopper Penguins preen on the foreshore after landing and prior to feeding youngsters waiting on the rocks above (far right).

Beauchêne Island.

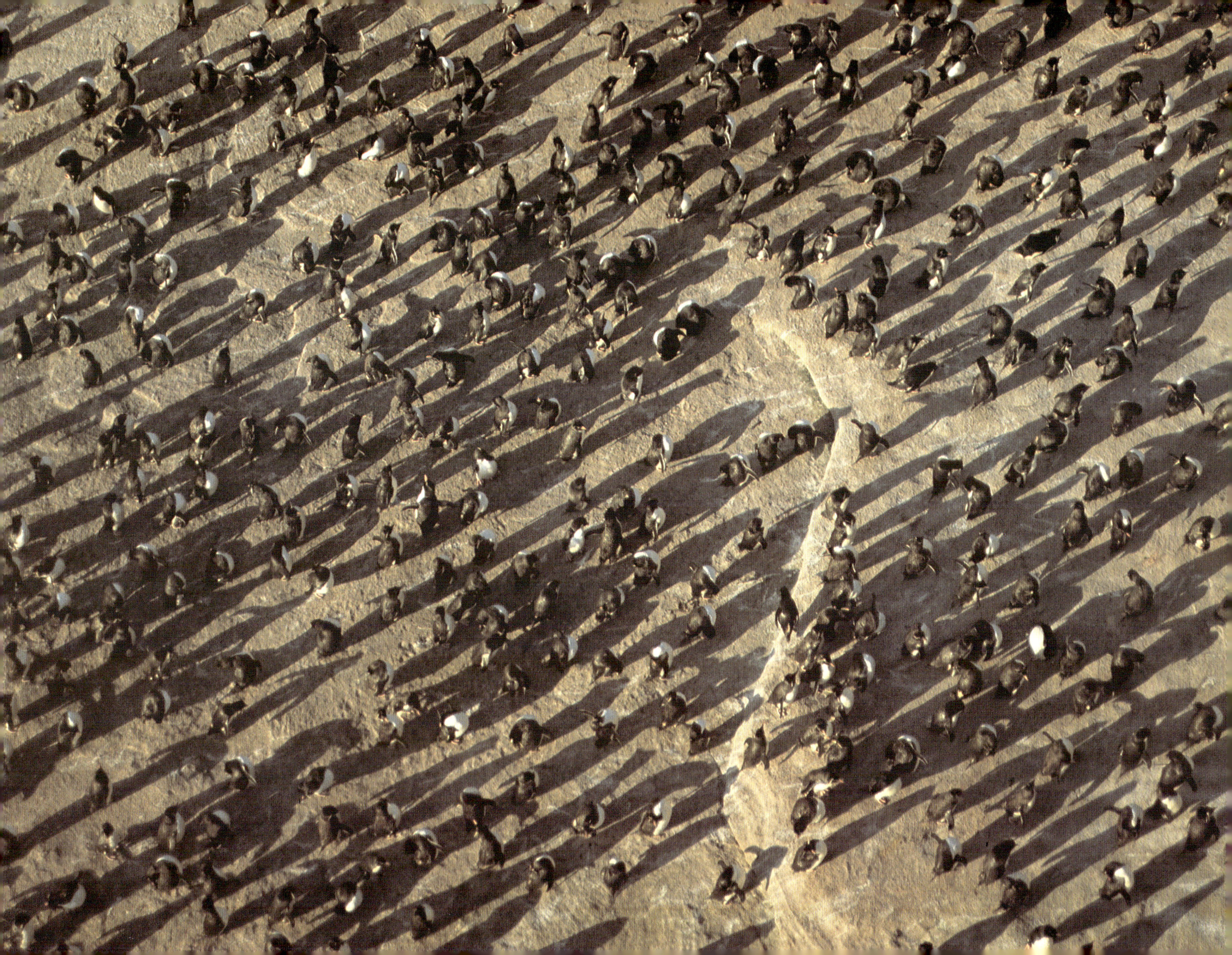

Rockhoppers

Egging, probably on New Island, in the early 1900's. Once popular, the licensed collection of penguin eggs each spring, for the larder, is now a dying tradition. When cooked, the 'white' remains transparent while the bright red yolk stares back up from the frying pan like a bloodshot eye. (Photo *Falkland Pictorial*)

This blood-drenched rockhopper barely kept its head following an early evening attack by a sealion on the nearby landing beach.

Every afternoon, every summer for a thousand years, rockhoppers have come ashore at this spot. Approaching the beach in bunches, they pop out of the breakers like champagne corks to land on a flat, shelving rock. Frenzied feet and flippers scramble to get them clear before the following wave arrives. The shore is completely exposed to prevailing winds and incessant pounding from the open ocean. Yet, so strong is the urge to reproduce which brings 'rockies' back here from their pelagic winter wanderings, that I have seen them battling to land in terrible gales when the sea is blanched with boiling surf and massive waves send sheets of spray 100 metres into the air.

Beyond the beach, penguins step, scramble and hop up traditional paths to the breeding colonies, wayside rocks polished and scored by centuries of clutching beaks and scraping claws. At the clifftop, from October to March, tens of thousands, together with mollymauks and king shags, fill a tussac-fringed natural amphitheatre and form a vast, clamorous and pungent avian assemblage. On quiet days, when a light northerly air brings mist from the sea, the reek and roar of the rookery is plainly apparent from outside our door a mile away. Arthur Cobb, farming on Bleaker Island in the 1920's, described the sound of the massed rockhoppers being 'as if thousands of wheelbarrows, all badly in need of greasing, are being pushed at full speed'.

Two centuries ago American sealers and whalers found New Island to be a fine source of shelter and food. The harbours became well known as vessels revictualled with barrels of eggs and salted penguin meat. When rendered down in a trypot one rockhopper, or 'jumping jack', was found to yield a pint of oil suitable for lighting and tanning. Consequently thousands were driven into stone corrals to be clubbed and cooked. This industry peaked in the 1860's when, with a potential profit of threepence per penguin, in excess of half a million birds were slaughtered in the Islands during a three year period. Thereafter the market slumped and, apart from a brief revival in the late 1870's, the roaring trade fizzled out.

However, the crude corrals still remain, though now overgrown and ghostly and from my window I can see a large iron trypot with a hole in its bottom, welded by rust to rocks on the beach.

Rockhoppers nesting 400ft above sea level on Precipice Hill, New Island (right).

Rockhoppers in the surf.

Jackass

If there is a sound which, more than any other is evocative of the Islands, it is the braying song of this abundant bird commuting from beach to burrow in the quiet of a summer evening.

Less romantic but almost as memorable is a small inelegant beast which lives amongst its feathers, for the 'Jackass' hosts a flea which shares the same den in the human memory as the midge, the mosquito and the bed bug. At any opportunity afforded by a hiker in jackass-infested tussac grass it will exploit the gap 'tween trouser and boot, gaining access to tasty ankles and tender toes with a bite that is large, lasting and extremely irritating.

Surprisingly little reference is made to these parasites in early literature, after their piebald hosts were first noted by Magellan in 1520 about 600 miles north of the Falklands. In 1578, when Sir Francis Drake's crew clubbed 3,000 jackasses for provisions in one day on Penguin Island, off the coast of Patagonia, the sailors must have been eaten alive by fleas. Likewise Sir Thomas Cavendish's men who stored three tons of penguins on board their ship nine years later. In 1592, after a series of storms during which he discovered the Falklands, John Davis sailed the *Desire* to this same island. With his crew mutinous and desperate for fresh food he replenished his stores with 14,000 salted down but insufficiently-dried penguins, reckoning that four men would eat five penguins each day on the voyage home.

But Davis was dogged by bad luck. Firstly, nine men died in a skirmish with giant, masked Patagones a dozen miles up the coast at Port Desire. Then, a final landing near Rio de Janeiro resulted in the loss of a third of his remaining crew when a shore party of thirteen was slain by locals as they snoozed in the heat of the Brazilian sun. A further attack by two boatloads of armed men forced the hapless Captain to hastily up anchor and away before filling his casks with fresh water.

Bound for Britain, they became becalmed in the tropics with only stagnant water to drink. As the crew succumbed to scurvy, groaning and aching, with spongy gums and swollen parts, so the penguins took their revenge. They started to rot and emerging maggots began to devour everything including the ship's timbers, even attacking the men themselves. On arrival at Berehaven in Bantry Bay, only sixteen exhausted members of the original complement of 76 were still alive. They were carried ashore by the townsfolk as the tiny harbour was filled with the stench of putrefying penguins.

Davis hitched a lift on a fishing boat to Padstow and returned home to Stoke Gabriel, in Devon, penniless. In his absence he had been deserted by his wife, Faith, and maliciously branded a villain by her lover, a muckraker called Milburn, well-connected amongst the jealous circle of Elizabethan navigators. For a while he turned to writing books about seamanship but two years later was once more under sail piloting a trading expedition to the Far East. In 1605, off the coast of Malacca, his ship *Tyger* encountered a Japanese junk full of smuggled rice and poor John Davis met his end impaled on the point of a pirate's sword.

John Davis (?1550-1605). Author, discoverer, inventor and penguin pickler, whose name is immortalised in a Greenland Strait and a Stanley Street. (By courtesy National Maritime Museum)

Jackass or Magellanic penguin outside its burrow in the tussac grass on Carcass Island (left).

Typical landing beach, Ship Harbour, New Island. Jackasses often gather here at dawn and perform curious group dances along the beach to the accompaniment of much braying and bill fencing.

Jackass penguins live at sea throughout the winter. They return to the Falklands to breed from mid-late September. Morning and evening their loud display calls echo around bays and harbours, heralding the arrival of spring. By the end of May, with the breeding cycle complete, they return once more to the ocean.

Gentoos

All penguins feed at sea, breed ashore and in between spend varying amounts of time on the beach. Different species prefer different types of shoreline. Gentoos, like people, tend to select gently sloping, sandy bays.

Each year with the approach of Autumn, they move down from their rookeries to gather at the water's edge. Some are adults, others youngsters, cautiously tasting the ocean for the first time (see far right). Such a massed baptism of debutantes acts like a lodestone to the old sealion who has patrolled here for many years. I watched him cruising just offshore, sometimes sitting in the wavelets just yards from the birds, occasionally making a short dash to try and grab one. But he was slow, with blunt teeth and a short future.

Younger lions are faster, devastating and spectacular predators. Usually alone, they stalk shorebound pods of penguins, the submerged and shadowy shape suddenly exploding in their midst to grab a victim and carry its broken body back into the surf. Within minutes all that remains is a skeleton with feet at one end and a reversed skin at the other being picked clean by scavenging 'stinkers', and afterwards just a patch of oil on the water.

I once saw a sealion make seven similar Gentoo kills in an afternoon.

Sealion with gentoo victim.

Kings

King Penguins were once heavily plundered for their eggs, oil and fancy feathers. Hordes were boiled in South Georgia and the few in the Falklands were exterminated during Victoria's reign.

Not until World War II was a chick again reared successfully at Volunteer Point.

Fifty years more have passed and today I am lying on the wet ground at 'Volunteers', dampness creeping into my knees and elbows. The 'Oakum boys' come waddling up, chirping and whistling, resembling bearskins at Buckingham Palace, only bigger and brown. One gently prods my boot with its bill. They are young Kings, charming and likeable, and there are now over 150 surrounding me.

A King amongst the Gentoos.

Gentoo penguin beach (right).

King Penguin chicks were called 'Oakum boys' by wooden-shipped sailors as their feathers resembled the oakum used in caulking deck seams.

18

Mollymauks

Beginning less than a mile from our house on New Island and extending north and eastwards almost continuously for six miles along the cliffs are a series of colonies and groups of Black-browed albatross. There are perhaps 10,000 pairs present during the summer. Altogether in the Falklands there are an estimated 370,000 pairs, which make up over 70% of the world's population of this species, the only albatross which breeds in the Islands.

They are known here as 'Mollys', a shortened form of mollymauk which, according to the learned commentator, Newton, in 1896, is a sailor's corruption of an English word corrupted from a German word, in turn corrupted from the Dutch. Apparently this name was first applied to the Arctic Fulmar, the vast flights of which resembled 'mallemugge' – the tiny midges around an oil lamp. To add to the confusion, mollymauk is a name applied by sailors of all nations to most of the other smaller albatrosses also. *Diomedea melanophris* is wide-ranging and circumpolar in the southern oceans and readily follows ships, benefiting both from updrafts caused by the ship's progress and from the scraps thrown overboard.

Sailors of yore, in addition to being familiar with the mollymauk as a pelagic companion, also knew about the nutritional value of its egg. The sealing captain, Edmund Fanning, noted in 1797 (no doubt with a view to the larder) that on New Island, the earliest eggs were laid on 10th October. A.F. Cobb, a sheep-farmer on Bleaker Island, remarked in 1933 that "a fried mollymauk egg will cover a dinner plate and together with a few mutton chops makes a good breakfast for a hungry man". Today the eggs are protected by licence.

Mollys may live for more than fifty years and tend to mate for a lifetime. Adults return to the same nest sites in late September each year, adding to the pedestal nest of mud and grass which may reach a height of half a metre. A single, irreplaceable, red-spotted white egg is laid and the first chicks hatch out around Christmas Eve. By February the grey, down-covered youngsters are large enough to be left alone while both parents go to sea to obtain food. During March the down is shed and the juveniles increasingly begin to exercise their gangly wings. They leave eventually by late April or early May to spend six or seven years at sea before returning as mature adults. At this time it is not unusual to find youngsters who have lost their way waddling about in their ungainly fashion in the camp, miles from anywhere. Once on the ground it is very difficult for them to take off again and many perish, although two people running along holding a wing tip each can sometimes get them airborne. Feeding largely on squid, small fish and jellyfish, large numbers congregate astern of the trawlers and jiggers working around the Islands. This new source of food has led to a recent rapid increase in local Molly populations.

Molly chicks, early February.

North Island ablaze. This remote virgin tussac island mysteriously caught fire in January 1988. Within days all the vegetation was burnt but the fire continued to burn into the peat, in places, for over a year. Amongst the flames and smoke is a large, mixed colony of Black-browed Albatross and Rockhopper penguins. Adult Mollys wheel above the ten feet high grass.

Young Mollymauk in March.

Mollymauks often follow in the wake of ships. These two have just been feeding on some gash thrown overboard from *Foam*.

Shags and Sea Hen

KING SHAGS are slightly larger than Rock Shags and breed in tightly-packed, cliff-top rookeries, often in association with other seabirds. Each pair builds a nesting mound of grass and muck just a hook-billed peck away from the next. The low pedestals are laid out with chequer board symmetry, each one crowned by a splendidly-dressed, slightly loopy-looking cormorant and ringed by spokes of greenish-white excreta. On warm days, in order to lose heat while incubating atop these compost heaps, king shags often sit with wings spread, beaks open and gullet vibrating.

The ubiquitous ROCK SHAG is a resident of the coastline but although commonly found in sheltered harbours and near human settlements it often remains as unnoticed as a shy neighbour. A rather weak flyer, it quietly potters in the kelp, making a living by diving for fish, and breeds in gulches and on cliff ledges all around the Islands, often nesting and roosting on jetties and wrecks.

Along the southernmost coasts of South America and Tierra del Fuego, Rock Shags were once hunted nocturnally by the native, and now vanished, Fuegians. The cunning Yaghan Indians would paddle their canoes beneath a shallow cliff where sleeping shags stood roosting, then wave bright torches of birch bark to and fro to dazzle the birds. Dizzy shags, toppling into the boats, were knocked on the nut with a stout stick. Another method was to creep up and seize the birds as they slept, head under wing, quietly despatching them with a bite through the neck.

The Ona Indians also made use of misty conditions and one famed cormorant hunter named Talimeoat would climb naked down a cliff using sealion hide thongs and grope silently along the bird-limed ledges to find and kill shags. His wife cooked the birds by stretching them out on sticks like kites to bake until crisp over an open fire. She carved with a knife made from a barrel hoop while gripping the bird's leg with her teeth and its head with her toes. Boiled or roasted in an oven, shag meat is said to be pretty awful, but prepared in the Ona way it is delicious.

King Shag.

Rock Shags nesting on the *Charles Cooper*, Stanley Harbour (far right).

Sea Hen or Antarctic Skua.

The Catharacta skuas are a genus of noisy and aggressive pirates which, in four specific forms, plunder the world's oceans. The Falklands play host to the smallest species, the Antarctic Skua, known locally as the SEA HEN.

The Rock Shag's summer is laced with intimidating images of this big, brown, dive-bombing thug, thieving eggs and nestlings and stealing fish which the shag has surfaced to swallow.

Sea Hens scare people too, especially around Christmas time, when their chicks hatch out and parents become very aggressively protective. Some sailors, stretching their legs on New Island, strayed unwittingly into a skua colony. Repeatedly raked fore and aft by swooping parents working in tandem, one of Her Majesty's mariners took flight and, falling into a penguin hole, broke an ankle. He returned to his ship by stretcher.

Near Spring Point there is a place mysteriously called 'Snaith's Point' where some sea hens breed. Sheep-gathering shepherds avoid it. The birds dive at your dogs, the dogs run under your horse, and the bucking horse leaves you sitting in the grass wondering if that was what had happened to Mr Snaith in the first place.

Stinkers

Southern Giant Petrel or 'Stinker'.

Nobody loves a 'Stinker', but I once met a Frenchman who liked them so much that he had devoted a considerable chunk of his life to their study. His name was Voisin and together we were passengers, casually looking out over the boat's rail at passing Giant Petrels just off Mengeary Point, when quite suddenly he began to leap about, grasping binoculars and muttering in French. One of a number of accompanying 'Nellies' was odd. Its bill was not green, but brown. It was *Macronectes halli,* the northern species, and the first ever recorded in the Falklands where the southern variety *Macronectes giganteus* is the norm. My friend's Gallic enthusiasm was catching, but for a decade since I have searched the waves in vain for another.

Giant Petrels, 'Stinkers' or 'Nellies' are ugly and uncouth sea-vultures with a wing-span of six feet and a massive bill capable of holing boot leather. Less graceful flyers than the mollymauks, they are nonetheless capable of sustaining a glide for ten minutes without a wingbeat.

At sea, they eat almost any animal food, dead or alive, from a crustacean to a man to the carcase of a whale. Their keen eyesight and sense of smell enables them to find food from afar.

Ashore they have been known to attack rats, rabbits and cast sheep. One was seen to emerge from the water, waddle clumsily up the beach and murder a moulting goose by grabbing the neck and throttling it. At dawn I have sat amongst 'Stinkers' which were bloated on a blood-bathed breakfast of baby Rockhoppers, unable to fly and surprisingly unaware of my presence merely a metre away. I was perhaps fortunate because at the nest they tend to vomit at approaching strangers.

After killing the weekly mutton on the farm, I dump the entrails into the sea and it is amazing how quickly 'Nellies' appear from nowhere in their haste to get at the guts. Along the beach by Stanley's Butchery and in places where the town's sewer pipes enter the sea, they have become quite tame in response to a constant source of easy food.

On land they are very shy creatures and breed only in remote places away from people. This is one such place (right).

Pintado

The Pintado is 'Beauty' to the Stinker's 'Beast'. A dapper, medium-sized, ship-following petrel with chequered plumage and fulmar-like flight. Well-known by sailors for centuries, they congregate magically whenever gash goes overboard in southern oceans. When feeding on fry, the petrel's feet paddle vigorously whilst it sits upright on the surface, characteristically pecking like a pigeon at its prey.

Pintado Petrel (right).

Nightbirds

Once or twice each summer, on nights when the mist is thick, the lights of our house attract numbers of flying petrels. White shapes ghost past the window, thumping into the building like snowballs. Most are Thin-billed Prions which nest in profusion here on New Island. Confused by the light and stunned by collision they congregate in corners, squabbling and cackling in the grass. Sometimes there is a flush of tiny storm petrels and, just occasionally, a diving petrel appears. I put one in the bath and watched it fly underwater like a miniature penguin. One morning I sketched a Wilson's Storm Petrel sitting quietly by a Corn Flakes packet on the kitchen table. It had flown into the porch on the previous night, dossing down in a Wellington boot. Wilson's is one of the commonest, and therefore most successful, birds in the world. Yet, like all burrowing petrels, its design, which has proved so successful for life at sea, has resulted in extreme vulnerability ashore. It is easy prey for terrestrial predators, falcons and skuas. To overcome this problem all these petrels breed in burrows on offshore islands, coming and going by night and navigating by the moon and stars and possibly the smell of their rookeries. Any bird flying away from its hole during daylight risks running the gauntlet and most are pursued, pounced upon and torn apart in seconds by gangs of skuas waiting around like muggers on a city street.

To be on such an island at night is like entering another secret world. As the sounds and colours of day fade, the deepening darkness is gradually filled with a weird cacophony of cooing, croaking and whistling petrel song. Unseen wings whirr and flutter by. Bodies crash into the tussac, sit for a few moments, then scurry off like mice. They fly into and climb over you, leaving an impression of soft feathers and that familiar, musky odour peculiar to petrels. It is easy to lose track of time and sit fascinated through the night so that by dawn, cold and tired, and with all the birds having disappeared again, it is like waking up from a dream.

Belcher's Thin-billed Prions (left).

Wilson's Storm Petrel (top left).

Sooty Shearwater (centre left).

Common Diving Petrel (bottom left).

White-chinned Petrel or 'Shoemaker' (below).

3 STANLEY

Stanley lies at the eastern end of East Falkland, a tiny city of immense charm, a living relic of the British Empire. It is a long thin town lining a long thin harbour, a patchwork sandwiched by Atlantic grey and moorland ochre.

Stanley became the capital when the seat of government was moved by Lieutenant Governor Moody from Anson (Port Louis) between 1843 and 1845, to the area formerly known as Port Jackson and subsequently renamed after the Secretary of State for the Colonies, Lord Stanley. The site was well chosen with shelter, fresh water, a land-locked harbour and 56 acres of nearby peat. A leading citizen of the day, J.W. Whitington, enthusiastically observed, "of all the miserable bog holes, I believe Mr. Moody has selected one of the worst for the site of his town."

During the 1850's, as sea-borne traffic around Cape Horn increased, vessels trading in Californian gold, Peruvian guano and Chilean copper began calling into Stanley for repair and supplies. Some vessels attempting to round the Horn were overloaded, some unseaworthy, and others simply unlucky. Many suffered severe batterings and limped back into port with the prevailing westerlies to lick their wounds and provide employment for the young town. A few lame ducks never recovered. Others were deliberately wrecked and their cargoes sold by unscrupulous dealers. The port gained a notorious reputation and a cast flock of worn out windjammers. Several are still stuck in the Stanley harbour mud.

By the last quarter of last century the islands had been divided up into large farming estates and sheep were nibbling every available pasture. As the centre of commerce and the only sizeable settlement, Stanley rapidly grew in importance. However, the decline of the Cape Horn trade route, the replacement of sail by steam, and the opening of the Panama Canal in 1914, left the colony totally dependent on its woolclip. Both the capital and the economy stood still and life changed but little for a lifetime until the war of 1982.

In the last few years, netfuls of licence money have poured in from companies wishing to fish within the Falklands Conservation Zone. Stanley has become a boom town and Mr. Whitington's bog hole today proudly boasts 1700 residents, a £13m school, half a dozen pubs and a fish 'n' chip shop.

Patriotic Islanders gather on Government House lawn, 1981.

Stanley 1991 (right).

Government House

"… the rain poured in …"
– Governor Allardyce 1904

"… it is convenient and workable, and has atmosphere"
– Governor Clifford 1950

"… a home to look back on with real affection …"
– Governor Haskard 1971

Head Gardener Gen Williams testing grapes in the conservatory at Government House (far right).

Government House.

Following his installation as Governor at Port Louis in 1842 Richard Moody established Bougainville's neglected stone chapel as the first Government House.

Soon afterwards, however, he received instructions from the Admiralty to remove the seat of government to its current position, and in 1844 constructed a single-storey wooden building (where today stands Cable and Wireless) to serve temporarily as the new 'G.H.'

Work began on the present House in 1845 to Moody's modest design which featured a north facing central block of three storeys (later reduced to two) and two matching single-storey wings east and west, all to be built of stone. During his period of tenure (1841-47) the eastern block was completed and thereafter used as the Government Offices until 1859 when Governor Moore, having finished the central block, took up residence. The western wing, as originally conceived, was never built. Since that time bits have been spasmodically tacked on or lopped off according to the requirements and whims of various incumbents and their spouses. Between 1881 and 1883 Thomas Kerr, with total disregard for Moody's blueprint, added a wooden, western wing consisting of four freezing bedrooms linked to the earlier part by 'an icy passage' which became known as the 'Straits of Magellan'. The 'Captain's Room' and the 'Bishop's Room', however, proved 'useful for male guests, as after a dull evening they could retire early, slip out of their windows and repair to the Colony Club for a poker session'.

By 1899, "nothing short of heroic measures were required," complained Grey-Wilson as he moved forward into the new century with six bedrooms and seventeen leaky roofs. So he added yet more and by 1904 'G.H.' had sprouted a new red brick wing (with three bedrooms and eight more roofs), some stables (just windward of the dining room) and two large heated conservatories. Since then another conservatory has been added, a porch moved, a cottage built, the stables converted and a few extra roofs popped on for good measure.

Today's rambling, palatial hotchpotch is saved from indistinction by the well-kept facades and, more especially, the surrounding trees, lawns and flower gardens. To the rear of the house is the oldest kitchen garden in the Islands, measuring three roods, which dates from the mid-1840's. Head gardener Eugene Williams began work here as a boy in 1949 and has watched ten governors munching his carrots and bolting beetroots. On April Fool's Day I found him behind the maids' quarters thoughtfully gazing into the bowels of a leaf-filled skip. He looked up with a seasoned eye.

"You don't often come around these parts." He paused. "Must be after something."

"Would you like to star with your vines in next year's calendar?" I asked, and was whisked *tout de suite* into the flower-filled conservatory where Gen's magnificent grapes dangled from the rafters.

"These vines came out when the Haskards were here, in '66 I think it was, from some friends in Monte," he said. "Where do you want me, old bean?"

I indicated the spot I had in mind.

"What, here?" said Gen in disbelief.

Clack went the shutter.

"You see, all this fruit takes a lot out of the plant," he expounded, ascending a step ladder.

The strains of an unfamiliar opera began seeping through the pelargoniums.

"So the earlier you cut them back, the more time they have to recover."

With the panache of a wine tester he sampled one from a particularly splendid bunch. I looked questioningly towards the open french windows into the Governor's sitting room remembering that I'd forgotten to ask if they'd mind me wandering about in their house.

"Is anybody er …?" I whispered.

Gen nodded.

"And if you disturb her that'll be the end of your grapes, sunshine."

He popped another large black pearl in his mouth and, as the Mecablitz let out a dazzling flash, a cultured female voice behind me said firmly: "Exactly *what* do you think you are doing?"

The Philomel Store

Philomel Store.

Des Peck's grave, Stanley Cemetery.

1972. In the bunkhouse at Fox Bay West, after supper, the navvy gang slouched in threadbare armchairs around an open grate, listening to the announcements on the radio. It was half past seven and I had been in the Islands just two days. Following the weather forecast and next day's flight schedules, came a curious advert.

"From the Philomel Store," began an ethereal female voice, and there was a stir of interest among the dozen dozing men. "Just received on the charter boat, finest Eskiltuna knives and steels from Sweden – buy now while stocks last. Quality cowboy hats in black or khaki. Also one only saxophone. Remember we are sole agents for Beefeater Gin, Chanel No. 5 and Homecharm Paint. Priority given to camp customers."

"That's Des Peck," said someone.

"Best knives you can git," said another, and from the back of the room a rude remark caused a ripple of chuckles.

Des Peck had opened the Philomel Store in the early fifties; no one could quite remember when. He was a man of forthright opinion and always wrote a 'pome' about any topical event of the day. He was known as the Falklands' Poet Laureate.

1982. One day after the Liberation I popped in to buy a guitar. An old-fashioned shop's bell jangled as I opened the door and, behind a mountain of cardboard cartons, there was Des flogging someone a fluffy penguin.

"See that? Can't get them in fast enough, son," he said when his customer had gone, "going like hot cakes".

We shifted the boxes of birds away from the door.

"Now what was it you were after?"

I told him.

"I've got just the very thing. Wait a minute, son, you just wait there one minute." His voice trailed away as he limped first into the office at the end of the shop, then disappeared upstairs. I looked around. Displayed in a case on the counter were ornamental candles from Guernsey, Zippo lighters and mugs with Lady Di on them. There was a creaking sound as Des rummaged somewhere aloft. A row of blazers lived in the corner above some first day covers from the Antarctic. Suspended from a shelf by drawing pins hung a series of white satin pennants with gold tassels, each bearing one of the bard's famous 'pomes' printed in blue script.

The noisy bell announced the arrival of two more penguin seekers and, in the twinkling of an eye, the old shopkeeper reappeared.

"Here we are, son, look at this one, see?" he said, handing me a jumbo and turned to serve the newcomers who soon departed, each with a stuffed bird tucked under his wing.

"What happened here?" I asked, pointing to a broken window pane. I'd heard the story before but Des's yarns improved like ageing wine.

"Bloody Argies," he fumed. "They broke in and stole all my invoices. Look at this." It was a bit of cardboard with a dirty splodge on it labelled *Genuine Argentine Footprint*.

I bought the guitar. "Hey, before you go, listen to this one, it's my latest, see what you think," he said, producing his own out-of-tune guitar from under the counter, and to the melody of *Jingle Bells*, sang this haunting refrain:

*"Oh Harriers here, Harriers there, Harriers everywhere,
What a pleasure it will be when-there's-no Skyhawks in the air.
So Harriers here, Harriers there, the Skyhawks are no match,
And in the first day's battle 22 of them went crash."*

1992. I went in the store again the other day. The door bell tinkled and there was Des's son, Burned, playing poker dice on the counter with a mate for sweepstake tickets. Nothing much has changed, except that Burned doesn't write 'pomes' like old Des, but then I don't suppose anyone else ever will.

Des Peck in the Philomel Store (right).

Organic Gardening

Des Peck loved to entertain. Brought up in the camp, he taught himself and many others to play the guitar, the mouth organ and various other instruments, and often performed in local dance bands. In his latter years he became famous for his poetry, which appeared on the radio, in the *Falkland Islands Times* and in *Penguin News* whenever he felt inspired. Des's 'pomes' were short, simple and often amusing. They contained references to 'our Prime Minister Margaret', Kaiser Bill and 'penwings'. Before he died in 1988, Des put many of his songs, 'pomes' and reminiscences on a tape from which I borrowed the following:

"In 1978 Mr Abbie Alazia and Mr Dolan Williams gave talks on the radio on what to do in your garden. These went on for weeks and weeks. Then, one night, a dreadful storm struck Stanley from the north-east. The animals all came into the town from the Common and took shelter behind fences, sheds and houses. One horse was by Mr Alec Bett's house and in the morning there was quite a heap of manure. So I composed a 'pome' and this is how it goes:

*"On getting up this morning
and going to the gate,
a horse was standing there all night –
you can guess what was my fate!*

*After hearing about the gardening news
I decided this was it.
So with my bucket and shovel
I gathered up every bit.*

*Now it's round my rhubarb
and some are ready to pull.
I sometimes wonder how high it would be
if that horse had been a bull."*
                                              Des Peck

Nelly Betts' house (far right).

Kay McCallum's garden.

Lawrence and Mally Blizzard's house (top right).

Rene Rowlands in her prize-winning flower garden 1992 (bottom right).

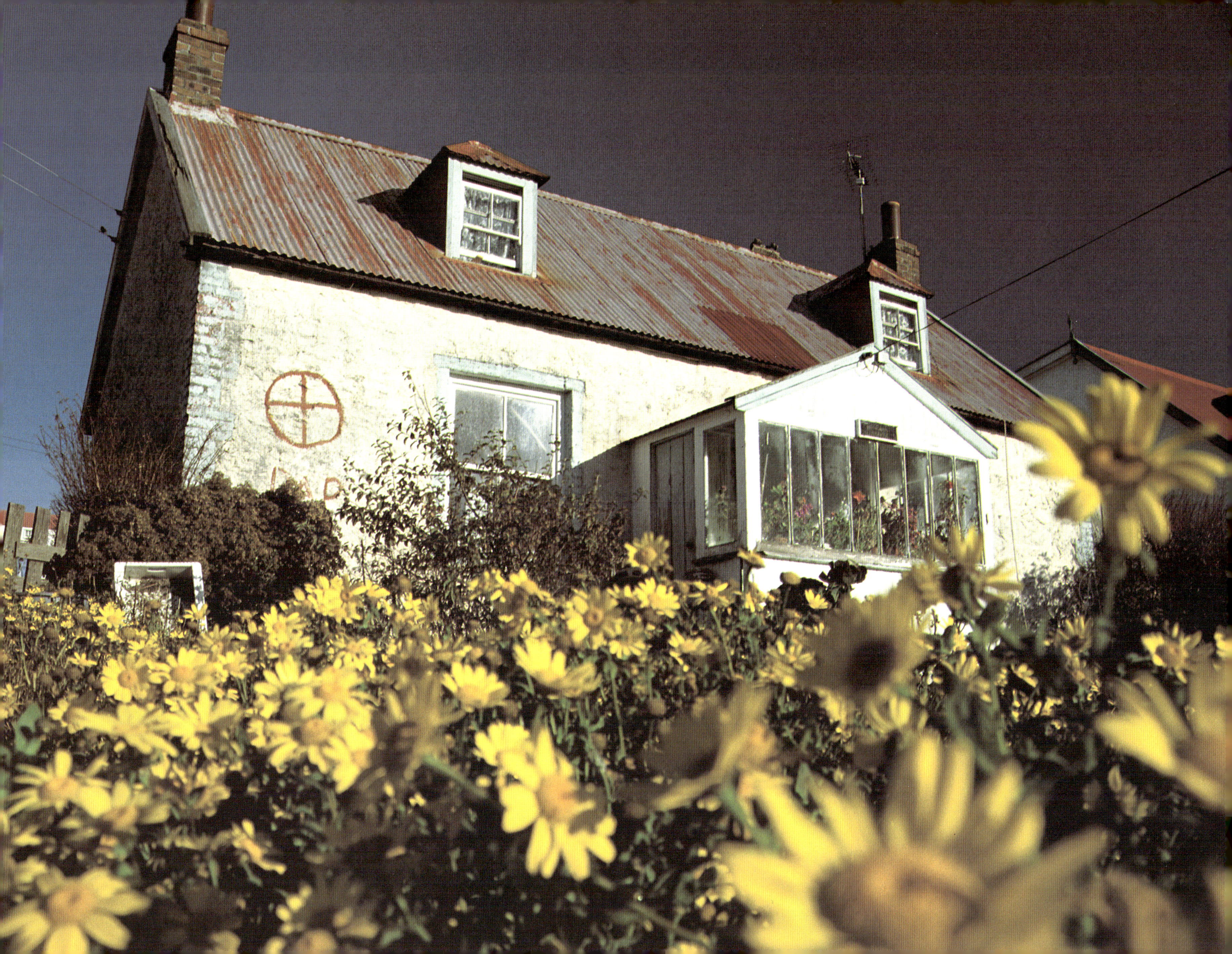

Christ Church Cathedral

The Chancel

Christ Church, though a small and rather plain Anglican Cathedral by European standards, is the best-known and most-loved building in the Islands. When consecrated in 1892 it became both village church and, for 85 years, Mother Cathedral to the vast missionary Diocese of South America.

Today it remains a focal point for the community, regardless of denomination or lack of it, especially at times of great sadness or celebration such as after the Liberation in 1982, when a concert was given by the band of the Royal Marines. They played magnificently, dressed in combats in the choir stalls, while we sat scruffily in the pews, all still under threat of air attack and feeling grubby from clearing up the streets. Harry Bagnall said a prayer and Harold Rowlands called for "three loud cheers for the Task Force". As *Rule Britannia* rang up to the bell tower, the congregation felt down for their handkerchiefs.

Before the Cathedral was built regular worship had taken place in the dockyard, the barracks and the *Speedwell*, but it was not always the vogue amongst a frontier community. The first colonial chaplain, the Rev. James Moody, was so popular that for one Easter Sunday service no one at all turned up, not even the Governor.

Eventually part of the impressive Exchange building was procured for worship in 1856. It became known as Holy Trinity Church, but was condemned 30 years later following the second peat slip. Services moved temporarily to a sail loft.

At that time the chaplain was a deaf, short-sighted but remarkable Irishman, Lowther Brandon. Throughout his 30 year incumbency (1877-1907) he tirelessly fought against widespread intemperance, while for children he opened a Sunday School, a savings bank and a library. Brandon's 'Camp Visitations' on horseback or under sail to every Island household became legendary, always carrying papers, mails and the famous magic lantern in his molitos. He raised cash for and supervised the building of the Cathedral, becoming Dean on its completion. In his spare time Dean Brandon also founded, edited, printed and distributed the first newspaper, the *Falkland Islands Magazine* affectionately known as the 'Squeaker'.

From the March 1893 edition comes this edited description of a fund-raising bazaar which he inspired in the Assembly rooms for the new Cathedral organ:

"Proceedings were opened by the Bishop. The room was tastefully decorated with flags and flowers and artistic arrangements of small arms. Among them a Nordenfeldt gun, gave piquancy and brilliance to the peaceful and busy scene. A novelty of a very interesting kind had been provided by Capt. Lang (*HMS Sirius*) which was nothing less than a real torpedo for the inspection of those who wished to see. The fishpond, over which the Judge presided, was large, the fish were abundant and fine. Pressure to get rods and lines was immense, nor did it cease until more than 400 imaginary fish had been drawn from the would-be lake, Mr Bailey had a more lively sort in a tank for, with the zeal and genius of a real fisherman, he had provided a supply of mullet still alive to be fished for by those who would. An electric battery provided many amusing incidents. Things went on merrily. Perhaps the most sedate feature of the bright and bustling scene was the microscope and its wonders…

"Two hours passed away and a great change has been effected. The tables, which at first were resplendent with all manner of charming things, are rapidly being despoiled of their beauty and within three hours the presiding ladies look down upon a desert of boards and mere fragments of a vanished splendour. Very lovely had been the flower stall but its glory had passed away. The magnetic skill of the lady sellers had told to the uttermost and the result of the sale exceeded £160."

A new, six foot steel cross is helicoptered into position in May 1991 as part of the Cathedral restoration project.

The Whalebone Arch, constructed in 1933 from Blue whale jaw bones, and recently renovated and reinforced with epoxy resin, stands alongside Christ Church, the world's southernmost cathedral.

37

The Horticultural Show
March 1992

Brian and Joe at the Horticultural Show.

I had just put a toe in the bath as the 'phone rang. It was Kitty to say that Roddy had rung and wanted me to know that a freak wind was blowing at over seventy knots from the south east on West Point and that his boat, the *Redwing*, was on the beach.

"Is the *Foam* alright?" she asked.

I was about to get out when the 'phone rang again, this time from Weddell where our boat was anchored.

"The *Foam*'s taking a pounding," said John, "but hasn't moved yet so I don't think she's going to. It's gusting 68 out here and the barograph's dropping like a stone."

Within ten minutes, from being virtually calm, Stanley Harbour was white with spray as the wind whipped up, and through the window I watched the old *Penguin* being tied off the Public Jetty for safety. Apprehensively I rang John but the *Foam* was still riding it out.

After lunch we went down to the Horticultural Show in the Defence Force Hall and outside met Bob.

"Bad luck on old Rod, eh? And Fenton's one, the *Tern*, she's on the beach too, at Golding," he said. "It's the worst gale since 1945."

We went inside, paid our 20 pences and bought some raffle tickets. Amongst the luxuriant pot plants – English marigolds, African violets and Californian poppies – I found Pat peering at Sarah's creeper and Terry's chrysanthemum.

"How's yer boat, Tone?" he asked with concern, adding gravely, "The *Tern's* a write-off, then. I haven't seen the like since '44."

A savage hail squall lashed the roof as Annie and I marvelled at the size of Harry's marrow and Shirley's beetroots. Brian was relieved. His enormous leek amongst "Any Other Vegetables" had won a prize. He had another in the cabbages.

Bill was worried lest the bad weather would keep people away from the Show.

"Somebody said it's blowing 160 knots up on the mountain and the thunderbox on Sedge has blown over," he said.

The first vegetable competition had been organised by the 'Improvement Society' in 1867. By 1905 the 'Flower Show and Industrial Exhibition' further included sections for hide gear making, wild bird stuffing, fleeces, flowers and photos. A recent request over the radio had brought forth a prizewinning snapshot of a mollymauk taken by G. Scott of New Island in 1908 and here it once again graced the wall, admired by the Governor, William Fullerton.

"Glad to hear your boat's alright," he said. "Did you know that the *Barbara E* has run aground in Mare Harbour and the anemometer mast on Byron bent horizontal with the windspeed at 115 knots?"

The cookery section filled a third of the hall. There were Swiss rolls, sausage rolls, buns, scones and tarts and a bright green dragon cake which had been delivered by the Doctor. Amongst the bottled preserves June's pickles were outstanding. In another corner stood Don, dressed in his chauffeur's uniform and dwarfed by a ten foot hydroponic pepper plant. Some of the red and green fruits had been knocked off on the way up the road and stuck back on with Sellotape.

"I hear some fallen trees have brought down the power lines at Port Howard," I said.

That's nothing, son," replied Don, "part of Rodney's house roof carried away and his hangar blew to bits. They say it's the highest wind since '46".

In the evening came the traditional speeches and the chairman praised the exhibitors on a magnificent show, proudly adding that entries were up 500 on last year. Finally, a lively auction ensued, by which time the gale outside was abating while inside the speed of rumours had risen to hurricane force. We eventually came home with a fortnight's supply of vegetables for fifteen quid and a hose which came up on the raffle.

Reg Lyse in his prizewinning vegetable garden 1992.

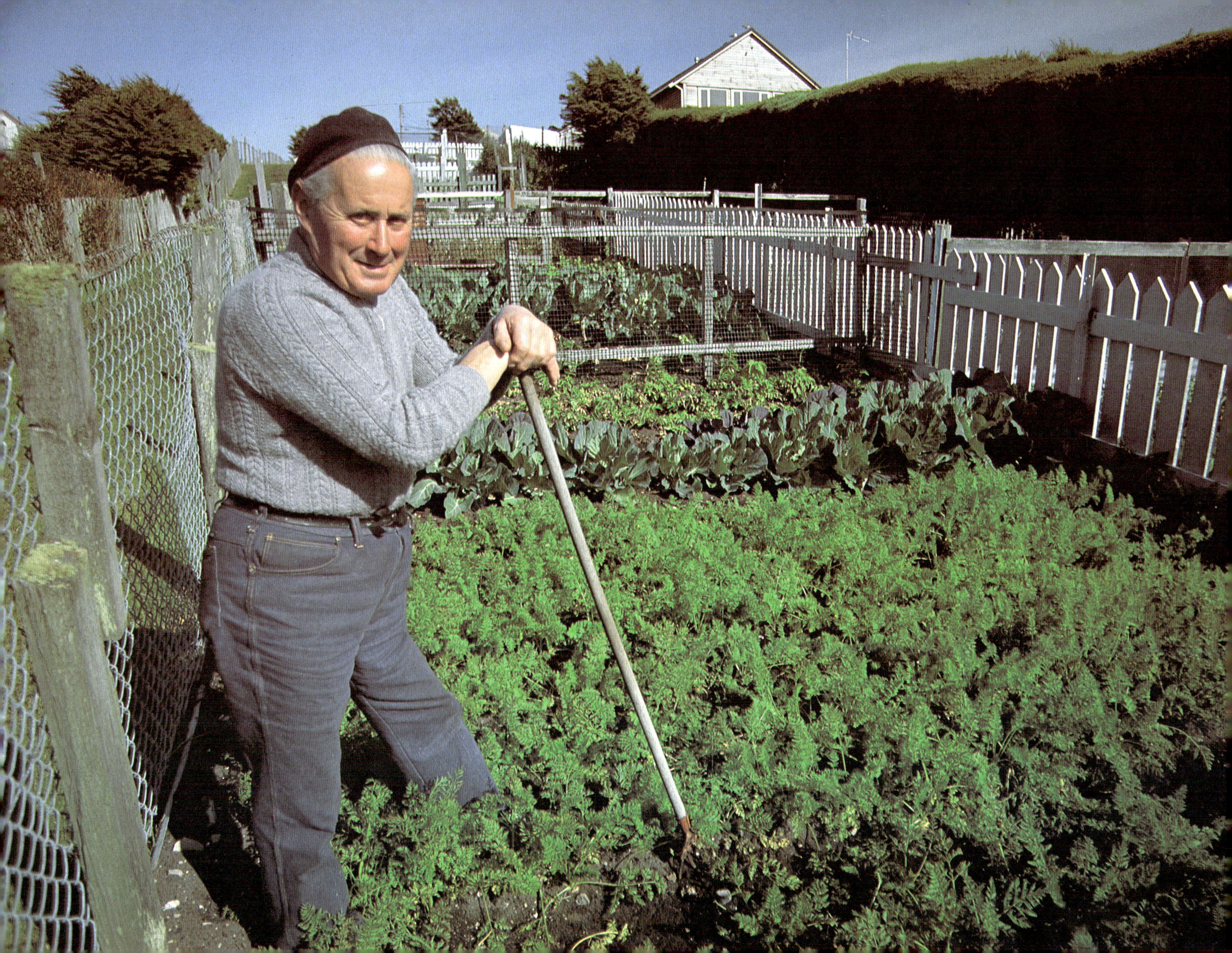

Sport

A Stanley boat racing crew in the 1930's. (Photo Bill Goss)

Stanley XI, 1983.

Extracted from *Flash Boats, Dollars and Cocks* by Vice Admiral B.M. Chambers and reprinted in the *Falkland Islands Magazine and Church Paper* (November 1925).

In speaking of boats and racing, I am inclined to think that I ought perhaps to give pride of place to the Kelpers of the Falkland Islands, at least in their home waters. It is said, whether truly I know not, that they have never been beaten by a man of war crew. Like many such traditions it probably rests on scant foundation. I have seen one such race, and that against a service boat of much more than average excellence. It was an interesting sight; on the one hand the shabby crew, their ill-kept boat lacking a much needed coat of paint, as opposed to the spick and span galley from one of HM ships, bright-work sparkling in the southern sun, bright-hued jerseys and racing flags, and the crew trained seemingly to the last ounce. It seemed hardly possible that such a scarecrow crew as the Kelpers could lower the pride of our champions. But the knowing eye of the expert could determine fine lines in the shabby old boat, selected from the ocean flotsam of a hundred wrecks. In its essentials the boat had all the good points which make for speed and lightness. In similar manner, beneath the worn blue guernseys, length of arm and firm, lean muscles promised speed and endurance, steel muscles without a pound of surplus flesh. When the race started there was something in the purposeful stroke, sweeping and long, which was different from anything in service use.

Before the race these wily Kelpers found lots of sailors who would stake their pound on the event, no Bradburys then but good red gold, if not at evens then at least at the very shortest of odds.

They won hands down, the flash boat was beaten, and the Kelpers had the dollars.

In March 1976 there was in 'incident' on the high seas near Stanley when *RRS Shackleton*, an unarmed Antarctic research ship was threatened by an Argentine gunboat.

"*Endurance, Endurance*, you are to proceed to the nearest Argentine port," demanded their captain, mistaking the ageing red and green vessel for the ice patrol ship *HMS Endurance*. *Shackleton's* skipper replied that he was heading for Port Stanley.

"Stop your engines or I shall open firing."

The 'Shack' remained on course even as the Argentines subsequently opened fire across her bows with a Bofors gun. Eventually, with both ships on the horizon within sight of the town, the gunboat broke off and steamed away.

It was a very disturbing affair for both the captain and his crew and the local population. Tension ran high and dockers refused to unload the Argentine freighter *Bahia Buen Suceso* which lay at anchor in the port.

By chance, the following day, there was an end of season cup final featuring a team of Argentine construction workers who had been building a fuel depot down by the rubbish dump at the east end of town. Ranged against them was the might of Stanley FC under the wily eye of manager and former chief policeman, Dolan Williams. The match suddenly grew in stature and inevitably became a showdown – the Falklands versus Argentina – with shades of the notorious World Cup quarter final at Wembley a decade earlier.

In a stiff breeze, a third of the capital's 1200 people lined the touchlines or sat watching from landrovers, as we played on the famous sloping pitch by Government House. The game was rough. After twenty minutes one of their blokes was sent off for aiming a boot at Bobby Charlton (or was it Les Biggs, the carpenter?) which might have saved our midfield maestro the cost of a vasectomy had he wanted one. Their entire team trooped off in protest and sat in the coach, the only one then in the Islands. After a while they came back and we carried on. Nobby Stiles (who with his teeth in could have been mistaken for docker, Terry Betts) took the ball down the right and crossed, and I slipped it in from six yards. One-nil. There was a tide of pandemonium, a sea of smiling faces, and an ocean of light blue shirts, and I thought I heard Jimmy Greaves say, "Great goal, mate", but perhaps it was just one of the sheep shearers.

Stanley scored again, but in the second half the 'Argies' came back at us, down the hill, with a following wind and a banana kick which deceived goalie, Terry Peck (the spitting image of Gordon Banks). In a gripping finale, we hung on to win by two goals to one. The country's dented pride had been restored and we all retired to The Globe.

Of course, all the great players of yesteryear have now retired. Some can still be found lurking in their gardens or supping in The Rose, ever willing to share their hard-won international experience with some up and coming whipper-snapper. Today we have to rely on a lesser breed like Billy Gascoine, James Lineker and Gonzo Barnes. Things just aren't the same any more.

There is a long sporting tradition in the Islands, often reflecting the working activities of the community. Boat racing and cricket have long since ceased but horse racing, steer riding, shooting, soccer and darts are as popular as ever. 1990 saw the opening of the Islands' first swimming pool and two years later the magnificent Falkland Islands Community School was finished as part of the same complex. It incorporates a multi-purpose gymnasium, squash courts and, at last, a level playing field for football and athletics. All these facilities are open to the public.

Steer riding at the Stanley Sports 1983. The idea is to stay on, use your spurs, and look as competent as possible for one minute, with just a rope to hang on to (above right).
Before the 'back to front race', Stanley Mini Sports 1992.

Peat

Peat is hard work. It needs to be cut, rickled, carted home and stacked before burning; the ashes emptied and dust cleaned up afterwards.

Twenty years ago every householder annually used 120 cubic yards of it to warm the home, boil water and bake bread. The majority of Islanders still prefer its smoky reek to the expensive convenience of gas, oil or electricity.

Present day peat began to form here over 9,000 years ago as plants colonised available areas during the post-glacial period which followed the Pleistocene Ice Age. Dead vegetation formed a mat which was gradually decomposed by water, compressed and partly carbonised, in many places accumulating to a depth of 4 metres.

Early French colonists at Port Louis, seeking fuel, at first made a fruitless search for trees. Then the padre, Dom Pernetty, wandering about with a mattock, hacked up some turfs and impatiently chucked them on the fire. Thus peat was discovered by a monk on 17 February 1764.

In 1842 Governor Moody was so impressed by the quality and quantity of Stanley's peat that he felt by using Lord Willoughby D'Cresby's compressing machine it could profitably be exported to Argentina. Things took a little time but eventually, by the 1970's, second-hand plastic bags labelled 'Genuine Falkland Islands Peat' and containing a few old nobblings for 50p became available to Argentine tourists from the Kelper Store.

In the early days the nearby peat banks above and behind Stanley were cut in a somewhat random manner. Bogs were destabilised and badly-drained and, twice, rivers of peaty slime spewed down through the town and into the harbour. The second 'peat slip' of 1886 killed two and stove in the church. Nowadays a peat officer supervises allocation of Government and private banks, one per household. New bogs must be cut two yards wide to avoid trapping livestock, although today there are few beasts around Stanley Common as, in 1982, the Argentines ate most of the milk cows, then littered the pastures with undetectable plastic mines.

John Henry Lee taught me how to cut peat during my first Spring at Fox Bay. In twenty minutes, using a sharp spade, he transformed two yards of sodden bog into 128 glistening black cubes arranged neatly on top of the bank to dry in the wind. Like many Kelpers, John had the knack of doing this heavy job with efficiency and economy. "Always keep the handle clean," he said, handing me the Bulldog and turning to his own bog whence, for the rest of the day, interrupted only by 'smokos', rolled out a steady stream of sods.

Down in my bog, sheltered from the westerly wind by a growing wall of peat, the sun got hotter, the heavy sods heavier and my blistered hands sorer. As each buttery cuboid was hurled out, I received in return a faceful of wind-borne peat mould. I clearly hadn't yet acquired the knack but instead soon became knackered. At four in the afternoon the ruddy-headed foreman returned with a satisfied grin. It was knock-off time and he had forty on the bank.

"How did yer get on, then?" chuckled John, surveying my untidy jumble of heaped peat.

I had managed only eight yards all day.

Old peat cutting exploits are legendary and the life-blood of many a bar-room dispute, giving rise to the theory that more peat has been cut on the 'Rose' banks than anywhere else. However, the record almost certainly belongs to Pat Whitney who marked and cut an extraordinary 108 yards during one day in 1975 and, with cutting becoming increasingly mechanised, it is an achievement unlikely to be easily beaten.

Evening. Peat smoke over Stanley (far right).

Carting peat home using a tractor and trailor (bottom right).

The author opening up a new bank. (Photo Annie Chater)

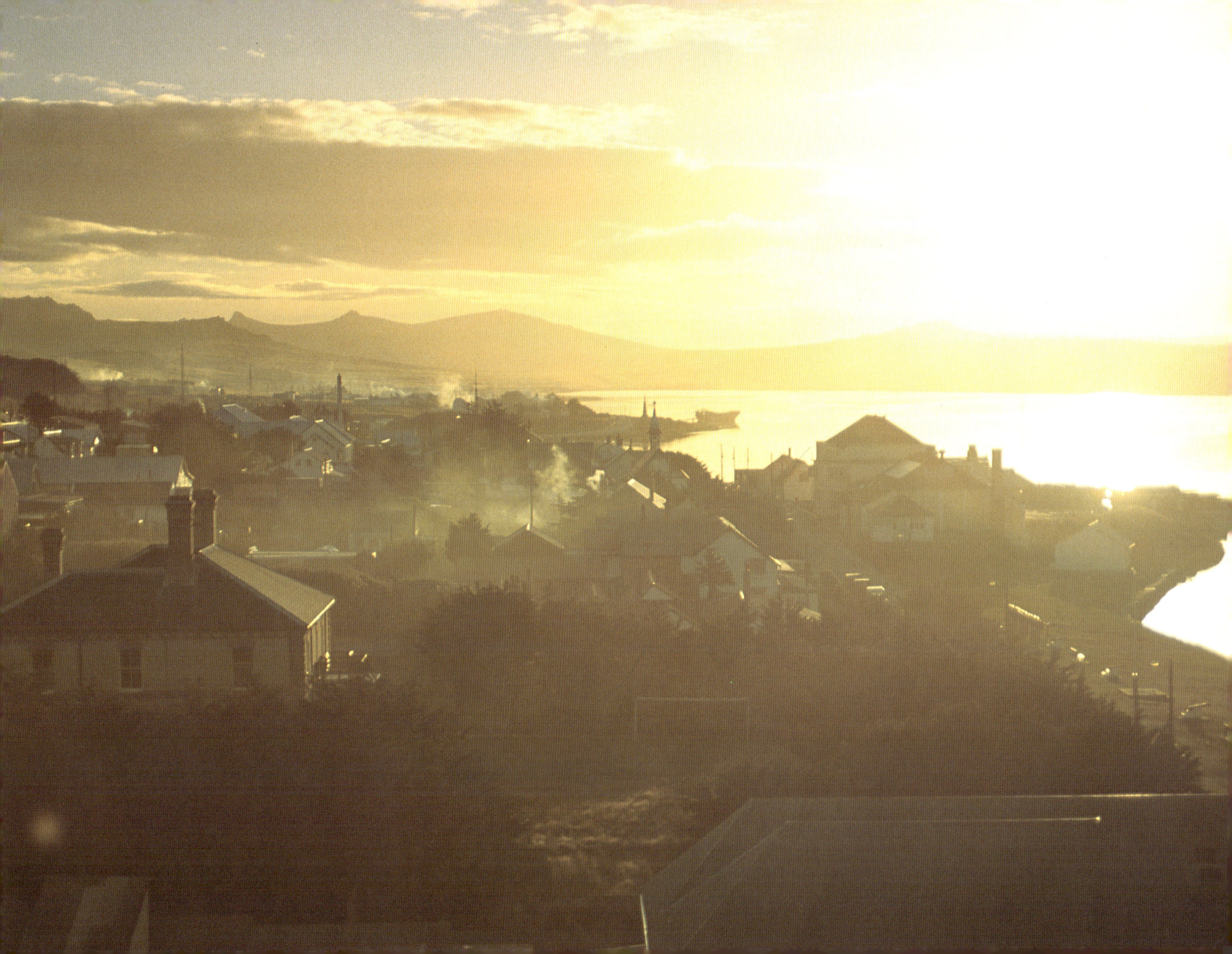

Architecture

Jane Cameron, the Government Archivist, who works for the Museum and National Trust in Stanley, is the leading authority on local architecture. She has generously contributed the following:

The beauty of Falkland Islands architecture lies not in grand or public buildings, but in the histories of individuals.

Arriving in a treeless land where the quartzite blunted the mason's tools and cracked into unpredictable forms, the early settlers resigned themselves to importing their building materials. The lightest and cheapest were shipped in: wood and galvanised iron.

Usually working to standard patterns from 'home', they constructed simple timber-framed dwellings to shelter themselves and their families. In this new settlement even the Colonial Surgeon had to sleep in a tent for three months while he built his own house.

Some examples, such as those erected in 1849 for the army pensioners on Pioneer Row and Drury Street, came in kit form. Advertisements for 'complete cottages' from England appeared in the *Falkland Islands Magazine* at the turn of the century, equipped down to the doorknobs, and costing a few hundred pounds. Two of the most attractive buildings in Stanley, St Mary's and the Tabernacle, were imported in kit form; examples of a thriving Victorian mail order trade, civilisation in flat packs designed to console pioneering settlers in the furthest corners of the Empire.

Shingles were a popular form of cladding in the early years but were rapidly superseded by galvanised iron, probably because the large sheets were so much quicker to apply. However, the older houses can often be identified by a fringe of shingles appearing at roof and wall edges beneath sheets of corrugated iron.

Although the timber-framed house became the common form, some people persevered with stone buildings and there are still a number of attractive cottages reflecting the solid traditions of the English countryside.

Most of the older Falkland Island houses have been gradually added to over the years, commonly by a lean-to at the back to accommodate a kitchen and bathroom, a porch at the front to capture sunshine and grow tomatoes, and dormer windows to bring light to attic bedrooms. The claddings, however, typically of weather-board, flat tin and various patterns of corrugated iron, have remained largely unchanged.

Paint was applied to protect the wood and iron from the salt winds, but became a medium of individual expression which today characterises the buildings. Colours glow in the brilliantly clear air, distinguishing each house from its neighbours and emphasising the decorative woodwork on barge-boards and porch trims; expressions of individuality and the pride of people in the work of their own hands.

The Tabernacle, in Barrack Street, was imported in kit form and erected, in 1892, by workmen from the Falkland Islands Company. It was designed by the Rev. C.H. Spurgeon, Baptist Minister of the Metropolitan Tabernacle in London, who specialised in 'planting churches' in far-flung places. In this case he even contributed to the freight costs.

Amongst a number of alterations made over the last hundred years was the re-siting of the main doors from the sides to the front of the porch to allow easier access for funeral parties.

With one exception the photographic montage (left) is comprised entirely of Jane Cameron's original and refreshing images of gaily-painted buildings in Stanley. Beginning at the top left-hand corner and proceeding anti-clockwise around Mrs Kitty Bertrand's yellow roof are …

Ray and Gay Robson's house
Eddie and Lizzie Anderson's house
The Fleetwing Shop
Stanley Cottage (bottom left-hand corner)
Gilbert House
Ken and Dot Keenleyside's house
Government House (bottom right-hand corner)
Jane Cameron by Fred Ford's Garage (photo Tony Chater)
Government Printing Works

Angus and Estelle Jaffray's house, Cemetery Cottage, Snake Hill.

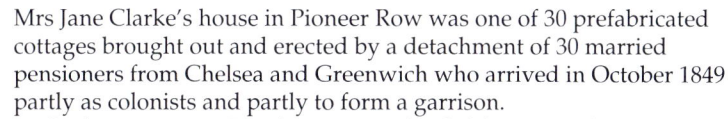

Mrs Jane Clarke's house in Pioneer Row was one of 30 prefabricated cottages brought out and erected by a detachment of 30 married pensioners from Chelsea and Greenwich who arrived in October 1849 partly as colonists and partly to form a garrison.

In the same year, 777 ships set out for California via the Horn or Magellan's Strait during the Gold Rush. Many came to blows with 'Cape Stiff'. Stanley was about to be transformed from a pioneering hamlet to a growing town full of shipwrights.

The Dockyard

The Government Dockyard is the oldest part of town. Begun in late 1843, it included a 'storehouse' jetty, three large storehouses, workshops, a jail, magazine and smithy all enclosed by an eight foot high fence of wooden palings. Atop a 40 ft high spar by the guardhouse hung a large ship's bell. It was rung in alarm, to announce the beginning and ending of daily work and to summons the settlers to worship in the early days, before a church was built, when services were conducted in one of the dockyard buildings. The bellringer earned sixpence a day.

Some of the original buildings are still used by the Public Works Department. The old jail is now the Carpenters' Shop and the No.1 Storehouse has become the Government Central Store. Tucked away, near the waterfront, is a charming stone building called the Blacksmith's Shop, resided over by a master metalworker, Ronnie Clarke. Originally the building was the smithy with forges, bellows and anvils; vice, drill and swaging block.

The Government Jetty, Stanley, 1980.

Ronnie Clarke in the Blacksmith's shop.

"It's more of a machine shop now", said the genial Ron, proudly surveying his arsenal of modern equipment. But when he first started there in 1961 there were still cinders on the bare earth floor.

Underneath the end of the Government Jetty rest the remains of the *Margaret*, a 615 ton Canadian barque which staggered into port under command of Captain Till in August 1850, six months and twenty-two days out of Liverpool. Leaking, damaged and overloaded with coal and cannonballs for Valparaiso, she was condemned and subsequently cut down to her 'tween decks, then filled with rubble to form the base of the pierhead.

The Government Dockyard, 1991 (right).

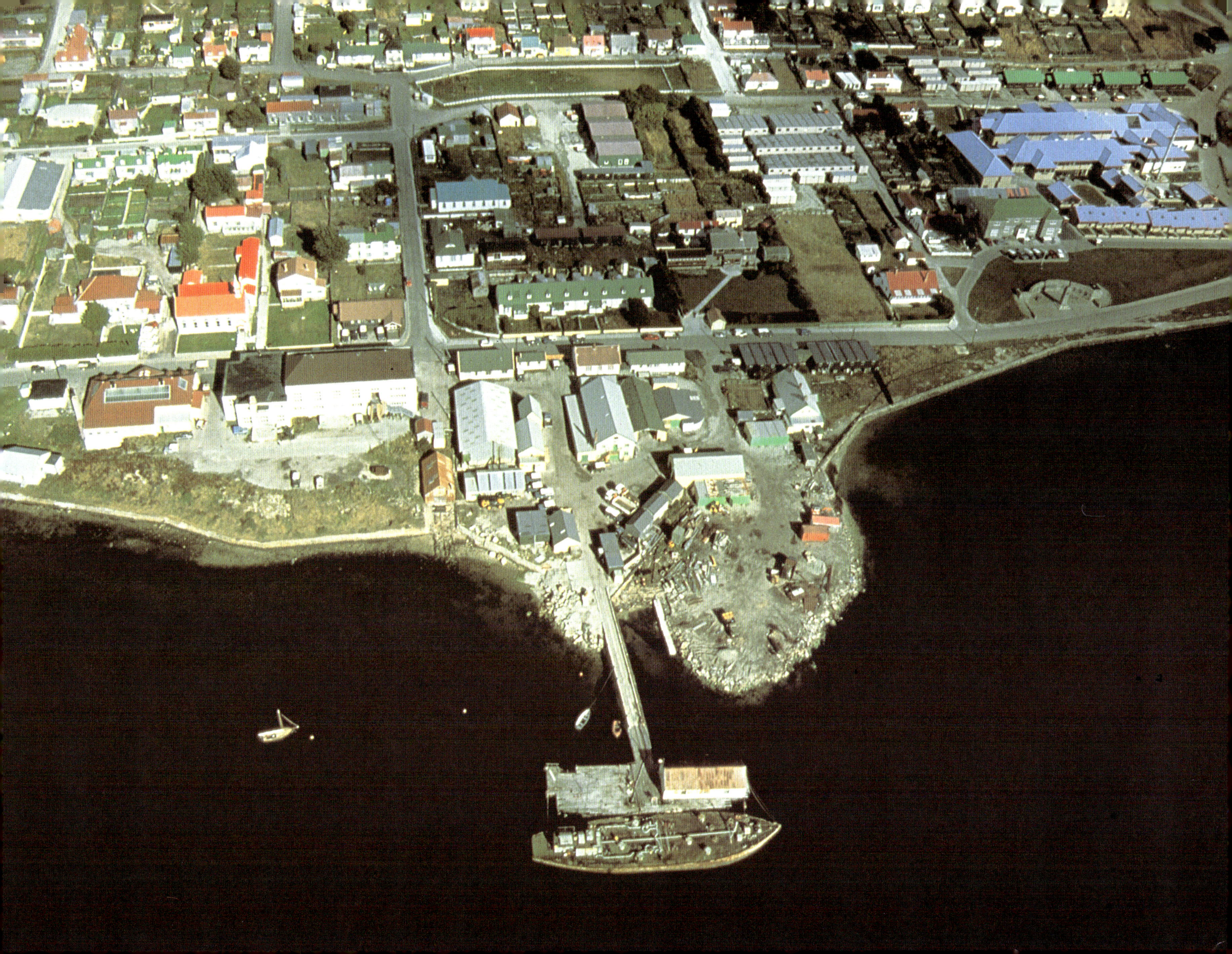

City Life

Governor William Fullerton, Lady Margaret Thatcher and Major Pat Peck at the Falklands War Memorial, 14th June 1992.

Chief Fire Officer, Marvin Clarke, and the men of the Falkland Islands Fire Brigade (top right).

The Pink Shop ('The Harrods of the Falklands') (bottom right).

The butcher delivers meat by the quarter, to Stanley households, twice a week. Laurie Butler (shown here) owned and ran the business from 1983 until 1988.

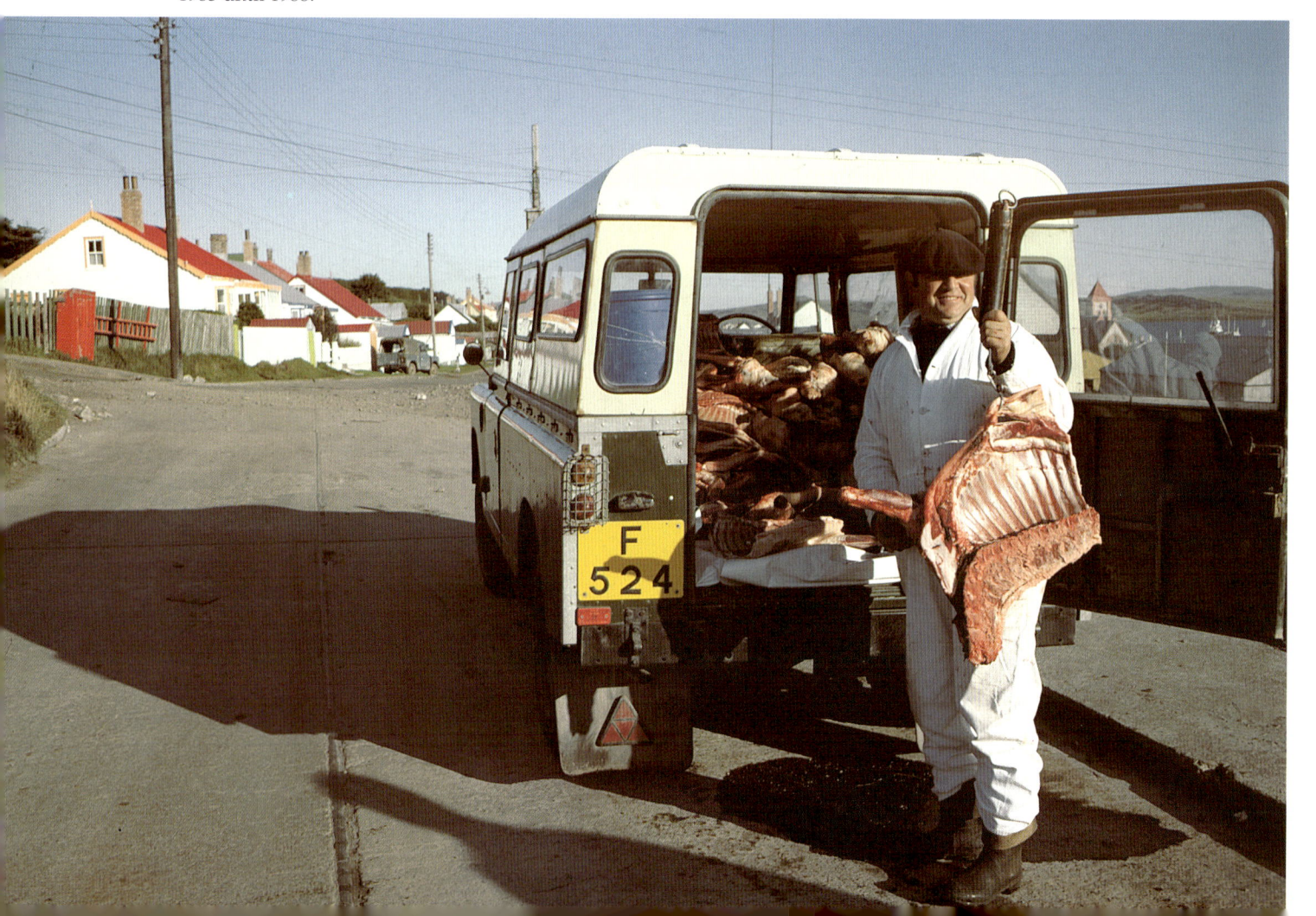

Bert Ford and Priscilla Morrison tripping the light fantastic at the 1993 May Ball.

Driving a flock of mutton sheep along Ross Road towards the Stanley Butchery, November 1989.

The Islands' 150th Anniversary Parade in 1983 (right).

Leona Vidal, deputy editor of the *Penguin News* (centre bottom).

The Speedwell Store, John Street (far right, bottom).

49

4 PREDATORS AND PASSERINES

Turkey Vulture

The Turkey 'buzzard' is the largest, commonest and most hated raptor in the Islands. In 1908, due to an alleged habit of killing sheep, Government placed a bounty of four pence per beak on its bald head. However, in twenty years, I have only once seen a turkey eat anything other than carrion, and believe the killing of new born lambs and other small creatures to be the exception rather than the rule.

Shy and largely silent creatures, they soar effortlessly on thermals, using acute eyesight and a sense of smell, unusual in birds, to locate food. On land, gathered around some dying creature, they look ungainly, like a bunch of hunchbacked, Dickensian undertakers, waiting for a sheep's tongue, a nag's eye or the chance to poke between the ribs of an old cow.

Carrion from the Islands' half a million sheep supports a large number of vultures, but they also eat dead birds and the excreta, placentas and bodies of seal.

Turkeys nest in crannies under rocks or in caves. The young ones are unusually aggressive and when walking through dense tussac grass it can be quite startling to be confronted by a rustling, hissing adversary, hidden below the waist-high canopy. They smell slightly fetid but in the 1920's a shipwrecked Arthur Cobb ate one "at 6.0am one cold winter's morning, on a tussac island miles from anywhere" after "a hungry couple of days and nights surrounded by sealions."

He reckoned it was "better than goose".

Scavenging Turkey Vultures gather around a dead sheep.

Cassin's Peregrine Falcon

Female Cassin's Falcon at nest.

Peregrines concentrate the senses like attractive women. They are immediately interesting whether sitting as an intriguing silhouette on a distant buttress, flickering away from a fence post, or as a screaming, chattering speck in the sky. Years ago, while I drove a cut of sheep through "Strawberry Hill", one hung hawking over the flock's fore-end, picking off finches as they flew up from the grass, disturbed by advancing hooves. Three times the falcon fell, on each occasion taking a victim from the air to pluck and eat on a trackside balsam bog.

At Fox Bay I had a young tiercel called Fred, and carried him about on a home-made gauntlet of boot leather, hoping he would bag a goose for Sunday lunch. By day he sat on a post with jesses and a hood made from a red leather mini-skirt my wife wouldn't wear. One afternoon he escaped and I received a blunt message from a neighbour five miles away. "That bird of yours is on my hen house." We brought him back in a Land Rover. Along the track someone got out to open a gate, slamming the door because the catch didn't work very well. Fred's talons tightened in a minute-long embrace, piercing both the gauntlet and my hand inside like butter. The following week he escaped again, but this time I let him go. He returned just once, exactly a year later to the day and briefly sat on our chimney pot, but after that I never saw him again.

We see falcons often on New Island, jousting amongst the clouds or dashing along the shoreline after duck or oystercatchers, though mainly they prey on the teeming prions. On a January afternoon I saw an eyass being taught to hunt. One of its parents took a freshly-dead prion up into the air, called, and dropped the body for the youngster to catch. He missed it and flew onto a gatepost, beak wide open, his panting clearly audible from where I stood six feet away.

Carancho

The resplendent but retiring Carancho is both resident and widespread though never common in the Islands. On the mainland of South America this subspecies ranges from Cape Horn to the Tropic of Capricorn, to be replaced further northwards by three other subspecies whose ranges extend to the southern United States. In Mexico, where it is the national bird, the aquiline features and brightly coloured head have earned it the name of the Mexican Eagle.

Continental Caranchos prefer arboreal nest sites but in the virtually treeless Falklands they use sea cliffs or inland bluffs. The nest is an untidy, often large and accumulative structure of twigs and bones lined with grass and wool. Two or three blotched, brick coloured eggs are laid in mid October. Chicks hatch out a month later and by Christmas successful youngsters will be flying.

Adults are shy and only at the nest is it possible to approach them. Sitting on a prominent rock or branch they repeatedly grate the alarm at intruders with a series of rich, raven-like croaks and a flamboyant toss of the head.

The Crested Caracara's diet includes invertebrates, rodents, nestlings and carrion. They will chase domestic chickens and readily kill young lambs, sometimes only for the eyes and tongue. Winter flocks up to thirty strong rake the turf like rooks for beetles and worms and one gang of 150 was seen at Roy Cove.

In 1908, following pressure from sheepfarmers, a bounty of two pence per beak was introduced by Government Ordinance and by the early 1970's it had risen to the princely sum of £1, although this figure was paid only by the private farms. However, the bounty had little effect on the wary hawk, which apparently proved a match for all but the very finest shots.

Johnny Rook

Young Johnny Rooks feeding on a dead lamb.

The swashbuckling Johnny Rook is noisy, sociable and extraordinarily tame. It is confined to the remoter parts of the Falklands and a few bleak Chilean coastal islands from 50° South down to Cape Horn and Diego Ramirez, often living around seal and seabird colonies. At New Island a flock of fifty, mainly youngsters, spend much of the year living off the large Gentoo penguin rookeries taking eggs, weaklings and excreta. A raucous crowd of them often gather on winter mornings outside our window at breakfast time waiting to be fed. We watch them squabble over scraps of mutton only an arm's length from our toast and tea.

As in the case of the Carancho, the Johnny Rook's beak was once worth tuppence but this more inquisitive hawk fell easy prey to bounty-hunters and was rapidly reduced. Since the 1920's it has been a protected species. The few hundred that live in the Islands today constitute an amusing, annoying and bloodthirsty band of rascals. I have watched them kill new-born lambs, peck out only the brains from goslings, pluck clean the mane of a horse and take out stitches from boat sails. In places they have become partially nocturnal, hunting night flying petrels as they return to their burrows at dusk. Sometimes they will follow people for a considerable distance with short flights and their jaunty, swaggering runs, picking up any interesting, unguarded objects. They specialise in watches and lens caps but will settle for taking the hat off your head. A few years back one of the little sods flew off with my cumbersome Russian binoculars and, from a few hundred feet, dropped them into the South Atlantic.

Carancho.

Johnny Rook.

Red-backed Buzzard

Adult female Red-backed Buzzard (right).

Fledgling buzzard eating a young pipit (far right).

Dark phase Red-backed Buzzard (female). As its Latin name, *Buteo polysoma*, suggests, this species occurs in different colour phases. However, adult females always have reddish-brown backs while the smaller males sport bluish-grey.

There is a ditch below East Bay House where Falkland Trout still run every September, as yet undisturbed by the larger, introduced Brown Trout which now dominates most suitable streams. One evening as I went down to fish, there was a loud 'quark' from a disturbed young Night Heron, rising with a sudden flap from under the bank at my unseen approach. From nowhere a pair of buzzards flew at him, low out of the sun like Spitfires, one after the other, forcing the fisher to land. Three times the flustered heron flew low from the ditch and each time the male attacked, with the more powerful female following in ten metres behind. Twice the youngster grounded and made defence behind a dagger beak and a frightened squawk. On the third attack the female hawk's talons grabbed the heron by the neck in mid-air and she carried it off over a salty creek. But the victim's weight was too great and together they lost height until, barely above the wavelets, the raptor released her grip and flew off, leaving the stunned heron to recover in the shallows.

Normally, buzzards take much smaller prey, hunting alone for small birds, insects, rodents and young rabbits, or eating carrion. They are a wide-ranging species, found throughout the Falklands and extensively in South America, north to the high Andes of Colombia. One of the reasons for their success is an ability to use different nest sites, from towering sea cliffs to coils of discarded fence wire. In 1977 I found a nest on the ground in the middle of a white grass flat, next to a telegraph pole which the adults used as a lookout. Pitching an old army bivouac tent nearby I left them alone for a few days before returning with camera and sleeping bag to spend the night. The picture on the opposite page was taken here after the cock bird, who did all the hunting, had brought back a fledgling pipit at first light.

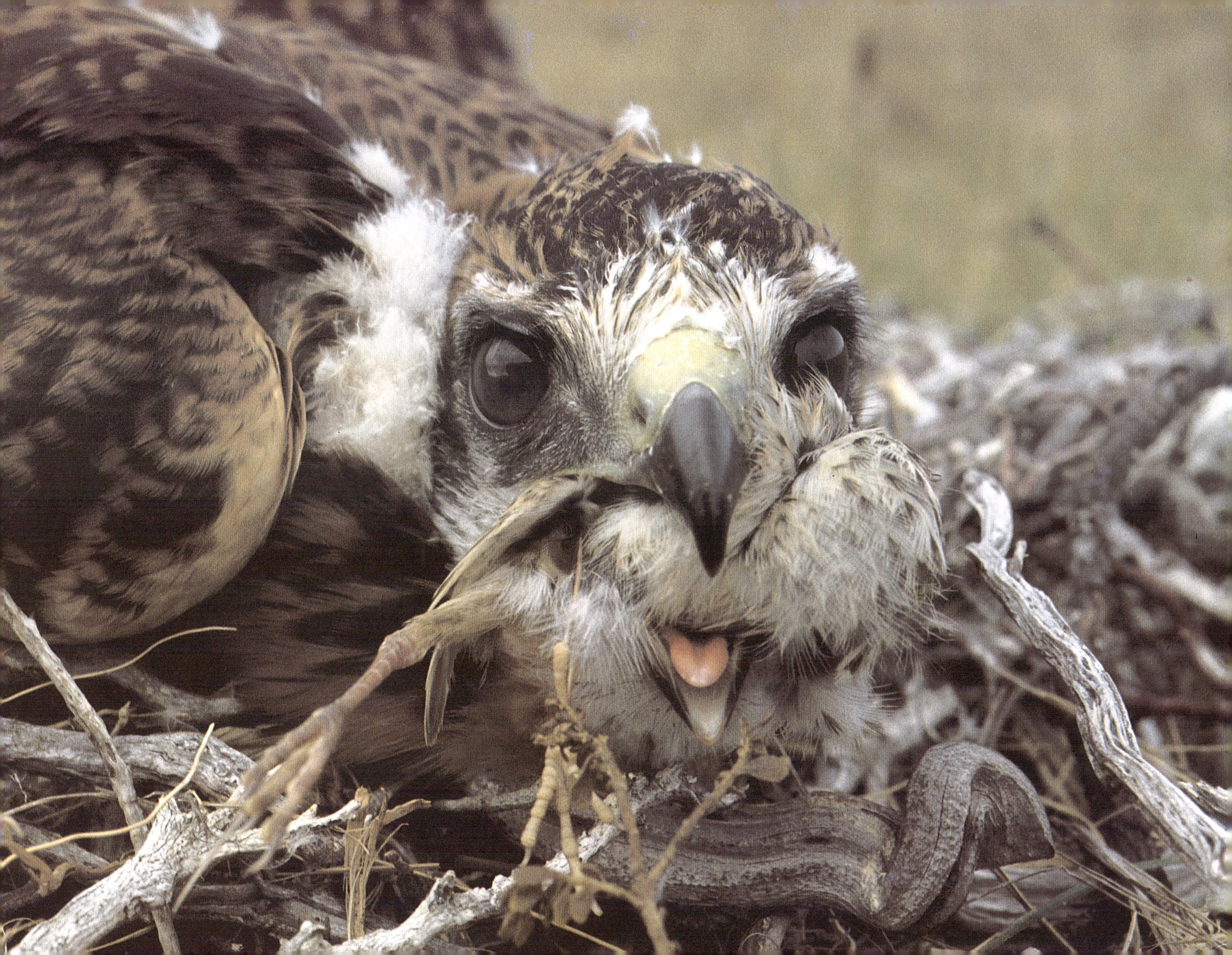

Songbirds

The Falkland Thrush readily nests in sheds and shanties (right).

The Falkland Pipit, springtime minstrel of the whitegrass plains.

Male Long-tailed Meadowlarks or Robins use fence posts, chimney pots or grass bogs as a stage for their strident and rasping territorial song.

Cobb's Wren hunts for shoreline insects amongst boulders and beachtop debris.

Black-chinned Siskins nesting in native boxwood, the largest native shrub.

5 SHIPS AND SHORELINES

The Jasons

The Jason Islands from the North-West.

Jason West Cay, the westernmost part of the archipelago. Mysteriously perched on the highest point of this tiny island is a section, measuring 60 ft by 25 ft, from an old wooden vessel. Some say it is from an Elizabethan pirate ship. Nobody really knows.

Grand Jason (nearest) and Steeple Jason from the South-East. Steeple hosts the world's largest rookeries of Black-browed Albatross (c. 166,000 pairs) and Rockhopper Penguins (c. 190,000 pairs) according to a survey in 1992/93.

The Jasons, a knobbly chain of reefstrewn, tide-ripped islands, stretch 40 miles beyond West Falkland north and west towards Patagonia. They poke out of the ocean like the giant vertebrae of a drowned sea monster, infested with seal, seabird and shipwreck. Outlying Grand and Steeple rise dramatically to 1000 feet, often capped by a blob of white cumulus, visible from twenty leagues, and were probably the first Falklands seen by man. 500 summers on they remain remote, seldom visited, and are owned by Richard Hill, a bird-breeder from the Cotswolds. Hill's late father, Len, bought the pair as a nature reserve for £5,500 in 1970 becoming a self-styled 'Penguin Millionaire'. Twenty years later I took Richard out there in the *Foam* from New Island across 40 unusually calm miles of ocean north to the exposed anchorage at the Grand. He wanted to install a telephone and collect penguin eggs to incubate, hatch and rear by hand in Gloucestershire. As we approached his islands, the wavetop air filled with scything wings of mollymauk and shearwater. Massed prions and stormy petrels fluttered like confetti in the orange evening. We dropped anchor at dusk in a northerly swell.

By dawn the wind was picking up, bringing in sharp squalls from the sou'west, and rolling down off the mountain at double speed, forming spray-whipping, spinning 'woolies'. Unable to land or leave we survived 48 hours of lousy stew and force nine stories.

"I've never been to a night club", I said innocently.

"Next time you're in London I'll show you one that'll make your hair stand on end", promised Richard with a wicked glint in his eye.

The anchor chain groaned as the boat heeled first one way, then the other. The gale whitened the sea and stunned the senses.

"I'm taking some of my king penguins to Hollywood," said Richard, "they're going to be in *Batman*

Returns". A bedraggled swallow, blown across from Chile, landed in the rigging. It disappeared into the fo'c'sle, found its way aft into the wheelhouse and perched on Richard's head. Later, when the birdman awoke from an afternoon nap, both wind and swallow had expired. So had our available time. We motored home to New Island, disappointed, having achieved nothing other than to join the ranks of past seamen who had taken on these moody outliers and lost.

From the late 18th century, itinerant sealers worked sporadically around the Jasons, leaving behind a few goats which later bred up on the Grand, but no-one ever lived here for long. The earliest resident, a 33-year-old sailor Peter de Clerck, arrived abruptly on the Grand just before dawn on 12th April 1858. His ship, the 1200 ton Belgian barque *Leopold* was bound for Callao with twenty men and a load of Welsh coal. Making about ten knots, while running before a dirty nor'easter, she struck hard against a steeply-shelving beach. Heavy seas worked over her, carrying away three boats and two men, who drowned attempting to swim ashore through the surf, each clenching a rope between his teeth. Legend has it that, as daylight came in, de Clerck, dressed only in an old shirt and a pair of drawers, was perched on the jiboom, furling a headsail, when the *Leopold* was poleaxed by a wave. He shot through the air like a rocket and landed in the tussac as the ship slid backwards and down with all hands. He searched the island, living on birds and seal and made a fire by rubbing a piece of wood with some rope for five hours. The smoke attracted Captain Smylie in his brigantine *Nancy* and de Clerck was found, rather deranged, after 23 days of solitude.

Stock were formally introduced by a Dane, Charles Hansen, who had arrived at Stanley in 1860 as one of a whaleboat crew forced to abandon their beaten and waterlogged ship near Cape St John. He leased Carcass Island, all the Jasons and several smaller islands in 1872. Charles taught himself navigation and using the schooner *Foam* based in Carcass, he gradually cleared the goats, by now several hundred strong, from the Grand, putting sheep there and on Steeple. To operate the Jasons under sail alone required guts, skill and a good boat. The Hansen family were to continue for over half a century.

As a young yacht, *Foam* had been sailed by Lord Dufferin to within 630 miles of the North Pole. In middle years she ran mails to Montevideo for the Falkland Government. Her days ended in fog on a rocky Carcass shore in 1890. A year later, returning from 'The Coast' in the heavily-laden *Result,* Charles fell overboard in heavy seas while taking a sight 50 miles west of New Island. With the schooner's dinghies full of cargo, and timber lashed on top, the crew looked on helplessly as mollys attacked the oilskinned figure. In twenty minutes he was gone.

The mantle of management eventually fell to his youngest son, Jason, who in 1910 bought the 36 ft *Golden Fleece,* built in Burnham-on-Crouch and the last working schooner without auxiliary power imported to the Islands.

Each season two, sometimes three, men would be dropped off from the 'Fleece' onto Grand or Steeple (both bought by Charles' widow, Sarah, in the late 1890's) along with dogs, stores and a fifteen foot open pulling boat called the *Queen.* They sheared and bagged the wool first on one island then, on a slack tide, rowed across the dangerous one-and-a-half mile channel to work the other. There are no safe anchorages on the Jasons so the little schooner would go back to Carcass, returning some weeks later during fine weather to pick them up.

In 1927, after a particularly hairy passage, caught out in a gale with men, dogs and woolclip on board, Hansen sold Grand and Steeple to Dean Brothers of Pebble. Using their own boat, Deans continued to run 2000 sheep there until it became uneconomic. The stock were slaughtered in 1968.

Jason Hansen passed away in 1952 aged 71 while driving his tractor on Carcass. The *Golden Fleece* outlived him by 38 years, slipping suddenly beneath the waves while under tow at night, five miles north of Salvador Waters in July 1990.

Charles Hansen.
(Photo courtesy Mrs Betty Miller)

Golden Fleece at Carcass Island, 1959.
(Photo courtesy Willy May)

Marooned

Scurvy Grass was used as an anti-scorbutic by early visitors to the Islands.

The adventures of the wooden-shipped whalemen of New England are preserved in chests of hairy tales and sprays of salty yarns, but few are as harrowing as the curious story of Charles H. Barnard.

In April 1812 Barnard was in New York preparing to command twelve men in an oaken sealing brig to procure oil and skins in the Falklands. On the eve of an embargo caused by impending hostilities between the Englands, Old and New, the *Nanina* quietly slipped out of harbour.

In September they dropped anchor in Hooker's Harbour, New Island, a familiar staging post amongst the close-knit whaling fraternity who would often rest and revictual here *en route* to the Southern Ocean or the Pacific. The crew turned to, preparing the ship for mooring and assembling a gaff-rigged sealing cutter, the *Young Nanina*, for use amongst the islands. They put ashore two sows and a boar as fresh food on the trotter and these joined the goats and cottontail rabbits already introduced by earlier foresighted sailors. For these fine harbours had been frequently used since the keels of Cape Cod and Nantucket first furrowed south to the Falklands in search of whale, 40 years earlier. During a summer of successful sealing, news reached Barnard from a passing American whaler that the expected conflict had indeed now broken out. He hastily re-rigged the brig and repaired to his secret anchorage of Four Island Lagoon on the Great Maloon, hoping to avoid the storms of war. From here, using the cutter, they continued to seek Fur, Hair and Elephant seal, occasionally nipping over to Swan or Beaver Islands where the ship's dog would hunt pigs for the pot.

In April 1813 while the *Young Nanina* lay in Fox Bay, they espied rising smoke to the south east. They made sail for Eagle Island and found 43 of the survivors from the wrecked *Isabella* which had come to grief by striking a reef in darkness nine weeks before. Although the people were English, Barnard offered assistance and a deal was struck whereby he would receive the wreck and in return give them passage in the *Nanina* to a mainland port. With winter approaching he returned in haste with some of the survivors to fetch the brig, quietly pondering over his new charges. For amongst the cast of mainly decent men, women and children he uneasily detected a roguish hardcore of thugs, sots and tarts.

By June they had moved the *Nanina* to New Island where they became temporarily storm bound. Although some of the Englishmen were anxious to return to their shipwrecked companions, Barnard elected to await better weather before returning to Eagle Island. One day, with four others, Barnard pulled across to Beaver for hogs as they were short of provisions, returning with some carcasses after dark. To their astonishment the brig had gone. They had been abandoned with no food, threadbare clothes, a dog and a 22 foot open whaleboat.

Angry and scared they set out for the wreck 80 miles away using Barnard's knowledge of the channels and short cuts to avoid the open sea. But, without a compass and with hunger-wracked bodies and cold-numbed minds, they became hopelessly lost. His companions were Jacob Green, an experienced black whaleman, and three Englishmen, James Louder, Joseph Albrook and Sam Ansel, an illiterate London bully. For a month they barely survived in the snow on a diet of seal, johnny rooks and "tushook" roots. Barnard eventually got his bearings, and once more tried to reach the wreck, but failed.

Somehow they made it through to the spring and, now clad in suits of seal skin, returned to New Island in case a ship should pass, and to collect mollymauk eggs. One day, without warning and under the tyrannical rule of Ansel, the others sailed off, leaving Barnard marooned and alone.

Heavy hearted, he sat down to contemplate. Eight years before he was disowned by his fellow Quakers. He had now been twice deserted within six months. They had taken everything – clothes, tools, dog and boat.

He plodded on alone, discovering flints to make fire, peat to burn and building a small stone shelter. After two months of spirit-sagging solitude, his shamefaced and remorseful companions returned from Eagle Island where they had found the wreck abandoned, the survivors' camp deserted and only traces of the departed *Nanina*.

The obnoxious Ansel, continuing to intimidate the others, was then brought up short by being himself marooned, on Swan Island, for seven weeks. Thereafter, for a year, the five men lived as best they could, never straying far except to make one scavenging trip to the wreck and occasional short excursions for pork, seal or driftwood.

Barnard kept a log book using the skins of sea elephant pups as parchment, and taught the now tame Ansel to read. They extended their stone hut, learned to snare geese and slept in feather-filled seal skin sacks. They made knives of barrel hoops and spoons from clamshells, and the entertaining Louder sang and played tunes on a small bone flute, probably made from the wing of an albatross.

Then, one chilly November morning, while Barnard, Allbrook and Louder were away on neighbouring Swan Island collecting the medicinal gum of hilltop balsam bogs, they were transfixed by the sight of two white specks on the horizon. Joining hands, their eyes filled with tears. They watched spellbound as two English whalers approached and anchored in Ship Harbour, New Island. Barnard put on his best, a sleeveless and tailless checked shirt, and the three pulled like men possessed across the seven miles of open sea, joining the other two bearded, stinking and skin-clad castaways on board *Indispensible*.

Two years later, following further adventures in Peru, China and on Robinson Crusoe's Island, a bankrupt Barnard arrived home in Hudson to his wife and three children.

NOTE
This is a précis of C. H. Barnard's own narrative. I have used his own place names although some have long since disappeared from common usage. These are Swan Island (Weddell Island); Four Island Lagoon (Double Creek); the Great Maloon (West Falkland); Hooker's Harbour (Tigre or Settlement Harbour, New Island); and Eagle Island (Speedwell Island).

Whilst these events undoubtedly took place, Barnard did not publish his account of them until 1829, thirteen years after he arrived home and there is some doubt as to the reliability of his version. For example, while he consistently put himself forward as a fair-minded, honest and Christian leader, others claimed he was an unreasonable and violent bully who had driven his crew close to mutiny.

The passengers and crew of *Isabella*, wrecked on 8th February 1813, were eventually rescued by the Royal Navy who arrived on 17th May after seven of the castaways had made an astonishing, five week long voyage to Buenos Aires, in a partially-decked, seventeen foot longboat, in order to raise the alarm.

The *Nanina* was arrested by the British when she arrived at Eagle Island on 16th June, becoming a war prize, and was taken to England.

Prior to departure from the Falklands, on 27th July, Lt. D'Aranda, *HMB Nancy*, organised a brief search for Barnard and his four companions (three of whom were English and part of *Isabella's* original complement) who they thought to be stranded on or near New Island. They found no sign of the men or their boat.

The full story of these singular events, set as they were against a backdrop of war between Great Britain and the United States, will forever remain partly shrouded in mystery.

Hooker's Harbour, now known as Tigre or the Settlement Harbour, New Island, where Barnard and his companions were marooned in 1813. Beyond are the hills of Weddel and Beaver Islands. The site of Barnard's small shelter is unclear but possibly that now occupied by a large, ruined stone building, at the head of the bay, built sometime after 1860 for sheep work and storage of wool and skins, tallow, penguin oil and guano.

Cottontail Rabbits were introduced to New Island, where they still flourish, by New England sealers in the late eighteenth century. They are found nowhere else in the Islands.

Whaling

A watershed in the fortunes of the mighty rorqual whales was marked in 1864 by the experiments of a wealthy and innovative 55-year-old Norseman, Sven Foyn. Mounted in the bows of the ex-sealer's new and revolutionary whaling schooner were seven trial harpoon guns. With the very first shot the harpoon line coiled around the old chap's leg and he flew over the side and nearly drowned but eventually the equipment was perfected. The speed and manoeuverability of these steam catchers, accuracy of their guns and potency of the exploding harpoon heads, plus new 'inflation lances' to keep the dead whales afloat, rendered rorquals at last within the whalemen's grasp. Thus armed with Foyn inventions, the Norwegians rapidly depleted northern whale stocks and, as the century turned, their catchers were steaming southward.

Alexander Lange from Sandefjord obtained the first Falkland licence and operated out of New Island in 1905-1906. With ss *Admiralen* as factory/store ship and two catchers, *Hanken* and *Ornen*, he managed a haul of 125 mainly sei whale. This novel industry inevitably attracted visitors, the Governor and the Dean among them. There was also a travelling teacher, James Wilson, soon to become the first Magistrate/Postmaster/Coroner/Customs Officer/Policeman/Jailer in South Georgia, who left us this description from October 1906:

"We were being conveyed back to the settlement (New Island) in one of the Norwegian Steam Whalers when the eagle eye of the shooter, who was at the wheel, discerned the blow of a whale outside the harbour. With a broad grin he shouted his orders. At once ropes and winches were got in readiness, the course of the ship was altered and away we went at full speed. On clearing the harbour not only did we see one but several whales. The shooter at this stage left the wheel in the hands of the second mate and went forward to stand by the harpoon gun. After some manoeuvering we got within twenty yards of our quarry. With a loud report the harpoon flew through the air, striking its victim below the great fin. The whale dived at once. Engines were stopped and rope allowed to run freely. After running out something like 100 fathoms the whale came up ahead but this time a red spout shot in the air which told us it was badly hit. The running of the line was at once stopped, engines reversed and the whale was gradually drawn alongside. As he still showed signs of liveliness another harpoon was fired deep into the body. After a futile attempt to dive, the whale gave a convulsive shudder and turned over quite dead. Our prize (a fin whale), which was about 60 feet long, was firmly lashed to the side of the ship and with considerable speed we steamed back into the harbour."

The initially illegal successes of Captain Larsen, the king of modern whaling, at Grytviken from 1904, sparked

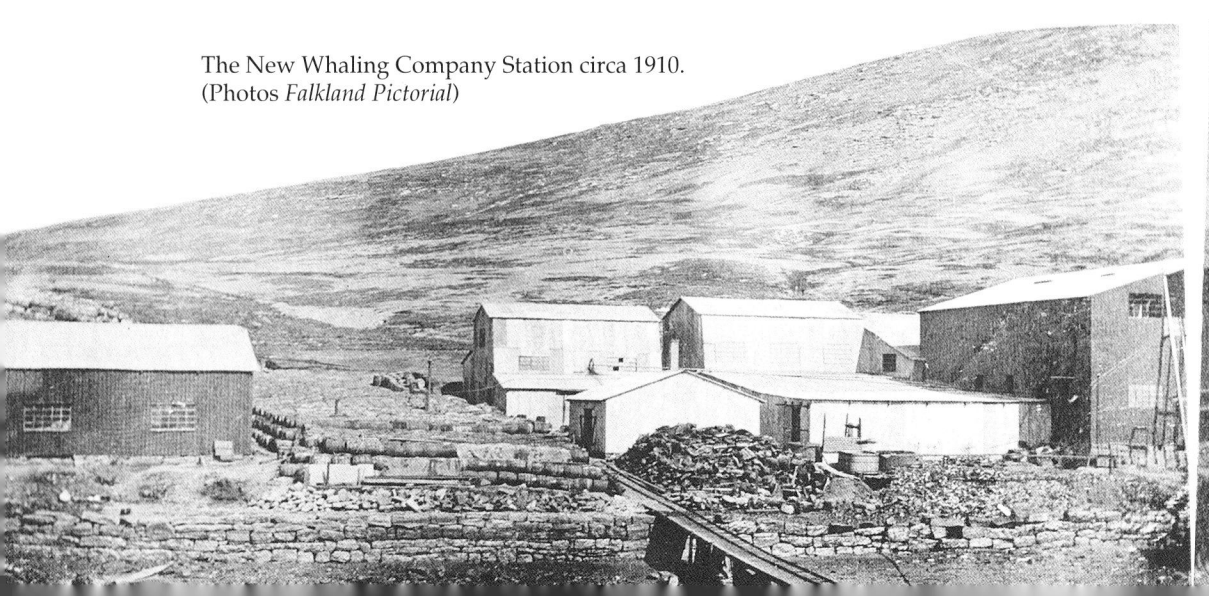

The New Whaling Company Station circa 1910. (Photos *Falkland Pictorial*)

A whale's scapula lies amidst the rusting remains of machine tools, winches and boilers (left).

Lambs grazing above the ruins of the whaling station.

a scramble for licences to join the whaling 'gold rush' in South Georgia. However, by 1907, Governor Allardyce had already issued three licences and, wary of over-exploitation, the enlightened Governor rejected an application from Larsen's great rival, Salvesens of Leith. Following Allardyce's alternative suggestion to establish an operation in the Falklands, Salvesen purchased, dismantled and shipped out a second-hand Icelandic station in the supply ship *Coronda*. With 60 men under Henrich Hendricksen, she arrived on Christmas Eve 1908 at New Island, a quiet and remote island sheep farm occupied by two recently-bereaved widows with their eight daughters and a single labourer, George Scott.

Hendricksen immediately set about levelling, laying on water and building at the 30-acre site in South Harbour, leased for 30 years from Fanny Cull, the farmer. On 16th January 1909 Gunner Edmund Paulsen opened the New Whaling Company account, harpooning the first whale from the steam whaler *Swona*. Throughout the eight seasons of operation Salvesen's provided the Falklands' community with a much-needed inter-island mail and passenger service using at first the 90 ft catchers, which were capable of up to twelve knots, and later an old rust bucket called *RMS Columbus*. New Island became a relatively busy port with its own post office and customs officer. The Lord Bishop arrived with his entourage to consecrate the cemetery, a world-rounding yacht was towed in for repairs and ships arrived to have their bottoms scrubbed.

By 1916, 1½ million gallons of oil had been sent to Scotland to make margarine, soap and bombs. Meat and bone residues were dried and ground to powder and 15,000 bags of it exported as 'guano' for fertiliser.

However the income was totally eclipsed by that

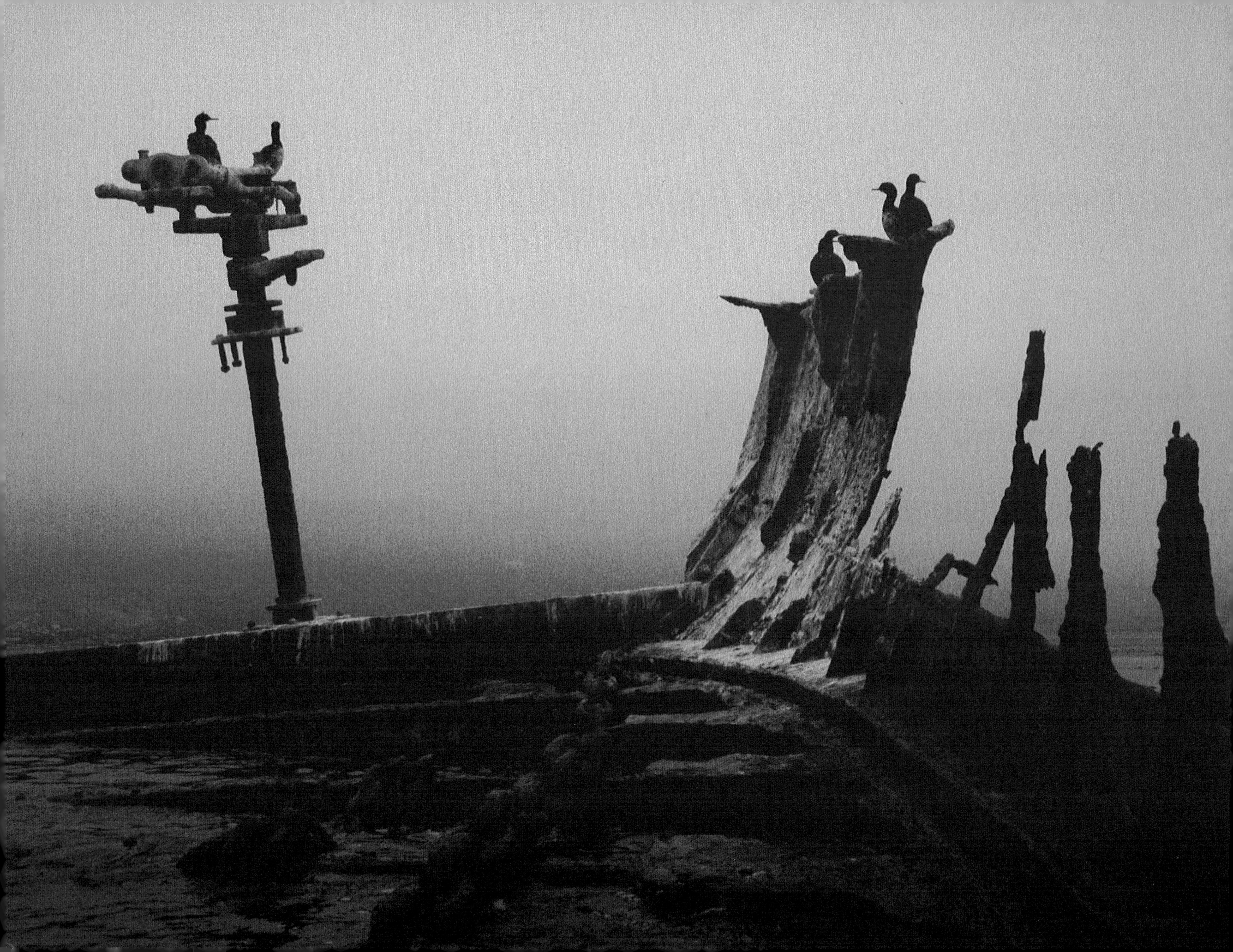

Glengowan

Flensing whale on the plan at New Island, *Glengowan* lies beyond (left).

Roosting shags aboard the *Glengowan* (far left).

Glengowan dawn

from Salvesen's other shore station at Leith Harbour which had been established in 1909 and was ten times as profitable. So in October 1916 the New Whaling Company station was closed, dismantled and shipped to South Georgia. The post office closed in 1917 and the remote tranquility of a pastoral existence returned to New Island.

I saw fin whales for the first time on a quiet grey March morning in 1990, one about 60 feet long, the other considerably smaller, perhaps a cow and calf. They cruised about the harbour in front of our house for several hours, occasionally surfacing to issue tall straight blows like yacht's masts and passing close inshore through South Harbour where time has turned the slaughter, sweat and stench of the station to a romantic memory. The rusting bedsteads, lathes and boilers are now overgrown with yellow-flowered sea cabbage. Sheep graze amongst giant skulls, bits of baleen and bleached and crumbling vertebrae, and the whalemen's graves lie untended and undermined by rabbits and petrels.

Salvesens ceased whaling a quarter century ago. Today they light pop concerts, sell oil booms to the Arabs and supply baleenless corsets to Marks & Spencer (1991).

The *Glengowan* was built of steel in Glasgow in 1895, having a displacement of 1801 tons. On 15th October she sailed on her maiden voyage from Swansea with a crew of 28 and a cargo of anthracite, coal and coke, bound for San Francisco via Cape Horn. By 15th December, a few miles south west of West Falkland, her cargo became dangerously overheated. Captain Doughty altered course for Stanley, anchoring in Port William two days later. The following day flames burst through the main hatch and surveyors recommended scuttling. She was driven under full sail onto the beach at Whalebone Cove, remaining there as a burnt out hulk for over a decade.

In 1910 she was purchased by the New Whaling Company, towed to New Island and used as a storage vessel until whaling operations ceased. Eventually, breaking her moorings in a southerly gale, she fetched up on the rocky shoreline where her remains now rest near the present day settlement.

Penelope

The late afternoon wind veered north easterly, increasing rapidly to 40 knots as ak *Penelope* motored up Brenton Loch from Camilla Creek. John Ferguson, the skipper, decided to anchor in a small bay under Cantera, a deserted outside shepherd's house with stone walls and a rusty red roof. On deck were 98 cashmere goats bound for Pebble Island 50 miles away, including five lecherous billies tethered by their horns to the bulwarks.

"Goats don't like getting wet", said John, as short waves slapped into the bow, sending spray over the animals. "Better wait here 'till the wind eases a bit."

His father, Bob, disappeared down the forward companionway, fed sawn-up logs to the Rayburn, and soon knocked up a delicious mutton stew with 'compo' potatoes, leftover tomatoes and a dash of Lea and Perrins. After supper we talked boats and goats while every now and then a brown-faced nanny stuck her head through the double doors above to peer down inquisitively into the fo'c'sle and shed a few hairs into the stewpot below.

The sixteen metre auxiliary ketch *Penelope* was built in Büsum, North Germany, for Dr Gunther Pluschow, a First World War flying ace, and was especially strengthened to withstand heavy seas using 40 cubic metres of carefully selected oak and extra thick glass. She was launched on 22nd November 1927.

The following year Pluschow sailed her south on a voyage of exploration and survey to Tierra del Fuego after which she had been named *Feuerland*. With him were five men, 1.5 nautical miles of unexposed cine film, a tiny, rapid-assembly Heinkel float plane, and his wife for good luck and to help maintain table manners.

Once in Fireland Herr Doktor completed a film and a book, both entitled *Voyage into Wonderland*, before falling out of his plane while photographing near Bariloche. The Germans built a monument to remember where he landed.

Feuerland was subsequently sold to John Hamilton who owned farming properties in Patagonia and the Falklands, including Weddell Island where she was to be based.

She arrived in Fox Bay in March 1929, a month after Pluschow's death, and was subsequently renamed after her new owner's daughter, Penelope.

For many years *Penelope* plied around the islands and across to the coast under Captain Schmidt, sometimes bringing over exotic animals for the eccentric Hamilton. Patagonian foxes today flourish on several western islands following their introduction in the 30's. Guanaco also thrive although only on Staats Island, and Fuegian otters may or may not have survived but his skunks, parrots, ibis and rheas have since vanished without trace.

Following World War II, *Penelope* was sold and has since had several owners and many jobs in addition to regular stock and cargo-carrying. When Government opened the first R/T service in 1950 she was used to transport twenty Berry twelve volt transceivers or 'Black Boxes' to isolated settlements. In the 60's she was a sealer, briefly; in the 70's a crabber, experimentally; and in the early 80's joined the Argentine Navy, temporarily. The Argies painted her black and she went to Fox Bay and was shot through the boom by a Harrier but not before Finlay Ferguson, her skipper for nineteen years, had used her to evacuate boarding school children home from Stanley to West Falkland.

In 1989 the *Penelope* returned to her first Falkland base at Weddell Island where boat and farm now belong to John and Bob Ferguson. She is still strong and sound, but these days her old decks leak a little after decades of shifting sheep with their trampling hooves and caustic urine.

Throughout the night, as we lay at anchor under Cantera, the gale continuing to howl and, with regular rain squalls lashing down, occasional drips found their way down onto my bunk. By morning the wind and rain had died and John was keen to move. Stock don't do well if they remain too long on boats and besides, smelly goat hairs were rapidly appearing everywhere – in teacups, turn-ups and sleeping bags. At first light the goat boat was again under weigh and, after lunching in White Rock Bay, we caught the strong rising tide through Tamar Pass

Skipper John Ferguson prepares a Sunday morning breakfast of mutton chops in the Falkland Sound.

and offloaded the stock onto Pebble Island jetty at dusk. (March 1992.)

NOTE
These goats were part of an experimental flock of 66 cashmere goats originally imported from Scotland to Goose Green in February 1991, the first fibre-producing goats brought into the Colony.

Bob and John Ferguson load mutton sheep onto ak *Penelope* at New Island (above).

Young guanaco on Staats Island (top right).

"Feuerland" shortly after launching in Büsum, Germany 1927 (centre, right). (Photo courtesy Deutches Schiffahrtsmuseum)

Anchor's up, signals Bob Ferguson, as we leave Cantera. Netting was hung around the bulwarks to prevent goats jumping overboard (bottom right).

Jhelum and Capricorn

The *Jhelum*, a 428 ton, three-masted, wooden barque was launched in Liverpool in 1849. Following her maiden voyage to Bombay she plied chiefly between Europe and South America. Outwardbound she would carry around 650 tons of general cargo, returning with either guano, nitrates or copper for the European market.

The guano came chiefly from the small, rainless Chincha and Guanape Islands off the Peruvian coast where millions of Guanay cormorants had been found nesting by Louis Antoine de Bougainville (the founder of Port Louis) in 1767. After the first small shipment was imported into Britain in 1839 it soon became fashionable amongst progressive farmers as an agricultural fertiliser. Vast amounts were excavated by convicts, trucked down jetties, loaded onto lighters and transferred into vessels sailing by way of Cape Horn to various euroports. It was a most unpleasant cargo; injurious to crews' health, corrosive to ships' ironwork and rotting to sails and rigging. Only watertight ships were deemed suitable as guano was very susceptible to damp. Prior to loading, holds were whitewashed and layered with dunnage and during the voyage they were vented to release fumes.

Thus laden, *Jhelum*, under command of Devonshire captain, J.L.C. Beaglehole, and with a crew complaining of the ship's unseaworthiness, set sail for the final time from Callao. After experiencing stormy seas around 'Cape Stiff' she put into Stanley in distress 37 days later on 18th August 1870, leaking and unfit to proceed, and was subsequently condemned. Today she sits at the head of the rickety Packe's Jetty opposite Sulivan House in Stanley.

A short distance to the westward lie the bones of the *Capricorn*, a smaller barque of 390 tons built in Swansea for the copper ore trade in 1859. En route from her home port in 1882 her outward cargo of coal ignited in heavy weather off the Horn. The master sailed her to Staten Island, where she was scuttled in shallow water to dowse the blaze then pumped out, refloated and taken to Stanley. She was condemned as unseaworthy and later used variously as a lighter, storage hulk and finally a jetty head for the military garrison during the Second World War. *Capricorn* was stripped for firewood in the late 1940's.

Jhelum (left).

Capricorn lies opposite the western end of Stanley (right).

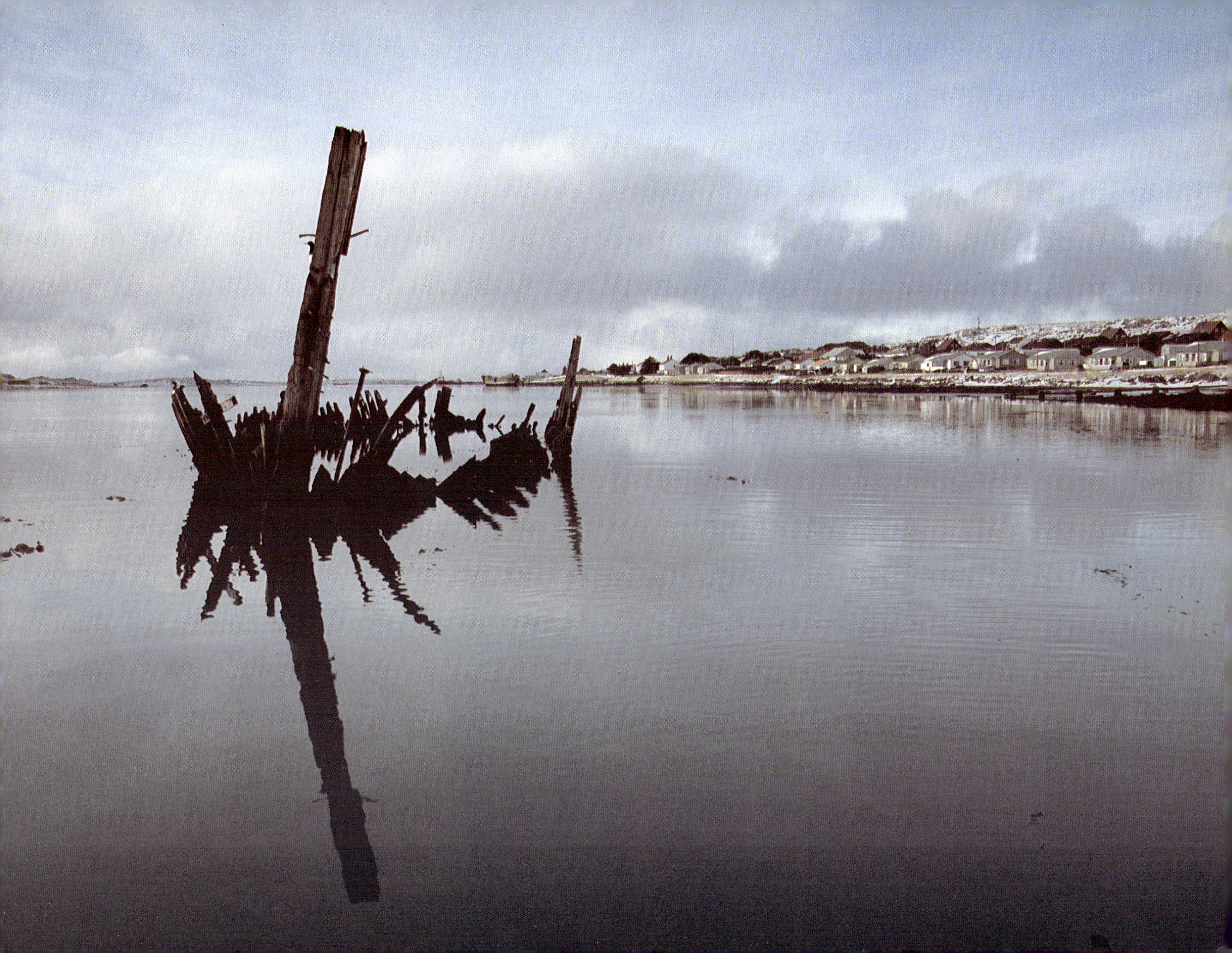

John Biscoe

Festooned with flags, *RRS John Biscoe* bid a final farewell to her home port of Stanley on 6th April 1991 after 35 years as an Antarctic research and supply vessel. The 'Biscoe' was built in 1956 in Glasgow as an ice-strengthened cargo ship although her main role in later years was as a research support vessel. On her maiden Antarctic season, 1956/57, she carried HRH The Duke of Edinburgh to some of the scientific bases. During her penultimate trip in 1989/90, she brought back an old fossil, a 70 million-year-old bird-hipped dinosaur from James Ross Island.

To an eleven gun salute and under command of Malcolm Phelps, her captain for eighteen years, she passed along Stanley's seafront releasing flares and balloons before going out through the Narrows accompanied by a flotilla of local launches.

The 'Biscoe' was replaced the following season by a new, multi-purpose logistic vessel, *James Clark Ross*, under command of Captain Chris Elliot.

RRS John Biscoe.

HRH The Duke of Edinburgh inspects the Stanley Boys Brigade on his arrival in the Colony on 6th January 1957. It was the first Royal visit since 1871. Following his trip to the Antarctic on *RRS John Biscoe*, Prince Philip had sailed to the Falklands on board *HMY Brittannia*. (Photo courtesy Mrs Grace Goss)

Copious

my Copious, a heavily-built wooden vessel of 49 tons, was built in Scotland as a fishing boat, but later converted for passengers. 70 feet long, gaily painted red and white and well-ballasted with Gordon's Gin, she was under charter for a season to 'Penguin Shipping Ltd.' to transport tourists around the western isles. It was a novel idea causing a larger-than-usual ripple of interest along drinking-room counters. She arrived in Stanley in November 1980, seven weeks out from home on the Hamble. But the accommodation was as yet unfinished and for days the sound of hammering and smell of sawdust greeted numerous curious visitors to the boat. By December no customers had appeared so *Copious* departed for the west on a 'recce trip' and on the third night anchored at Carcass Island. There were five on board plus myself as the naturalist guide, barkeeper and chief sandwich-maker.

"You might have to be careful if the wind comes into the south", said farmer, Rob McGill, thoughtfully, sitting in the ship's saloon. He had lived amongst boats and little islands all his life and owned Carcass. "You know, Tone", he said, "that chain looks awfully light to me for a boat of her size and er . . . what size anchor did you say she has?"

But skipper, Mike Tuson, a retired English bank manager, was confident that his boat's 'fisherman anchor' would afford him a good night's sleep in the bay. The McGills departed shorewards shortly before midnight, disappearing into the darkness in a dinghy with Rob still worrying about southerlies and the weight of tackle on the seabed.

At first light we awoke to an ominous thump. Six underpanted, bleary-eyed figures shot out of their bunks. The sun was rising, tide falling, wind southerly and *Copious* was stuck fast on a ridge of rock in Carcass Harbour.

Fortunately we got her off unharmed on the following tide but the whole project was continuously crippled for the rest of that summer by bad luck, bad management and a scarcity of bird watchers.

In addition, all air movements to and from the Islands were then via Argentina and the Argentines refused to co-operate with flight bookings unless they had a stake in 'Penguin Shipping'. Permission for this was understandably refused by Falkland councillors.

Copious returned to England, accommodation still unfinished, in February 1981. Tagged 'another disaster' she had cost Falkland Islands Government £23,000 and attracted just one overseas tourist, an elderly widow from Bournemouth.

The ship never came back to the Falklands. In 1988, after hitting a rock off Spitzbergen, she sank.

5.0 am December 1980. *my Copious* lies alongside Stanley's Public Jetty. Beyond in centre harbour, and tied together at anchor, are the Royal Research Ships *Bransfield* and *John Biscoe*.

Gentoo

The Canâche is a land-locked lagoon at the eastern end of Stanley harbour where square-rigged cargo ships were once beached for cleaning and repair. Lying there now, like a pair of ugly sisters, are the corpses of two drab North Sea drifters, *Golden Chance* and *Gentoo*.

The 55 ton *Gentoo* was built in 1921 and used to fish for herring before being bought by Dean Brothers, then as now owners of Pebble Island. At that time Deans also owned Grand and Steeple Jason, Keppel, Golding, East and various smaller islands, altogether running 22,000 sheep. Prior to sailing to the Falklands, the *Gentoo* was extensively altered in England for sheep-shifting. She arrived in Stanley via Rio in February 1927.

Bill Goss was the ship's mate in the early thirties. "We used to shift 6000, mainly young sheep, around the islands each season. They'd come out to the ship in a scow, up on deck by a race, and slide below down a chute – they don't like going down hill, of course. There was a raised layer of gratings in the hold so we could get more in, as she was narrow and deep. We'd put 100 sheep down below in four pens and about 150 on deck. When it came to get them out, the slide was turned over. It had slats on the other side so they didn't loose their footing."

Gentoo was the first local vessel to be equipped with a radio transmitter so that the crew could keep in touch with Jim Peck Betts, the Island's earliest radio ham, who had begun operating on Pebble Island in 1925. This link was particularly valuable when working the remote and dangerous Jason Islands. Jim's set worked on 32 volts supplied by a turbine. This in turn was wind driven by a twelve feet diameter aircraft propeller fixed up on a post. On board ship, Sturdee Betts, wedged in between a wash basin and a table, sat on the 'power pack', steadily cranking a handle with his left hand, for power, while tapping out morse signals with his right.

Gentoo ran cargo for over 30 years before being replaced at Pebble by the *mfv Malvinas*. The old steam drifter was sold in 1965 for £500, taken into Stanley and variously used to shift sheep and beef carcasses to town.

In the late sixties Bill 'Becket' Hills hatched up a plan to retrieve some treasures which, by legend, lay in shipwrecks in the Falkland Sound. In 1867, the 484 ton *Coquimbana* had left Valparaiso bound for Bristol loaded with copper ingots and barley, only to come to grief in the shallows at Tyssen Patch. Eighteen years later, the Italian barque *Luigi Y*, while carrying statuary to Chile from Genoa, had similarly taken up permanent residence on the ocean floor near Ruggles Island.

Bill and his mates, Bob Ross and 'Underwater' Fred Hetherington, formed the 'South Atlantic Salvage Company', purchased the *Gentoo* as flagship, and set a course for Tyssen Patch. But… someone had got there first and the ingots had gone. A few miles to the south, protected by a jungle of kelp, the *Luigi Y* yielded only a fresco of the Last Supper and that was scattered in a thousand marble pieces across the seabed.

Gentoo spent her sunset years swinging on a mooring in Stanley harbour. In 1980 she was bought by retired pilot, Dave Emsley, as a houseboat. He took her down to the Canâche but before he could move in, we were invaded. During the occupation she mysteriously ran aground nearby, rolled over on her side with the ebbing tide and filled with water. There she has remained ever since.

The *Gentoo* (top left).

Hussy being lifted out of the *Gentoo* at Grave Cove, 4th April 1936. (Photo Mrs Kitty Bertrand)

Jiggers

The Taiwanese *Chieh Man 1* thumps through the Narrows dribbling rust, smoking diesel and bedecked with lights, lines and scaffolding like a floating fun fair. Her 758 tons, 92 jigs and 21 men are typical of the migratory fleet of Far Eastern jiggers which gather here each autumn harvesting the Argentine Short-finned Squid. *Illex argentinus* is the most important resource amongst the vast and only recently-exploited biomass of saleable Falkland seafoods which overnight have caused a tenfold boom in a previously hungry and woolblind economy. *Illex* live for just one year, migrating southwards into the area from late summer and reaching a peak weight before disappearing by June, to spawn and die.

At night they are fatally drawn towards prowling jigger packs by massed lights so intense that they can illuminate the sky for 60 miles. The swarming squid, caught by barb-less hooks along jerking jig lines, are frozen alive into blocks bound for the Orient. They re-appear in restaurants as disembowelled tubes of grainless white flesh; eaten raw in Osaka, sauteed in Taipei, with chips in Sydney or stuffed in Singapore.

200,000 metric tons of *Illex* are caught here each year, half the total Falkland fisheries catch. Another smaller squid, *Loligo gahi*, and various finfish comprise the rest, trawled mainly by Spaniards and Poles for the European market.

Fishing within the surrounding 70,000 square miles of ocean, declared as an economic exclusion zone by Whitehall in 1986, is tightly controlled using patrol ships, surveillance aircraft and seagoing scientific observers. For the privilege of operating within the zone, a restricted number of around 200 vessels annually pay the Falkland Islands Government a total £25m in licence fees.

Chieh Man 1

The lights and jigs of *Hamazen Maru 58*, a typical Japanese jigger.

Horse Block and *Foam*

A remarkable and well-known marine landmark, which lies a mile to the south-west of Pillar Bluff, Weddell Island, the Horse Block is 67 metres high and from certain angles appears not so much as a horse, but more like a Scottie dog. Close to, it can be seen to have four 'legs' and the possibility of going through in a dinghy has often been discussed by daring seafarers. However, conditions are seldom favourable due to the oceanic swell. This is apparent here, although there was little wind on the day we passed by in the *Foam* bound for New Island from Cape Lagoon.

Our 11.2 metre auxiliary ketch *Foam* was built in Aage Walstead's famous boatyard in Thurø, Denmark, in 1958. Commissioned by Cecil Bertrand, she was the last small work-boat purpose-built for the Falklands. The *Foam* is built of oak on oak with pitch pine decking and mahogany deckhousings and carries over 500 feet of sail. She is beamy, at 3.5 metres with a large cargo hold amidships, draws 1.5 metres and displaces ten tons.

The Horse Block seen from the *Foam* (far right).

Loading sheep on the *Foam*. We carried 30 down below and 32 more on deck from New Island across ten miles to Weddell (right).
(Photo Annie Chater)

Beefeater II

Chay Blyth departed Port Stanley on 2nd November 1984 in his five-ton trimaran *Beefeater II*. He was trying to better the record of 89 days 21 hours set by Josiah Creesy in his clipper ship *Flying Cloud*, sailing from New York to San Francisco at the end of the last century.

A week later Blyth and his shipmate, Eric Blum, were picked up by the Chilean Navy after sitting for 27 hours on the upturned hull in 'once-only' suits off Cape Horn. They had been knocked over by a huge beam wave, sawn their way out through the boat's bottom and were located thanks to the vessel's automatic distress signal.

Some time later, *Beefeater II* was spotted at sea from a Hercules, still upside down and floating eastwards past the Islands. She was never seen again.

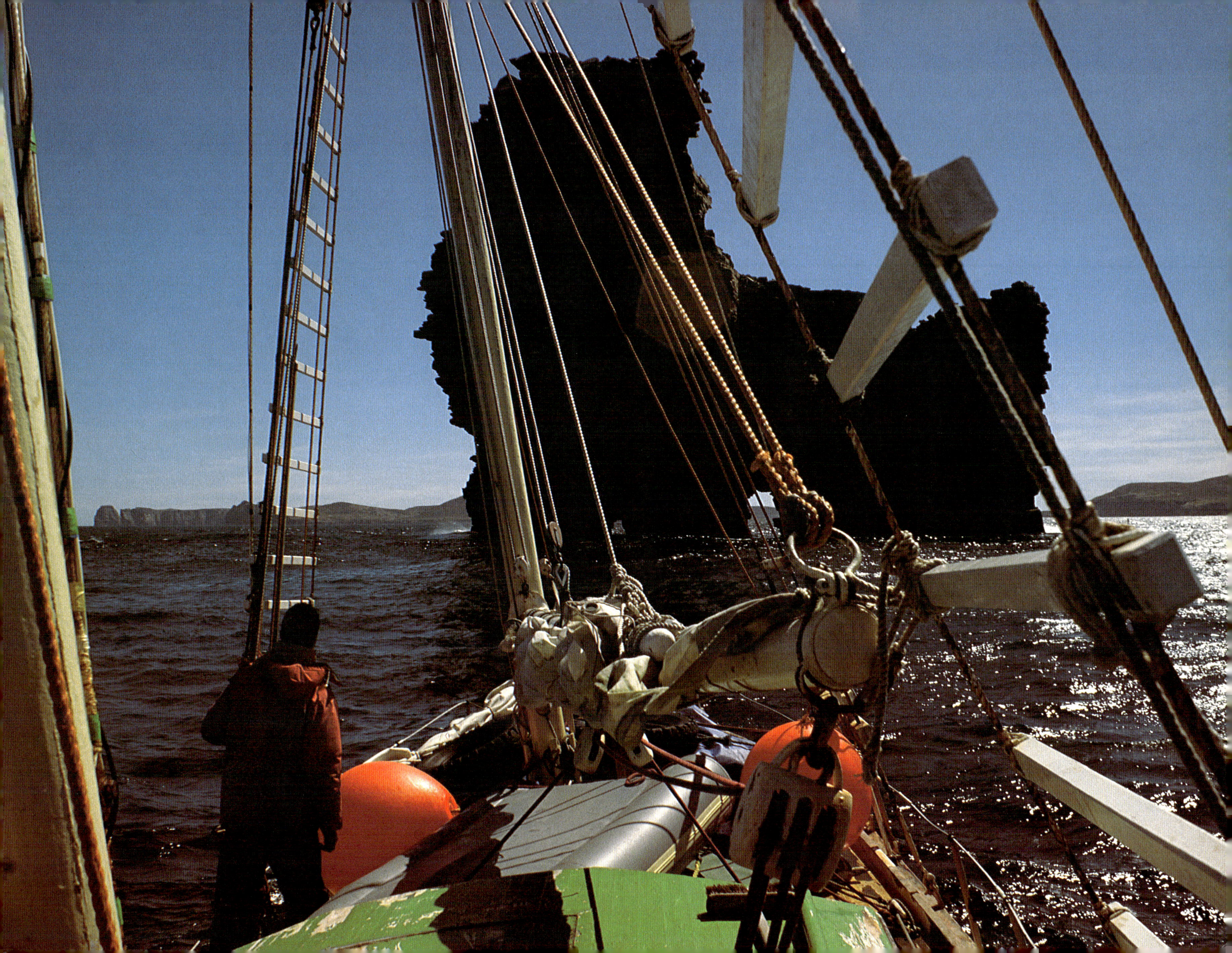

Lady Elizabeth and Samson

The 'Lady Liz' sits cradled in sand at Whalebone Cove, a dark silhouette seen from town, a stranded red carcase from above. Amongst Stanley's assortment of dead sailing ships, she alone retains her masts and grandeur. The others require imagination and a romantic eye to transform them from discarded junk into clippers, barques or brigs.

The 223 ft *Lady Elizabeth* was built of iron in Sunderland in 1879. She made several visits to the Falklands and during one, in 1889, brought bricks and cement for the new cathedral and wood for the Tabernacle.

In December 1912, under Captain Petersen, she sailed on her final passage with Oregon pine from Vancouver bound for Delagoa Bay in southern Mozambique. Severely battered by gales 300 miles southwest of Cape Horn, with her deck cargo and four men washed overboard, she put into Berkeley Sound on 12th March 1913. At the northern entrance she struck the Uranie Rock, was holed, and lost a section of keel. Three days later the barque was towed into Stanley by the tug *Samson*.

"We hear that she will be refitted … and will be able to continue her voyage", cheerfully announced the local

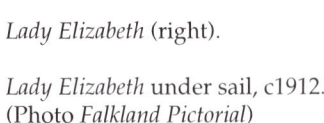

Lady Elizabeth (right).

Lady Elizabeth under sail, c1912.
(Photo *Falkland Pictorial*)

ss Samson in Stanley circa 1914 with passenger load of sailors. These men are probably from *HMS Cape of Good Hope* which visited town in mid-October 1914 and was sunk with all hands in the Battle of Coronel on 1st November.

newspaper. But the *Lady Elizabeth* never sailed again. Instead she was condemned and sold to the Falkland Islands Company, together with her valuable cargo, for a mere £3350. Her sails were cut up to cover calf pens at Darwin and she lay alongside the East Jetty as a timber warehouse for three years, thereafter spending a further twenty moored in the harbour as a storage hulk.

On 17th February 1936 she broke her moorings in a gale and drifted to her present position close to Stanley Airport.

Nine years later the 'Lady Liz' was once more joined by the *Samson* when the ageing steam tug broke adrift in the great gale of 1945, becoming a total loss on the beach nearby. The 94 ft *Samson*, built in Hull in 1888, was brought down by the Falkland Islands Company in 1900 following mariners' demands for a powerful tug in Stanley in the aftermath of the *City of Philadelphia* disaster.

Her value was shown in November 1912 after the PSNC liner *Oravia* had struck the Billy Rock near the entrance to Port William. At night and in heavy seas Captain Thomas took the *Samson* alongside the stricken vessel, disembarking over 150 passengers to safety.

But until she was converted into a lighter in 1924 her stock-in-trade was towing in an era when much of Stanley's shipping was still under sail. Her importance is shown in this edited extract from the *Falkland Islands Magazine and Church Paper*, January 1911:

> The *Wavertree*, a large vessel of 2100 tons, left Cardiff on 16th June 1910 for Talcahuna. When 58 days out she was about 200 miles south of Cape Horn, when a violent storm caused her to carry away all her sails. Being practically without canvas… she had to run back to Montevideo where she was refitted and left with practically a new crew.
>
> "At the beginning of December the ship encountered weather so severe that the mainmast snapped in two almost flush with the deck and smashed two lifeboats and the main pump. The wreckage tore holes in the deck, and through these a great volume of water poured into the lower parts of the ship. The water tanks were just under the damaged part of the deck and, through great carelessness on the part of the carpenter, had been left uncovered. Salt water, pouring down into the hold, filled these tanks so that the water become quite unsuitable for drinking purposes. The carpenter has sinced developed mental trouble and is under medical observation in Stanley gaol.
>
> "Five of the crew were endeavouring to make the deck watertight by covering the damaged parts by a sail when a heavy sea swept the men off their feet and dashed them against the wreckage that was everywhere strewing the deck. So violently were the men hurled that three had their legs broken and two ribs of another were fractured. The fore top gallant mast came down from aloft and did further damage to the deck while shortly afterwards the mizzen top-mast was carried away. The ship was now helpless and fortunately drifted towards the Falklands. She was towed in from near the lighthouse to Stanley on 24th December by the *Samson*."

ss Samson

Coastal Shipping

Since the time the earliest settlements, Kelpers have relied on the sea as their main highway. Today, although a simple road system is slowly snaking across East Falkland, the five hundred campers, most of whom live mainly on coastal sheep farms, still rely almost entirely on seaborne transportation of their woolcrops, fuel and supplies. For two decades these cargoes have been shipped to and from the camp and Stanley by two coastal vessels, mv Monsunen and mv Forrest.

Danish built in 1957, the 230 ton Monsunen arrived from Gravesend in September 1972 to become the backbone of Coastal Shipping Limited. For twenty years she visited each of the 43 scattered, sometimes tiny ports, every other month. At some she could tie up alongside a deep-water jetty but in many places she anchored off and used a shallow-drafted, fibreglass sea truck to ferry goods between ship and shore.

Monsunen was taken over on the morning of the invasion in 1982 and Captain George Betts and his crew displaced at gunpoint by the Argentine Navy. Her new masters applied a coat of black paint and for seven weeks used her to supply their own forces. In the early hours of May 23rd she was attacked by Lynx helicopters from HM Ships Brilliant and Yarmouth and ran aground in Seal Cove with a rope around the propeller and a gash in the bow. She was towed back to Goose Green by the Forrest, which had also been commandeered. By early June Monsunen had been recaptured by British forces following their assault on Goose Green. With Finlay Ferguson at the wheel, Mike Robson as engineer, a concrete plug in the bow and a hold full of Ghurkas, Monsunen began ferrying troops forward to Fitzroy during their advance on Stanley.

Following the conflict she returned to her normal duties after a dry-docking run for repairs 1000 miles north to Montevideo, skipper Bill Goss steering a course 260 miles off the Argentine coast while maintaining virtual radio silence throughout the trip.

In July 1992 Monsunen completed her last inter-island voyage to Port Howard and Salvador Water ports. During her Falkland years she had logged over a quarter of a million miles and carried 150,000 wool bales into town. Two months later she was purchased by a Chilean company, renamed Navi Sur and finally left the Islands on 25th September.

Forrest, an 86ft motor fishing vessel of 144 gross registered tons, was built in Wivenhoe, Essex, for the Falkland Islands Government at a cost of £60,000. She arrived in Stanley on 8th November 1967 and was named after a popular Tabernacle minister, Forrest McWhan. The new ship was able to carry 100 tons of cargo or 400 sheep and also 360 tons of diesel oil. For fifteen years Forrest was skippered by Jack Sollis and for much of the

Lifting wool bales from the sea truck onto mv Monsunen at Fox Bay West, 1977.

mv Tamar, under Captain Stephen Clifton, taking on sheep at Speedwell Island, 1993. (Photo Dave Hall)

time was under charter to the Ministry of Defence for use by the small detachment of Royal Marines at Moody Brook barracks. Later she came under the command of Nutt Goodwin.

After the Falklands War, during which she was extensively used by the Argentines, *Forrest* filled a support role for the ageing *Monsunen,* carrying coastal freights and making occasional trips to Punta Arenas in Chile for timber.

Coastal shipping operations were taken over and modernised in October 1992 by a new company, Byron Marine Ltd., for whom the replacement coastal supply vessel, *mv Tamar*, arrived in Stanley four months later. The 59l ton *Tamar* was built in Norway in 1979 and can accommodate 4 passengers, 700 bales of wool and chill 100 mutton carcasses. She is ugly but effective and her crane will lift a bulldozer.

Seamen traditionally respect omens, so was it just by coincidence that on her very first visit to New Island *Tamar* was slowly piloted into port by a fifty-foot-long Right Whale? How apt and how odd that the same vulnerable beast that first enticed bloody whalers to this very harbour over two centuries earlier could now idle, apparently without fear, like a monstrous, black inner tube just a harpoon shot in front of the ship's sharp and steely bow.

NOTE
In January 1993, the same month in which *Tamar* arrived in the Islands, a Bill was passed by the Islands' Councillors giving, for the first time, total protection to all marine mammals within Falkland waters.

mv A.E.S. being loaded with wool in Stanley for onward shipment to Gravesend in Kent. The entire Falklands' woolclip annually amounts to around 8500 bales. Tied up alongside are *mv Monsunen* and *mv Forrest*, 1987.

mv Forrest alongside the jetty at New Island, 1988.

6 WADERS AND WILDFOWL

Upland Goose

Flocks of up to one thousand non-breeding 'shedders', mainly young birds, gather near ponds and beaches in early summer, simultaneously moulting all their flight feathers. Brown females cackle; white males whistle.

Walter snored amongst a pile of rolled up, freshly-shorn fleeces in the cosiest corner of the woolshed, enjoying his lunchtime forty winks. As a young man he had been a renowned hand shearer, now, at 70 or thereabouts, he had offered to help me on the farm for the summer. He awoke at five minutes to one, ready for the afternoon spell.

"What do you fancy for supper, mate?" he said. We were alone on the island and fortunately for both of us, Wal had taken over the role of cook. I knew he had something in mind. There was a pause while a mischievous twinkle appeared, magnified by his glasses. "How about Kentucky Fried Goose?" he said.

A few minutes later there was a roar as Wal, dressed in boiler suit and deer-stalker, with a rifle slung across his back, zoomed past the shed door on my unsilenced trike and disappeared over the hill, all the time in first gear.

The Upland, or Greater Magellan Goose, is a large, tame and endemic sheldgoose found here in abundance. It grazes on stamps and coins, roosts in freezer bags and roasts in ovens throughout the Islands. Goose wings sweep around people's peat stoves, goose fat softens rawhide horsegear and goose eggs help Campers' cakes to rise. On New Island they hatch out and grow, court, breed, fight and die all around our house.

The Upland Goose is the most numerous of the four local 'geese'. In the early part of the century, with sheep numbers declining due to overgrazing, farmers needed a scapegoat and fell upon the goose. Concern was voiced about grazing competition between beast and bird and a bounty scheme was introduced. Government agreed to fork out ten shillings for every hundred beaks handed in. During the seven years from 1905 half a million birds were shot, although with little apparent effect on overall numbers. The project was scrapped in 1912. However, most farms carried on privately and it was still common to see a string of beaks hanging in a shepherd's outhouse only a few years ago. In 1976 further pressure from 'big farm' managers, trying to explain their falling profits to overseas directors, led to a scientific investigation into the matter. Sixteen years, a quarter of a million pounds and three highly qualified 'goosemen' later, the geese are as numerous and happy as ever but most of the large farm estates have gone out of business and interest in the 'goose problem' has waned. The study concluded that geese only really compete with grazing livestock in late winter and early spring, and recommended the possible use of battery-powered, propane gas guns with flashing lights to scare birds away.

The Stanley area is now a bird sanctuary and while the *Goose Report* gathers dust in the Agricultural Department, birds graze quietly outside the door. In recent years the Upland Goose has taken to nibbling also on Victory Green, in central Stanley, only a beer tin throw away from the famous hotel which bears the bird's name.

The female Upland Goose (left), incubates five to eight eggs for thirty days, leaving the nest briefly each day to feed and covering her conspicuous, off-white clutch with down. Adult pairs raise an average of just under two chicks each year. Most chick and egg losses are due to hawks, skuas and gulls. Only the Cassin's Falcon is capable of killing a healthy adult, although it is unlikely to happen often because at 3300 grammes, the goose thrice outweighs the hawk.

Upland Geese grazing above Stanley.

A goose's digestive system is simple and relatively inefficient compared to that of a ruminant, so they eat for much of the day. Each grass blade, berry or seed head is nibbled by the soft, serrated-edged bill, ground with grit in the muscular gizzard and pops out, largely undigested, at the other end a couple of hours later. A grazing goose produces one dropping every four minutes, often gobbled up by sheep or horse. As there are an estimated 350,000 birds in the Islands, the total population produces well over 50 million turds a day.

Wal returned by and by from the hunting trip, still driving in first gear, with downy feathers in his beard and four plump and plucked goslings tied onto the trike. That evening we ate them 'Kentucky Fried'. Extreme attitudes towards the geese vary from the most red-necked farmer to the romantic bird man. To me their value far outstrips any minor conflict with man's livestock. They represent a massive wealth of wildfowl, deliciously tasty yet worth far more than just their weight in golden breadcrumbs.

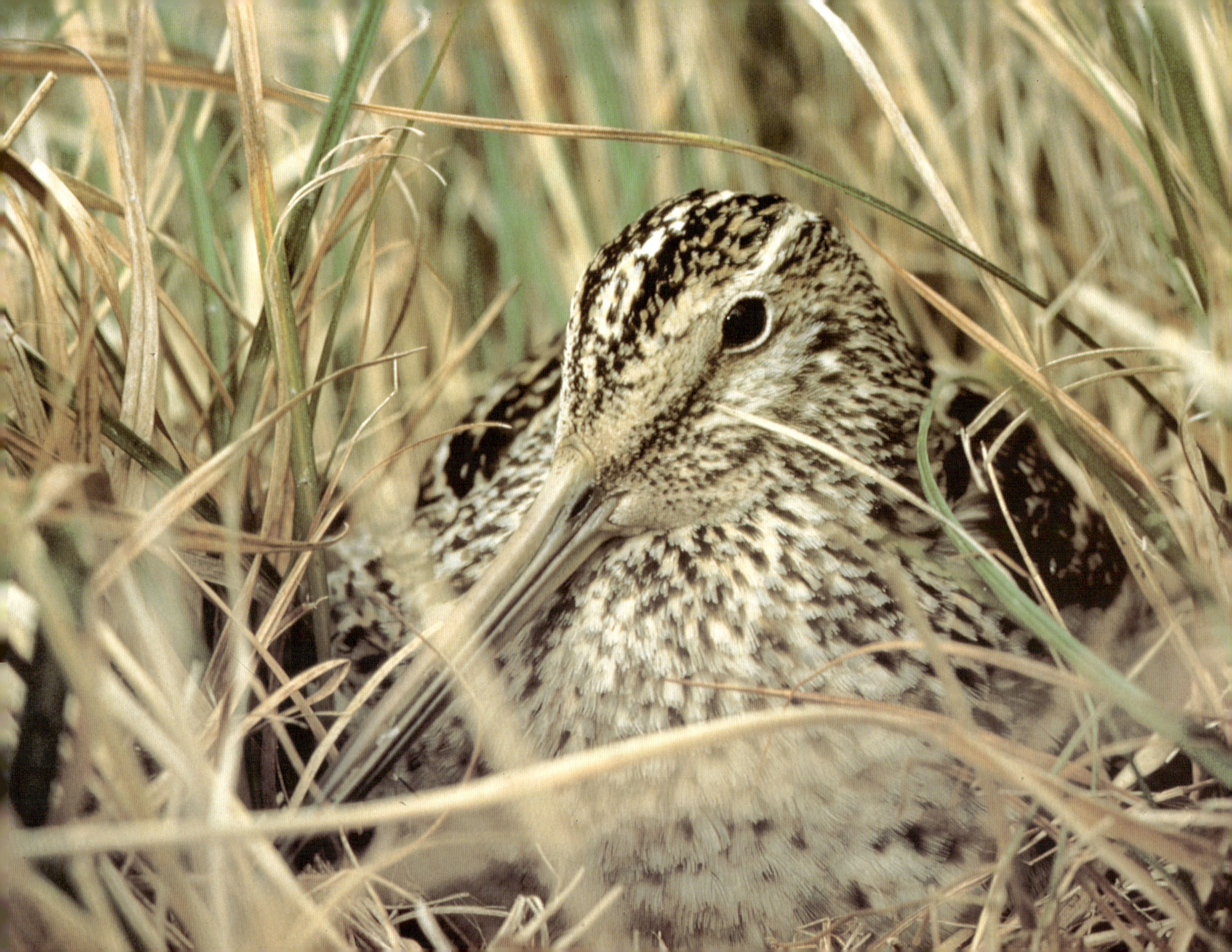

Dotterel, Plover and Snipe

The RUFOUS-CHESTED DOTTEREL (right) is a common summer resident whose return in September marks the beginning of Spring. Its 'clicking and wheezing' aerial display flights and plaintive, tremulous calls breathe life into the sombre heathlands. In summer, Dotterel incubate two eggs in a scrape in the lee of a grass or diddle dee bog. The pictured nest is in the parent's shadow. After breeding the adults fall silent and their bright colours dull. Most migrate north over one thousand kilometres to Argentina, Chile or Uruguay, while a handful remain here amongst wintering bands of ringed plovers along the beach.

The small and plump TWO-BANDED PLOVER (right) nests in a scrape on dry, often sparsely-covered ground amongst stones, diddle dee and lichen. When flushed from the nest it darts away quietly and mouse-like, or feigns injury to draw the intruder's attention from eggs or chicks. Sometimes they breed near Pied Oystercatchers, which produce similarly-coloured, though much larger, eggs. I once watched a broody plover mistakenly return to the wrong nest. For a few moments it perched ambitiously on top of one of the seapie's enormous eggs before realising its mistake and returning to the correct clutch nearby.

A long-billed prober of the peat bogs, common amongst rush and whitegrass, the MAGELLAN SNIPE (left) is often flushed by horse's hoof and motorbike. At dusk and during the night in springtime, snipe perform curious acrobatic displays using their tail feathers to make the distinctive and eerie-sounding 'drumming'. Their nests are notoriously difficult to find, often hidden deep in the grass. When accompanied by young, snipe can become extraordinarily tame. On Stanley Common I watched one catching and feeding worms to a single chick only feet away from my resting peat spade. All the time the adult bird, with a strangely disembodied voice, repeated its familiar, monotonous call, 'Cut peat, cut peat, cut peat'.

Quark

The 'Quark' or Black-crowned Night Heron is the red-eyed stabber of rock pool, kelp bed and ditch. Hunting, they stand motionless or stalk victims with feline stealth, striking with a lightning thrust of dagger beak. Disturbed, they flap off with a loud squawk and the disapproving air of a disturbed scholar. Night Herons spend the day snoozing amongst the branches of box bushes, on a beam in the hold of a scuttled ship or under jetties. They like to hunt after dusk, feeding mostly on small fishes, but taking almost anything from molluscs and spiders to mice and ducklings.

Quarks, though silent and solitary killers, are raucous and communal breeders. Their colonies reek of fish and rasp with croaks, hisses and cackles. They nest amongst shoreline tussac, lakeside reeds and famously in the settlement trees at Carcass Island, laying two or more pale blue eggs. Adults feed the chicks at first by regurgitation but later just dump food in the nest and let them get on with it. Ten weeks after egg laying, successful chicks can fly.

The Black-crowned Night Heron is extremely widespread through the Americas, Africa, Europe and Southern Asia and represented in different parts of the range by four separate sub-species. The race *Nycticorax nycticorax falklandicus* is endemic to the Islands.

Heron nestlings. (far right).

Adult Night Heron

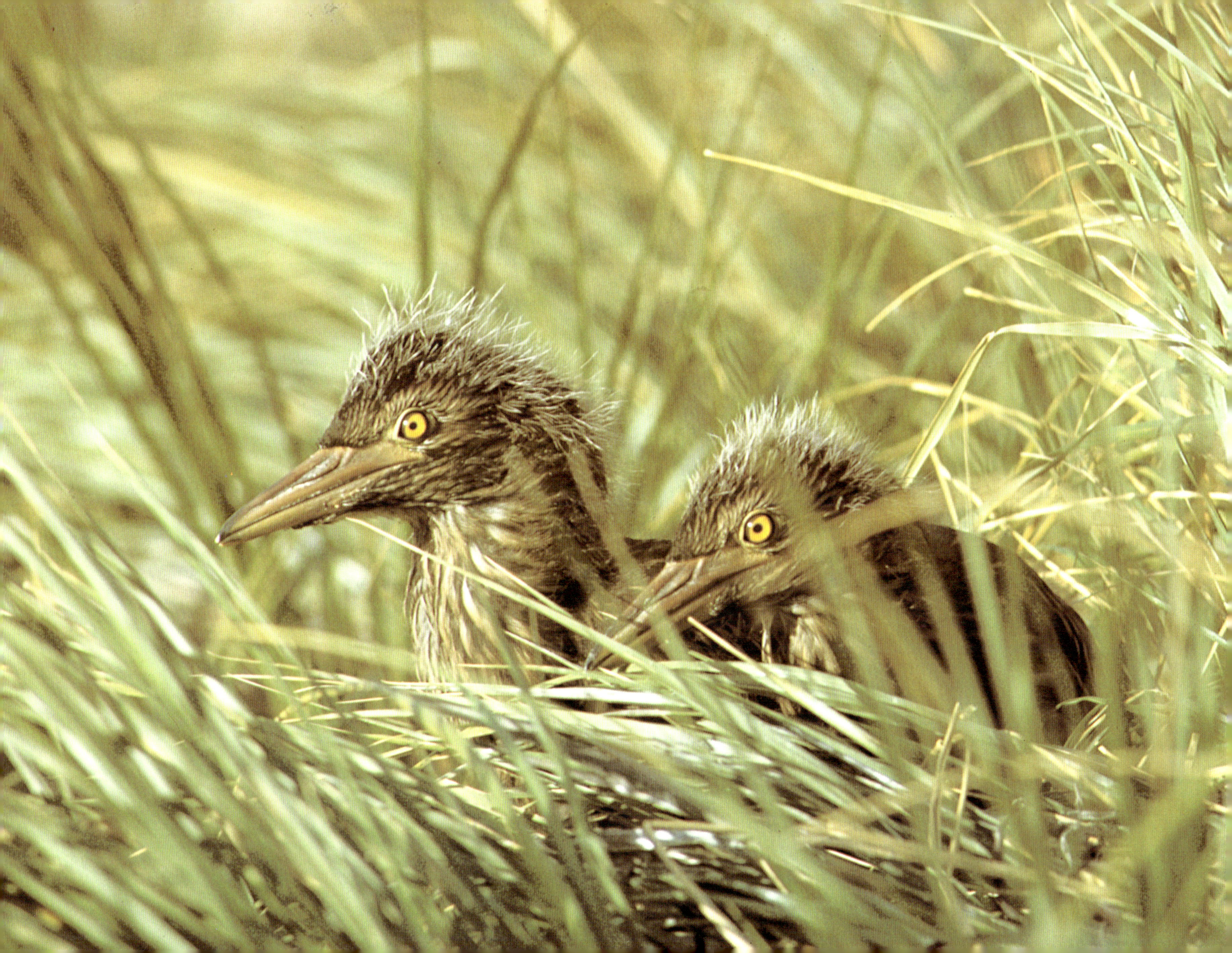

Oystercatchers

Young Black Oystercatcher (right).

A winter flock of Magellanic Oystercatchers, also called 'Black and White Curloos' or 'Seapies' (far right).

Black Oystercatcher nest.

Two of the world's eleven oystercatcher species, known locally as 'curloos', live along the Islands' shorelines.

MAGELLANIC OYSTERCATCHER

The 'Black and White Curloo' is the pied piper of sand beach and coastal green, prodding the turf for beetles, levering limpets from rocks and probing for worms along the lines of each receding tide. It lays two eggs in a scrape often behind the beach, by a bleached piece of driftwood, a sea cabbage, or an old sheep skull. Like most waders, hatched chicks leave the nest almost immediately. Parents become noisy and conspicuous when their nesting areas are threatened by intruders. Terrestrial predators such as man are led away by injury-feigning, whilst an aerial threat from a passing hawk or skua may precipitate a spectacular dog fight and I have seen them both attacking and being killed by falcons. In winter, seapies gather in flocks of up to a hundred, every so often breaking into a discordant chorus of long, wavering whistles.

BLACK OYSTERCATCHER

The Black 'Curloo' lays its eggs in a shell-lined scrape just above the high water mark on exposed, rocky or pebbly points along the shore. It is quieter and stockier than the seapie with a deeper, more melodious voice. On still evenings and during summer nights its bubbling flight calls echo around the settlement bay at New Island. Black 'Curloos' dine on rock-bound mussels and limpets at low tide.

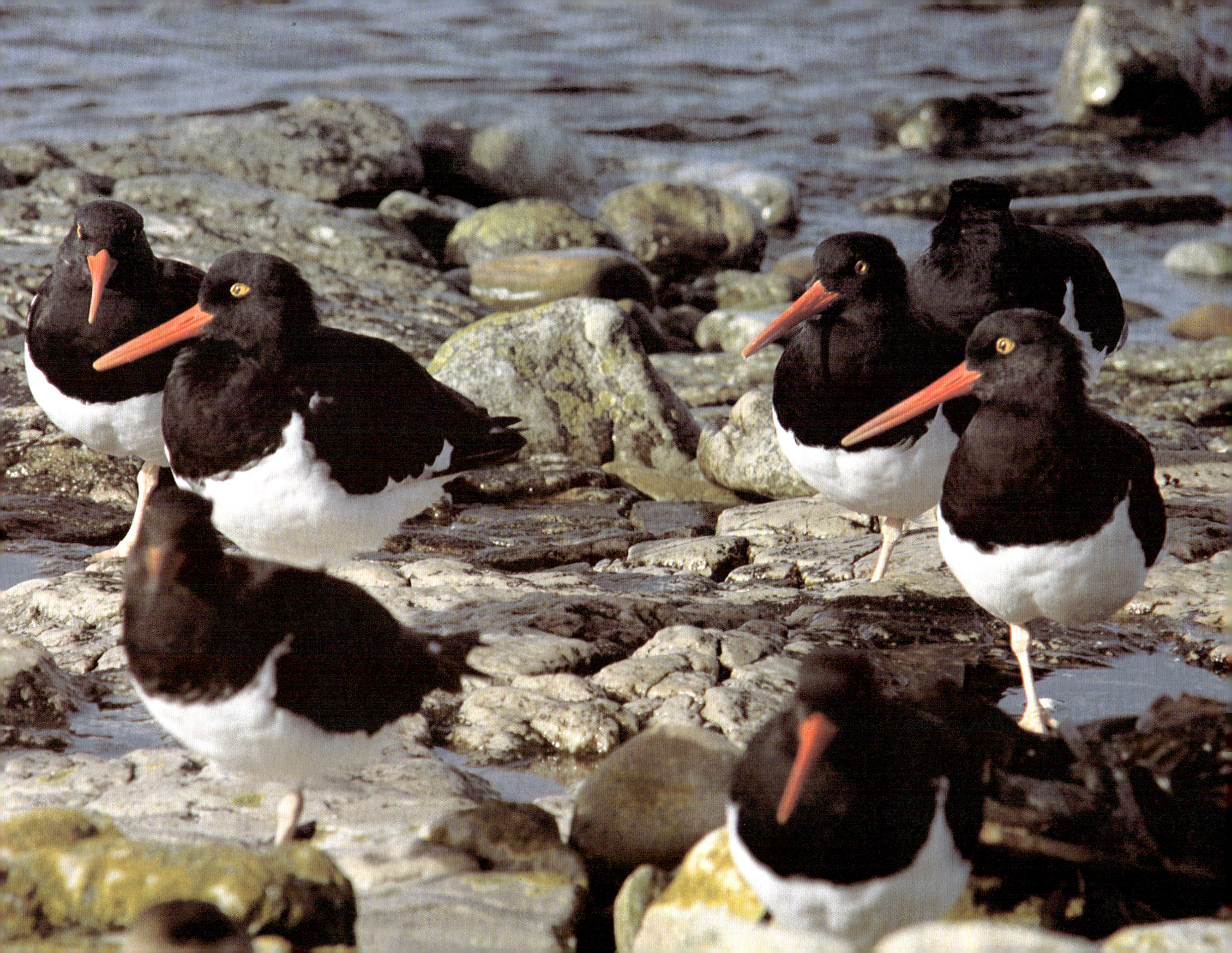

Pampa Teal

Shy and thinly distributed, the Pampa Teal (right) is a smallish dabbler of weedy pond and reedy lagoon.

They often go unnoticed through the breeding season but form flocks during the winter, and become a familiar sight on favoured ponds such as here on Bleaker Island or on the fairway to the 7th hole at Goose Green Golf Course. There are three races of Pampa Teal of which only the southernmost *(Anas versicolor fretensis)* is found in the Islands.

Grey Duck

An elegant, slender species found along coasts, in creeks and on many freshwater ponds. In Spring Grey Duck are noisy, aggressive and demonstrative, full of quacks and wheezy whistles. As summer goes on, they have an unusual habit of joining broods so that often a dozen ducklings of widely differing sizes will waddle along in a line accompanied by four or five adults.

Grey duck dabbling for invertibrates along the receding tide line. (far right).

Logger Duck

A massive and flightless sea duck, the Logger or Falkland Flightless Steamer Duck (bottom right) is endemic to the Islands and resident along every sheltered coastline. It is the world's second largest duck; only the closely related *Tachyeres pteneres* of Southern Chile is heavier. Loggers feed on marine invertebrates like worms, sea lice, snails and limpets by upending and diving in the shallows. When not eating they loaf; when not loafing they fight. They fight a lot. Each pair remains together and defends its patch of shoreline throughout the year. They approach trespassing neighbours underwater and at speed like twin torpedoes. Rival males lock onto each other's throats with formidable vice-grip bills while trying to beat one another into submission using the bony knobs on their elbows. The victor finally chases the vanquished away, both splashing furiously, running over the water with wings wheeling like the big paddles on a river steamboat. In summertime, when the frosty-headed drakes are particularly pugnacious, these scraps are frequent, sometimes epic, and very occasionally fatal. Sometimes the wives cross swords as well but mostly they just pose about the ringside croaking like bullfrogs in support, or shepherd the ducklings a safe distance from their crusty neighbours.

While collecting zoological specimens in 1834, Charles Darwin found the Logger Duck very difficult to kill and added, "their head is remarkably strong and their beak likewise". A thump from his big geological hammer only just broke the skull.

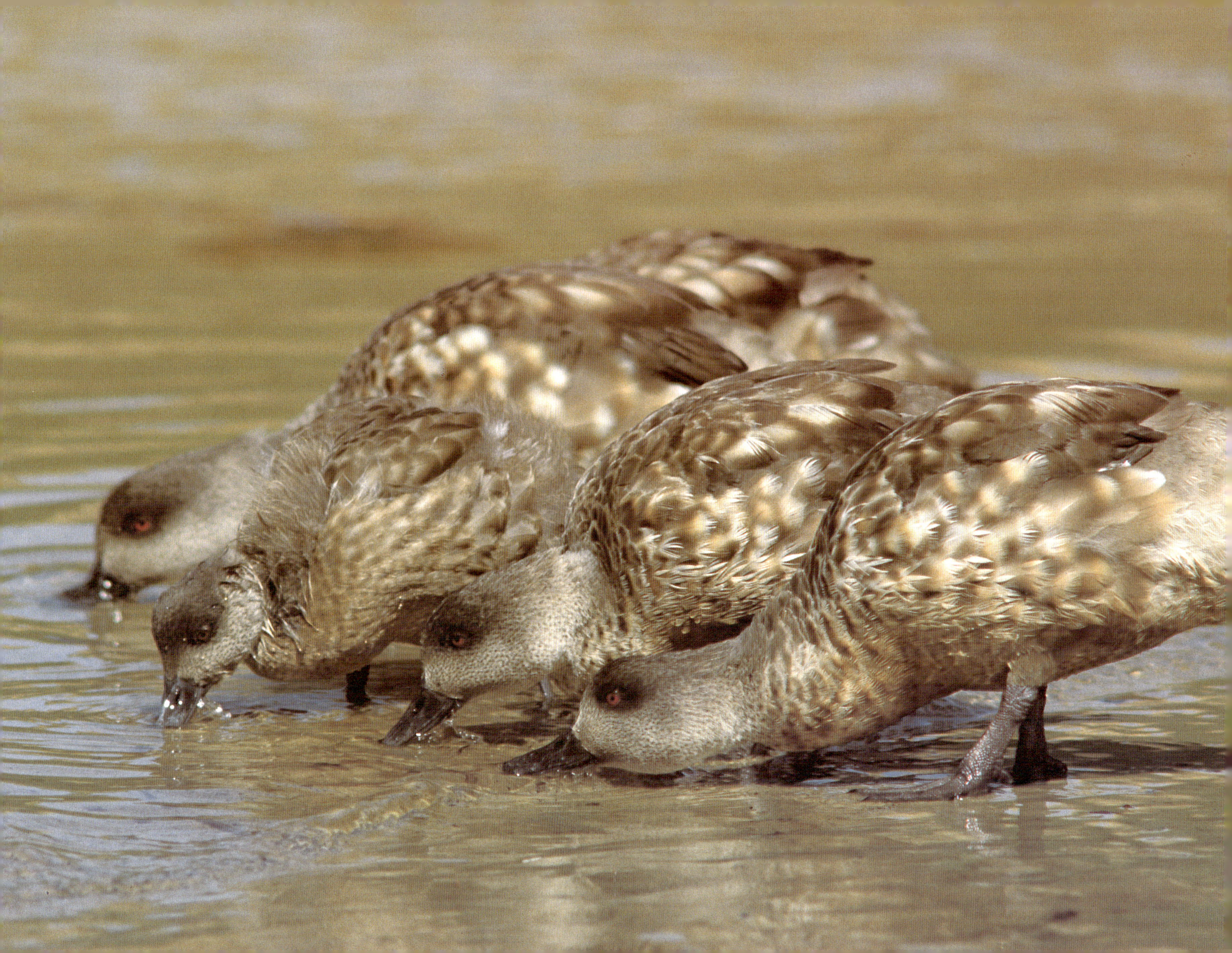

7 CAMP AND THE CAMPERS

Drafting sheep, New Island (below). (Photo Annie Chater)

Chartres was established as a sheepfarm in 1868 by New Zealander James McClymont. Today, owner Bill Luxton runs 17,000 Polworth sheep across 100,000 acres and produces 80 tonnes of greasy wool a year (bottom right).

The three million acres of outback, outside of the two small towns of Stanley and Mount Pleasant, are collectively known as the 'Camp'. This huge area is inhabited by just 500 sheep farming 'campers' who work by 'camp time', talk on 'camp telephones', travel along 'camp tracks' and divide their often vast ranches in sheepruns known as 'camps'. The word is a bastardized echo from Hispanic rule in the early 19th century when gauchos sucked yerba at Puerto Soledad (Port Louis) and called the surrounding countryside 'campo'.

1993 spawned a new tag – 'camp television'. In early April a friend rang up at suppertime. "Bill was watching *Eldorado* the other afternoon at Chartres, colour was excellent", he said. "Don't know if you'll get it out there on New Island, though, too far away from the transmitter. At Saunders they got it by plugging the two-metre aerial into the video."

I tried mine. Terry Wogan appeared in mono-chrome, miming in a snowstorm. It nearly put me off my meatballs.

From the time when the Camp was opened up in the 1860's, until the war of 1982, sheep ranching for wool produced the Islands' main and often only income. Although livestock had been first introduced by the French settlers at Port Louis in 1764, farming did not really begin until after the British regathered the colonial reins in 1833. By then de Bougainville's original importation of two bulls, seven heifers, some pigs, sheep, poultry, three horses and a baby goat had swelled to become large ferral herds, notably of cattle, horses and hogs roaming around East Falkland. But the future lay not in beef but wool and while itinerant bands of bolas-swinging cowboys galloped the plains after wild cattle for meat, hides and tallow, shrewder businessmen were queuing for real estate. Huge properties were created at the stroke of the Governor's quill across an Admiralty chart and, by 1869, virtually all the land had been carved up, dished out and leased to a handful of sharp-witted, mainly English prospectors. These pioneers established the Falklands' sheep farming industry and were to indelibly stamp their Victorian ideals on generations of camp culture.

In the beginning there were about thirty estates, the remotest lying several days by schooner from Stanley. Conditions in Camp were primitive and accommodation had to be built from scratch. Food shortages were commonplace and single women almost non-existent but grog, when available, was cheap. The new ranchers, young and enthusiastic, found solace in hard work, large profits and the thought of returning 'home' for a spell of wife-hunting in the off-season. As time passed the more successful became wealthy and influential, living in mansions and sending their offspring to English boarding schools. Labourers lived in cottages and bunkhouses talking, working and eating sheep while their wives milked cows or served at the 'Big House' and their children often had little or no schooling.

From 1874, when the colony's occupation was first officially described as 'sheep farming', there was a century of prosperity for the elite but social stagnation for the rest, during which land ownership altered hardly at all. As time passed and the early estate owners retired to the old country, many employed farm managers. A pattern of absentee ownership developed which, in time, became justifiably despised by the Islanders for whom there appeared no way of obtaining a stake in their own land. It continued until the late 1970's when competition from man-made fibres and higher wage demands forced the demise, sale and subdivision of most of the big farms.

There are now nearly one hundred smaller spreads, typically owned, occupied and worked by single Falkland Island families. Almost overnight the feudal era has vanished but unfortunately, with the collapse of the world's wool markets, so have the profits. Today's farmers form a colourful, often outspoken and independent society but lack the economic clout enjoyed by yesterday's wool barons. They have to be content playing second fiddle to the booming fishing industry while sharing amongst themselves a generous agricultural subsidy and a growing addiction to *Coronation Street*.

Saunders Island, the site of the earliest British settlement (begun at nearby Port Egmont in 1765) is now owned by Tony and David Pole-Evans. They run 9500 sheep over their 30,000 acre island farm (above).

Port Edgar, home of Tex and Mandy Alazia, was one of five farms created following the sale and subdivision of the Falkland Islands Company estate at Port Stephens in 1988. The Alazias run 7,500 sheep on their 50,000 acre farm but, as the picture shows, they had to begin their new and isolated homestead almost from nothing in the manner of the old pioneers (top left).
(Photo Lucy Ellis)

Fencers, Mandy McRae and Lucy Ellis, building a wire gate.

Shearing

Removing fleeces from the Islands' 600,000 shearing sheep is a demanding job performed once a year by travelling gangs, but twenty years ago the task fell upon the resident workforce on each Camp station. During the 1960's, after a century of woolsheds echoing to the rhythmic clacking of handshears, most farms had turned to mechanised shearing for speed and efficiency. When I first stuck my nose into a woolshed many of the older hands, while using electric machines, were still practising various "traditional" styles. A few knelt down on one knee, others sheared "cack-handed", while some swopped the handpiece from left to right. The handyman got on better than most, producing a steady flow of 'pink' sheep, while constantly sucking a dog-end through the cigarette holder which protruded from the midst of his bushy red beard.

Each finished fleece was picked up and thrown onto the wool table by a crotchety and barefooted old German called Bert, a former American P.O.W., who had been captured in a Cairo Bazaar while posing as an Arab in 1942. "Dis rotten, stinking sheep's grease vill kill me," he growled repeatedly through false teeth. Bert was a vegetarian who disliked many things but hated the shearing shed most of all. All through the heat of the day he chewed, breathed, sweated and farted raw garlic, claiming it kept him "aloive". "You must chew every mowtful fifty toimes, mench," he advised and his shiny dentures had been made extra long to cope with all chomping. He looked like a horse and lived amidst a huge pile of monkey nuts, in a garden shack hung with gaily-painted tools which mostly belonged to other people.

One man in the shed stood alone. The squat, swarthy figure of foreman Dave Bonnet might have gone unnoticed selling onions by the Seine. He wore a beret, thick glasses, a neatly trimmed beard and had a sticking-out bottom but *he* was the "gun" shearer. It was Dave's last season of a seven-year contract to the Falkland Islands Company and he was determined to be the first man in the Falklands to shear 200 sheep in eight hours. After each sweaty day in the shed he would enthusiastically lead us beginners to the dance hall where, with curtains drawn, we would study a short 16mm film "Wool Away" featuring a powerful black-clad Kiwi called Godfrey Bowen. He was the world's best shearer and spoke of "long blows" and "the last side" and every night near the end of the movie would say, "Keep his head up Harry" to some lesser mortal struggling with a sheep further down the board. In February, having perfected the Bowen style, the heroic Bonnet finally managed 208 ewes in a day, then left the islands. I've never heard of him again.

Peter Goss led the first private shearing gang in 1972 with other top shearers Keith and Tony Heathman and Trevor Browning, and Peter's wife Margaret as wool girl. The idea took off and, as demand for contractors grew, itinerant overseas professionals began to pop up each spring like returning penguins. The result was a rapid improvement in speed and technique. Today there are a number of local shearers in the highest class, notably many times West champion Robbie Maddox and local record holder Peter McKay who achieved 401 at Harps Farm in 1992. However, New Zealander Steve Cochran heads the way with a fantastic 421 ewes shorn in eight hours at Goose Green in 1990.

Handshearer from around the turn of the last century.

Kiwi Daf Coulter shearing a big wether at New Island (right).

The shearing board at Fox Bay West, 1977.

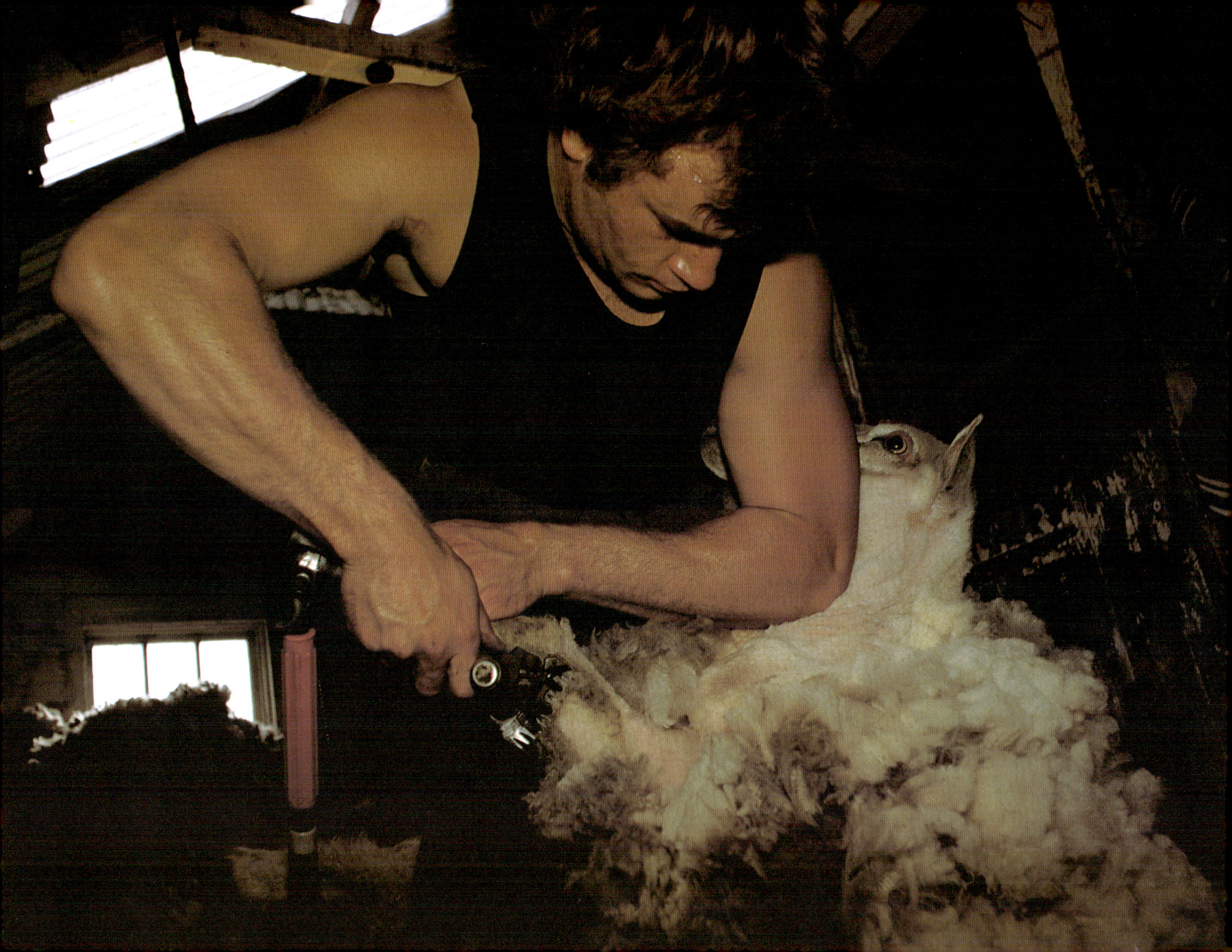

Droving

Fred Coutts riding a horse called Donkey behind a drive of 6,000 lambs on the track from Fox Bay West to the 'Plains'. With the carving up of the 'Big Farms' and Hondas replacing horses, scenes like this from the seventies have virtually vanished (far right).

Les Morrison, Head Shepherd at Port Howard, with his prize-winning sheep dogs May and Bounce (right).

Welshman Danny Limburn, Head Shepherd at Fox Bay West, driving 7000 freshly-shorn ewes across the 'Centre Camp' towards 'Diamond Corner'.

Shortly before Christmas 1973, after a year on the farm, I took my first solo drive of 300 newly-shorn rams eighteen miles from Fox Bay West to a camp called the 'Neck' at Queen Point.

I always looked forward to a night at Queen Point Shanty. It was a remote and seldom-used shack which stood in the middle of a whitegrass flat, near an exposed shoreline where ocean surfs roared day and night. Inside, a blackened kettle hung suspended from a piece of number eight fencing wire over the open grate. Whenever the fire was lit, and someone opened the door, peat smoke billowed back down the chimney. A pile of dog-eared Westerns, enjoyed by mice in our absence, lived on the dusty mantlepiece. On the table was a blue plastic bowl used for cleaning hands, frying pans and teeth. Our water came out of an old iron bucket, in turn scooped from a forty gallon drum which was filled by a pipe from the gutter, with rain drained off the roof. Three double-tier bunks, each with an unyielding straw-filled paliasse, lined the walls. Candle remains, resembling waxy white stalagmites, perched on the head of each iron bed frame. They were a dribbling reminder of the most recent occasion when a full gang of shepherds had overnighted and shared out a dozen threadbare World War II blankets from the chest behind the door.

On a fine morning, riding Annabel, a fat, broken-winded mare, and with three dogs, I set off behind the sheep. Rams are good sheep to drive, generally plodding along at a steady pace and seldom complaining. Unfortunately, going through the very first paddock gate, my flock got tangled up with a cut of 'double-fleecers', the last sheep known to carry ticks on the farm following a countrywide eradication scheme. Annabel waited patiently as I cursed and sweated, first catching then lifting each of twenty or so 150lb 'roughies' over a wire fence before continuing.

Towards evening, after six hours on the track, with dogs tiring and hungry sheep spreading out, the air became still and heavy as the sky darkened with menace. I put the flock in a paddock and arrived just as the first raindrops began, at Fish Creek, a shanty with less character but more comfort than Queen Point. It was freshly-tarred black, with red windows and inside it had the luxury of a stove, a sink and two chairs. Another shepherd, Danny, also looking for shelter, had just arrived from Spring Point. Almost immediately our roof announced the arrival of hailstones, ice on iron. It sounded at first like someone using one finger on an old-fashioned typewriter then suddenly exploded to a deafening roar.

There followed a devastating and still talked about three-hour storm during which newly-shorn sheep died in droves on farms Islandwide. 500 were lost at Fox Bay West that night and over 800 amongst the gorse hedges at Port San Carlos. Unable to help, we heard the news over the camp telephone.

Later, sitting in an armchair by the Rayburn, I felt ticks crawling creepily up my back. They had come off the roughies encountered earlier in the day. Dan picked them out and killed them with a lighted candle, each little blood-filled beastie quickly, quietly going pop in the flame. The next day dawned fine and tickless so I carried on droving the rams to the 'Neck' and spent the night at Queen Point Shanty.

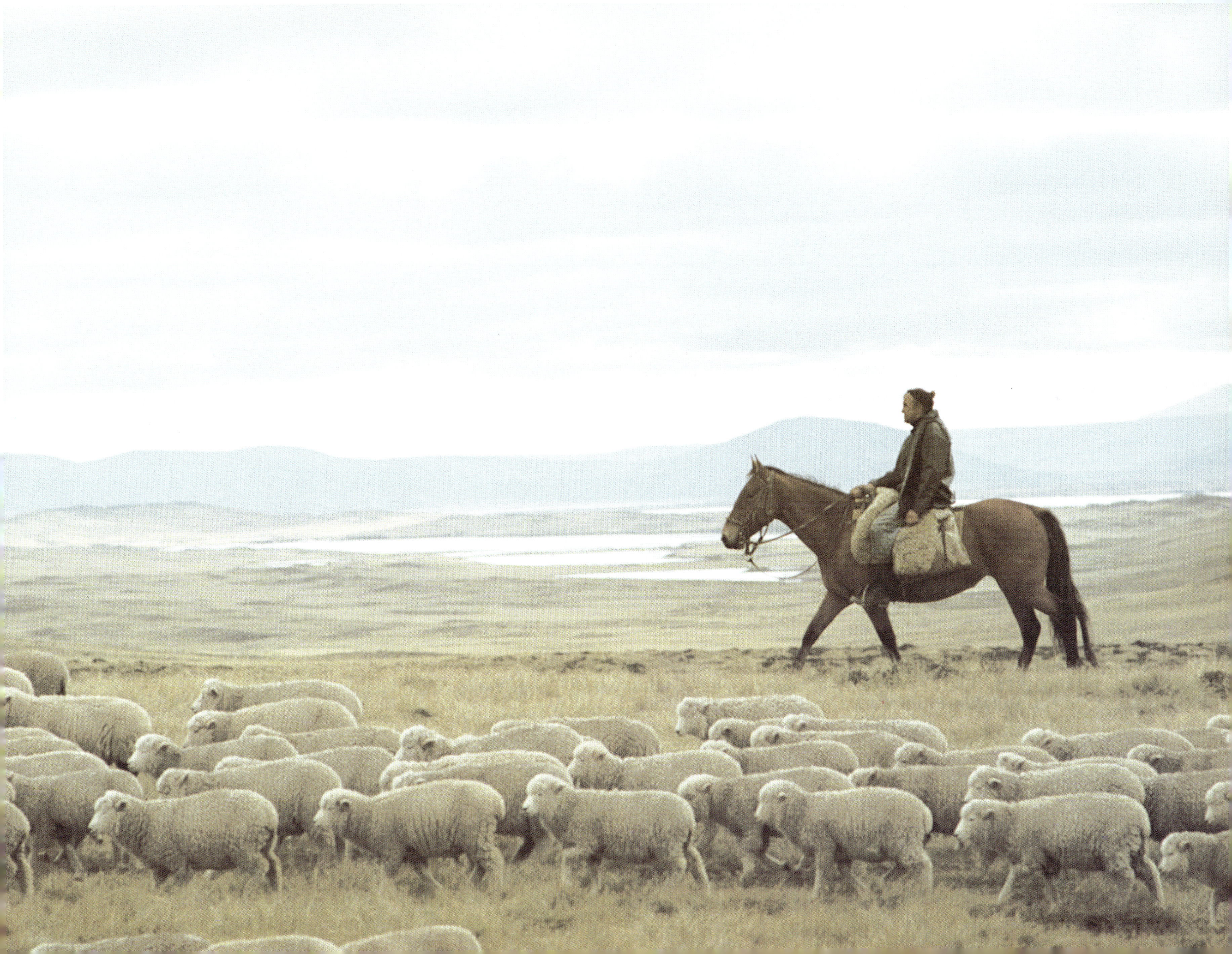

West Point Island

The ancient privy (which blew down in the great south-easterly gale of 1992).

Roddy and Poppy in the cowshed.

West Point has been in the same family ever since the opening up of West Falkland in the late 1860's. Originally part of the Shallow Bay Estate, it was set up and run as a 3630 acre sheep farm in 1879 by Arthur Felton, the great uncle of present owner Roddy Napier. Today Roddy and his wife Lilly live here with their granddaughter Poppy. West Point is extremely fertile, enabling the Napiers to run 1500 fine-wooled sheep at around 2.4 acres per head, easily the highest stocking rate in the Falklands.

Once known as Albatross Island and a haunt for sealers and penguin boilers, the island guards the strongly tidal, northwestern sea passage to the westernmost parts of the Islands, the Wooly Gut, which runs between West Point and West Falkland. Just around the corner from this pass, in the snug cove of West Point harbour and tucked under the hill, is the settlement.

Roddy is a raconteur in the finest island tradition, blessed with a remarkable memory, an impish wit and an uncanny ability to foretell weather. In the evenings, slumped in his favourite armchair by the stove, he recalls ringing albatrosses at the Devil's Nose, his younger days under sail aboard inter-island schooners, the pet guanaco or the occasion when he happened upon a septuagenarian lady guest who had taken to the sun in his vegetable garden.

Spring mornings on West Point hum with gorse blossom. Cows bellow to be milked and pet lambs bleat to be fed to the rhythmic thump of the same single-cylinder Lister generator that has given light to the settlement for 25 years. It drives the milking machine and the cream separator. It charges Rod's telephone battery and runs Lil's dishwasher and Poppy's video.

Lal and George Halliday, in about 1910, sorting out geese and mullet caught over at Grave Cove. These were smoked and sold to Norwegian whalecatcher crews who came here from the New Island whaling station for fresh water during the dry summer months. Behind is the shearing shed, still in use, with the sealion's head above the door. (Photo courtesy Roddy Napier)

On the slope above the settlement and near the grass airstrip stands Roddy's most remarkable acquisition, a lime green, single-decker Welsh bus for taking tourists to the penguins, and from somewhere down among the sheep pens comes the crowing of the only cock pheasant in West Falkland. Tirelessly he flirts with the chickens, drilling out their cockerel and chasing him around great uncle Arthur's shearing shed, watched by a century-old sealion whose skull hangs nailed above the lintel.

A disused and lopsided privy rests nearby. The door came from the barque *Actaeon* which has lain in Stanley harbour since 1853. Lilly told me that there are rude poems and things written in pencil inside. I looked, but passing time, salt air and sunshine has made them difficult to read.

West Point settlement in spring.

Roddy Napier, with Mount Misery (1211 feet) beyond.

Carcass Island

Carcass settlement (right).

Valley Cottage was originally built as a shearing shed in the 1870's.

Carcass settlement lies seven sea miles north-east and across the strongly tidal Byron Sound from the nearest neighbours at West Point Island. On a quiet spring morning we motored across in *Foam* to pick up mail and some young tomato plants delivered by aircraft from Stanley. *Foam* was returning home for the first time in a decade since the late Cecil Bertrand, who had her built in 1958, and his wife Kitty left the farm to retire in town. Cecil had worked in the great southern whaling fleets in the '30's so it seemed a good omen when a Southern Right Whale crossed our bows during the short passage. Three times its great black flukes rose above the sea as the monster slowly sounded and moved quietly westward.

We anchored near the jetty in Port Pattison, where the boat had spent much of her youth, and pulled ashore through a maze of kelp to see Rob McGill, the owner. He was standing on the beach in front of his house, which was hidden by a dense copse of cypress. A raucous colony of night herons squawked amongst the branches. Rob's round, sun-reddened face glowed against his turquoisy tee-shirt. A line of printed penguins scrambled across his chest.

"Would you care for some lunch, gentlemen?" he asked, rustling up some spam, salad and tea. We swopped news and gossip in his spacious orange kitchen. Rob talks slowly. Like the island he lives on he is quiet and serene, the latest in a line of caring farmers that have kept Carcass, almost uniquely in the islands, free of the scourges of rodent, cat or rabbit. Consequently this settlement twitches and twitters with small birds flickering from fence wire to fuchsia to gorse. Introduced shrubs and trees and surrounding green pastures give an almost sub-tropical feel. On a slope overlooking the bay I sat between two friendly horses, Dusk and Dawn, grazing lazily amongst the daisies and yellow violets.

Before returning to West Point we signed the Visitors Book and Rob poured us each a couple of 'wee snipes' with which to toast the Empire. Our course home may not have been quite as straight as it ought.

Rob McGill.

Dusk and Dawn at Carcass.

Inter-Island Flights

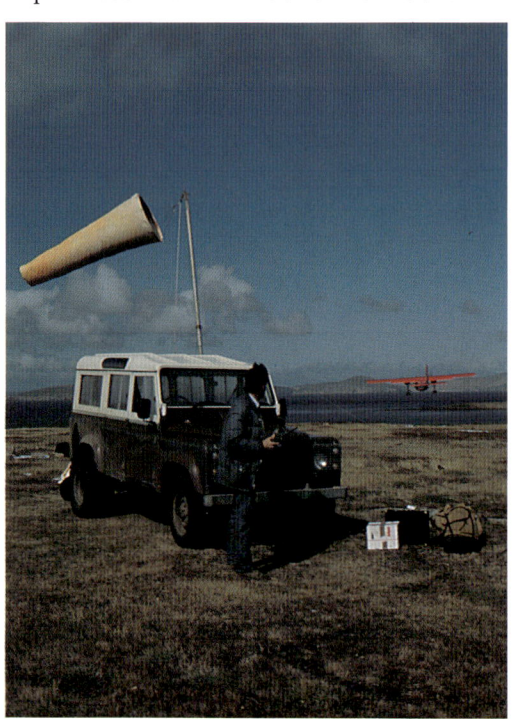

Every evening the radio station broadcasts the 'Announcements', an assortment of notices beginning with the weather forecast and including job vacancies, raffle winners, lost cats and funerals. But most eagerly awaited by Camp listeners are the nightly 'Flight Schedules' of the Falkland Islands Government Airservice (FIGAS) which give out who is going where (and with whom) on tomorrow's inter-island flights.

The airservice began in 1948, inspired by Governor Miles Clifford, when two ex-military Austers were purchased for £700 each. "He'll break his bloody neck", said the cynics as pilot Vic Spencer finished the inaugural test flight with a spinning nose dive before landing on the racecourse as sweetly as a goose. Five days later the little aircraft proved her worth when Spencer flew sixty miles to North Arm where 10-year-old Sandra Short needed urgent hospital treatment. The landing area was marked with sheepskins and wind direction indicated by smoke from a small fire. When Sandra and her appendix successfully parted company in town a few hours later, FIGAS was born.

In the first year there were twenty-eight passengers with priorities then, as now, first medicals then mail, passengers and freight. It soon became apparent that although every settlement was near to a sheltered harbour, creek or pond, few farms could readily conjure up an airstrip. So, before long, the Austers were converted to floats, thus extending the service to all outlying communities.

For three decades from 1953, the backbone of FIGAS was the de Havilland DHC2 Beaver seaplane – a noisy, cramped little aircraft which operated from the west end of Stanley harbour and could land just about anywhere there was a long enough stretch of water. The pilots became folk heroes with the control column in one hand and a sandwich in the other. They flew naturalists to remote outliers, buzzed startled tractor drivers in the middle of nowhere and knew the names of every camper's children.

At take-off the engine sparked up with a throaty cough, cowlings shuddered and a thousand rivets chattered nervously. "Everybody O.K.?" enquired the captain reassuringly and passengers nodded, grinned and glanced to check there was a sick bag in the back of the seat in front. As the throttle increased, the engine gave a lion's roar and away we went, gaining speed like a train, bucking swells and finally clipping a couple of wavetops before lifting clear. From then on conversation was limited to signals and shouting behind a cupped hand into your neighbour's ear, or bursts at the next settlement jetty. Men needing to water the donkey could do so, partially hidden, off the after-end of the float, preferably after landing. Women had to nip behind someone's shearing shed.

A feature of the Beaver days were the mail drops, giving passengers a rare glance at remoter settlements. During a slow pass low over some isolated homestead the pilot would toss the hessian sack, containing letters, out of the window and waggle his wings at the folk waving below. On one occasion the bag landed on the float and was lost in the sea, but generally there was a high standard of accuracy. A complaint from one farmer, who objected to having to walk too far for his mail, brought the sack screaming through his glass porch roof and onto the doorstep. Another mail bag landed in the back of a moving Land Rover.

Captain Derek Clarke at the controls of an Islander (right).

Captain Geoff Porter takes off at New Island.

1979 saw the beginning of a transition to larger, faster and more comfortable land planes with the arrival of the first Britten Norman Islander BN2. The floatplanes were finally phased out six years later.

FIGAS now operate five Islander aircraft. Two are adapted for maritime surveillance of the fisheries, whilst three others provide the internal passenger service using a network of thirty-seven prepared grass strips island-wide. The furthest away, at New Island, lies 131 nautical miles due west of Stanley.

Over 7000 customers and a variety of livestock and freight are transported annually. Passengers of recent note include several pedigree rams and muzzled dogs (bathed and in bags, please), an ex-Prime Minister, two Dukes, an Archbishop and a bull calf.

Islander aircraft overflying Sapper's Hill (top right).

Beaver floatplane alongside jetty at Fox Bay East, 1979 (right).

FIGAS is born as Vic Spencer carries Sandra Short away from Auster G-AJCH at Stanley racecourse after the first medical flight on Christmas Eve 1948. (By courtesy of V.H. Spencer)

Fox Bay West

I arrived at Fox Bay West in the summer of 1972 and stayed for a year and a bit. There were eight other single blokes working on the farm who lived in the bunkhouse, a large austere white box with peeling paint, rattly windows and corridors which smelt of stale tobacco, armpits and rum.

I was shown my room. It was glossily-painted a delicate shade of seasick green and furnished with an iron bedstead and a bare light bulb. A ring of woodworm-sized holes at head height, where some previous occupant had missed his dartboard, made one wall mildly more interesting than the others. I tried the lightswitch but nothing happened.

"Power goes on at six in the evenings," said a cheerful voice in the doorway. "Dick's the name."

He brought in a mattress.

"Bloody cold on this side in a south wind," he said. "When Jake leaves you'd best grab his pit, it's over the stoke hole."

Jake was a fiery-haired Scotsman about to finish his contract and return to the glens. Friendly Dick came from somewhere in Sussex.

"Can you do me a favour?" he tentatively asked later, in his room, eyeing me over a steaming pint of tea. "You see, I've all these letters from different girls and ... well ... I can't read."

I sat on a chair chewing a slab of cake speckled with currants and tasting of sheep grease. A pile of carefully-opened envelopes lay on the bed. Some were perfumed and contained photographs of dusky Latin damsels wearing various bits of almost nothing.

"If you can read 'em out loud, I'll pick the one I like

Farm Manager Jimmy Robertson and 'Chestnut'. Jimmy was in charge of Fox Bay West for twenty years in the days when stockwork was still done on horseback (right).

Charlie Robertson, the boss' father, an old-fashioned stockman whose father, Jim, had arrived from New Zealand as a Stock Inspector in 1895.

best," said Dick, "then you can reply for me, see, 'cos I can't write neither."

He grinned conspiratorially. I noticed that one of his yellow fangs was missing. Dick thrust a dog-eared print my way.

"We'll send her me portrait too."

The unknown face in the bromide was remarkably more handsome than his own.

"You can have all the girls I don't want," he added with a flourish. The deal was struck.

NOTE

For every two unattached girls in the Camp there were then at least four men, so the cookhouse boys had slipped an advert into the 'lonely hearts' column of the *Buenos Aires Herald*. "Girlfriends wanted by lonely men on remote island" sort of thing. The weekly airmail had brought a barrage of replies which snowed under Stanley's sleepy Post Office as a galaxy of prospective mates were shared out amongst the delighted shepherds.

Fox Bay West. This morning, in July 1976, was so exceptionally cold that the mile wide harbour at Fox Bay froze over and the cook's ducks walked across the ice to the neighbouring settlement at Fox Bay East. The coldest night on record in the Falklands was that of 1st July 1992 when a temperature of −21.2°C was recorded at Little Chartres, West Falkland.

Roy Cove

William and Katherine Bertrand, 1913.
(Picture by courtesy of Mrs Kitty Bertrand)

Roy Cove settlement 1991.

William Wickham Bertrand was born in 1841 in Dominica where his family had owned two sugar plantations since the 1770's. As a young man he went gold prospecting in Australia, hunting pig in India, farming in New Zealand and travelling in Argentina before hearing, with interest, of the prospects for sheep ranching in the Falklands.

He arrived in 1868 and with his partners, Ernest Holmstead and a jovial German called John Switzer, acquired a licence to operate one of the last available large tracts of land on West Falkland. Leaving the others to organise the new farm around a sheltered cove called Shallow Bay, William got a job managing the large FIC sheep farm at Darwin Harbour. He performed well, drawing on experience gained in New Zealand, and during a two year appointment constructed both the most modern shearing shed and the first dipping trough in the Islands. The dip was 30 feet long and, using an evil-smelling brew of boiled tobacco leaves and sulphur, he began to combat the curséd scab which was then ravaging Falkland flocks. "I can scarcely find words to express my astonishment and delight at the change Mr Bertrand has made," wrote his employer in 1869.

In late 1870, now married to Katherine Felton and with one child, Bertrand moved to Shallow Bay to assist Holmstead after Switzer had been summonsed back to New Zealand to face an arson charge.

Bertrand was a dynamic, fiery and deeply religious man who, it was said, would dress for dinner if only he had a sardine to eat. Holmstead was a staunch Anglican non-conformist. After each hard day's work the Bertrands, Holmstead and two or three navvies all retired to one small and leaky wooden house at Shallow Bay where they ate, slept and shared a tin bath eighteen inches across and five inches deep. Tensions inevitably grew and before long the partners agreed to divide the estate. Holmstead's share was larger, but Bertrand had the better sheep country and only a short boundary, which he later double fenced to guard against scab.

In 1872 William founded a new settlement in a creek named Roy Cove, 157 nautical miles by schooner from Stanley. He continued to run the farm himself until 1908 when son-in-law Howard Clement took over as manager. Bertrand left for England in 1913 and died in Colchester the following year.

The 76,000 acre farm remained in the family under the company name of Bertrand and Felton until 1981, when it was sold to the Falkland Islands Government for £220,000.

Government in turn organised the division of the land, stock, buildings and plant into six individual farm units, due to be signed over to the successful applicants on 2nd April 1982. Governor and Mrs Hunt, together with a large party, were scheduled to fly to Roy Cove for the occasion. However, by 8.0am that morning, when the plane would normally have been preparing for take-off, Stanley Airport had been closed due to a seaborne invasion of several thousand Argentine troops on a nearby beach. The ceremony had to be postponed until after they had gone away again.

Hill Cove

In the English spring of 1873, 22-year-old Robert Blake was at a loose end. Legend has it that while driving a dog cart near the family home at Bridge, Somerset, it was suggested that he might make his mark sheep farming in the colonies. His companion, Fred Cobb, the Colonial Manager of the Falkland Islands Company, had just married Robert's elder sister.

The Falkland spring found Blake rowing ashore from a schooner towards a small cluster of buildings at Shallow Bay. He had been invited to the West by Ernest Holmstead, son of an Essexshire doctor, who was struggling with a 100,000 acres grazing called Adelaide Station. Holmstead needed money, Blake a challenge. The two became partners.

By 1882 both men had made successful spouse-seeking forays to the homeland and returned, each with an English wife, and needing his own space in which to raise a family. Blake chose to make a new home twelve miles away, at Hill Cove where " … the French Hills will shelter me from all the bad winds and the sun pours down hot". He imported a large wooden kit house, a cook and a gardener. Dora, his wife, brought her piano so they could all sing hymns.

In 1889 the Holmsteads, with their two children, returned to England and the whole farming operation moved over to Hill Cove where the new settlement was complete. Perhaps their departure unsettled the Blakes? By now Dora also had a growing brood needing schooling, while Robert, who was suffering rheumatism and wanderlust, sought a new challenge. In 1892, having installed a farm manager at Hill Cove, Dora and the children moved to Manchester for two years, while Robert joined the speculative string of keen-eyed Kelpers looking for land to develop in the Argentine. Eight days ride northeast from Punta Arenas, Blake joined two penniless Scotsmen, both former Hill Cove shepherds, and invested in 75,000 acres of dust, scrub and pumas on the Patagonian coast. By 1898, having helped establish San Julian, like Hill Cove, from a wilderness to a highly profitable sheep ranch, Robert Blake was in failing health and retired with Dora and their eight children to South Petherton in Somerset.

Hill Cove remained under the company ownership of Holmstead and Blake for a further 90 years. In 1987 it was sold for subdivision. One of the eight sections, called "The Peaks", now belongs to Tim and Sally Blake. Tim is Robert Blake's grandson. They still live in the house he built 120 years ago.

The 'Top Settlement' at Hill Cove. Robert Blake's house is the large building in centre picture. The Hill Cove forest, the most impressive stand of trees in the Islands, was begun in the 1880's but substantially enlarged in 1925 by a government forester called Reid. It contains many species including pines, spruces, poplars and Patagonian beeches.

The Point Settlement, Hill Cove. Situated two miles away from the 'Top Settlement', the 'Point Settlement', was the working hub of the 100,000 acre Hill Cove sheep farm for over a century until the farm was sold and subdivided into eight smaller farms in 1987. Today the settlement is run as a co-operative village, permanently occupied by four families. The sheep handling and shearing facilities and jetty are still used each summer by five of the section-holding farmers (top left).

Tim Blake in an RAF Hercules, on his way to represent the Islands at the United Nations in New York in 1982, as an elected member of the Falklands Legislative Council.

A Farmer's Life

Linda McRae milking at South Harbour Farm, 1993. On many farms this is still done by hand. Afterwards, the milk is separated, and the cream turned into butter. (Photo Bill Chater)

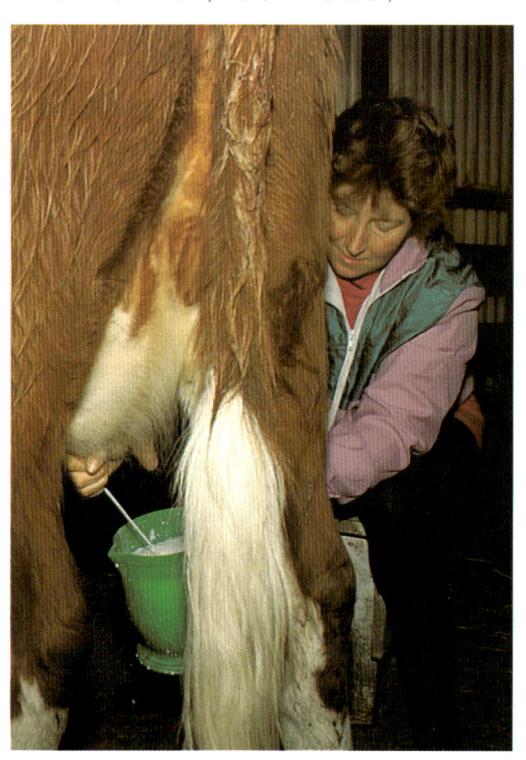

Veterinary Officer Michael Reichel, assisted by Kristin Wohlers, artificially inseminating a selected ewe with semen from 'Rokeby Admiral', a superfine Tasmanian merino ram. New Island, May 1992.

Kevin Kilmartin eyelocking at Spring Point, April 1977. Where necessary, lambs are eyelocked at about six months. This prevents them becoming woolblind, a condition which impedes feeding and increases the risk of them falling into ditches and streams in the winter (top right).

Marking lambs at Queen Point, November 1977. When the lambs are about six weeks old, ewe flocks are gathered into a lamb marking pen, often out in the camp. The lambs are drafted off and each one has its tail docked and an age and station mark put in its ear; right ear for males, left for females. Unwanted rams are castrated (right).

Camp Sports Week

The camper's year pivots around the main annual job of harvesting wool for export and the end of the busy shearing season is marked traditionally, on East and West Falkland, by two major race meetings held during Camp Sports Week.

The original idea probably sprouted from impromptu races between shepherds riding home after a day's sheep work and as early as 1875 there was a course at Goose Green. By 1889 the Darwin Harbour Sports Association was holding its "usual meeting on New Year's Day" on East Falkland. The same year, on the West, a Saturday afternoon challenge race, in April, between two rival horsemen along a Hill Cove sandbeach, drew a crowd of 30 onlookers. Two years later, the "Easter Saturday Races" had become so popular that the settlement was packed with visitors. There were "20 or more people sleeping in the house and about 50 in the men's quarters", wrote Robert Blake. "Between 60 and 70 horses ran and such a collection of men and animals had never been seen at Hill Cove before".

As the years passed the meetings grew into major events on both sides of the Falkland Sound, each held on different farms in rotation, and each attracting riders from afar. On the West, it has now become easily the biggest social gathering of the year.

In early March 1992, the population of Port Howard increased tenfold as 250 people turned up for the Sports by boat or plane, in Rovers or on horseback. So many folk assembled that a helicopter twice flew in with emergency supplies to keep the bars and dances alive.

There were sheep dog trials, shearing and steer riding contests, children's sports and a gymkhana. There was running, jumping, golfing and gossiping. There were mountains of sausage rolls at the beginning and mountainous hangovers at the end. Grown men, astride a greasy pole, tried to knock each other off with stuffed sacks. A flush of giggling girls chased somebody's cock around a field in their efforts to "catch the rooster".

Tuesday was the day of the races. Even the Archbishop of Canterbury was there to watch 'Shadow' win the Governor's Cup and Raymond Evans retain the title of Champion Jockey for the fifth successive time. On Wednesday a 70 knot gale whipped up at dusk, rain lashed the throbbing dance hall and Uncle Joe lost his false teeth in the gloom.

The next day everyone went home, and most agreed that it had been a "bloody good" sports.

Dancing to Terry Taite and the Chays at the Port Howard Sports, March 1992 (left).

Champion Jockey Raymond Evans on Natasha (nearest) winning the 600 yard Maiden Plate Open by a nostril from Dae Peck's Sudaña, at the Port Howard Sports, March 1992.

The Minstrel of Many Branch

A few miles north of Port Howard, surrounded by rolling whitegrass plains and overlooked by the Six Hills, is Many Branch House, home to generations of the Lee family.

I arrived to find my old friend, Les Lee, standing by the gate like a huge garden gnome, wearing a trilby and brandishing a peat axe.

"Gate wouldn't close properly," he said. "I had to chop a bit out of the post."

We looked at it, swung it, and stood back to admire the job.

"I'll paint him later," he said, and we went in for tea, but had a dram instead.

Les' great grandfather, Jacob John Lee, a 28-year-old Surrey shepherd, was employed in October 1856 by the Falkland Islands Company and during the three month voyage south from London, on the barque *Nithsdale*, he tended a flock of pedigree Cheviots and a racehorse. By the time the ship berthed in Stanley he had earned £9. 2s. 3d. but lost his heart to a young English governess, Grace White, also on board and bound for Valparaiso. Within three weeks they were married and went to live at Darwin, where Jacob received 27 shillings a week as a stockman.

In 1868 he became farm manager at New Island and they arrived in the spring with three young sons, on the schooner *Fairy*. But poor food and accommodation caused Henry, their eldest, to contract tuberculosis and after a year the family left for Shallow Bay. It was a bad move and following a drunken row with his new boss, Ernest Holmstead, Jacob was sacked.

"Best thing that ever happened," said pioneering landowner James Waldron, because the Lees then settled on his large estate at Port Howard and passing years saw the family grow and take up various positions around the farm. Many Branch, where Jacob and Grace lived, became an important outside shepherd's house and was to remain so for a century.

Following the Argentine occupation of 1982, during which several Port Howard families temporarily moved out of the settlement to live at Many Branch, the house fell into disuse and it was eventually sold. It now belongs to

Jacob and Grace Lee.
(Photo courtesy of Les Lee)

Les leans over the vegetable garden fence, Many Branch House beyond.

Les and his family, who come out from Stanley each summer to spend time in the Camp where they grew up.

Les took his guitar from a corner of the kitchen, fretboard gouged by years of use and bass string wound down to D. He taught himself to play by listening to 78's of Jimmy Rogers and Riley Puckett on a wind-up gramophone his parents had. In the blue of the day he sang a country song from the 30's or the 60's, or somewhere in between, and then we all listened to a tale about his grandfather, whose name was Alfred but everyone called him Joe.

Jacob's third son, Joe, married 16-year-old Hannah Simpson at Shag Cove in 1890 and the newlyweds settled at Port Purvis House, away in the back of beyond. So when Hannah gave birth to their first child, Nelly, they were completely alone. Joe took a sheepdog up the hill, attached a note to his collar, and cracked his stockwhip in the air, sending the startled dog shooting off towards Many Branch, nine miles away, with the news. "There were no telephones in those days you see," said Les.

He played a few bars of *Take Me Back*, his own song. "I had a Dobro once," he said, "but it got run over by a tractor at Pebble Island Sports and the front all bent in. So we took it over to Cinty Betts' place and straightened it back out and I played with it at the dance that night. It sounded good with an accordion."

Old Jacob died in his sleep aged 85 at Many Branch in 1913 having sired nine children with stockmanship in their veins. Today, one of his great grandsons, Rodney, runs Port Howard, the largest farm on West Falkland, while brother Robin manages Falkland Landholdings, the largest company farming on East Falkland. Together they control a third of the Islands' sheep.

In the stillness of evening I sat on a bank by a shock of rhubarb, watching ram hogs with red-ruddled rumps contentedly chewing their cuds. In the garden a patch of vegetables growing in tidy seams bordered an aggressive tangle of dog rose and couch. An ancient apple tree, dwarfed and withered by wind, rustled over a cluster of overgrown raspberries, honeysuckle and harebells and all was almost enclosed by a rickety-pickletly fence of weather-beaten battens and rusting iron. A little way away at the house someone had lit a Tilley lamp and the gentle strains of *Back in the Saddle Again* drifted out of the window and across the paddock.

The telephone at Many Branch. Most of the houses at Port Howard and the other farms were linked by a party line. To call any individual house it was necessary to signal the appropriate combination of rings with a series of sharp turns on the handle. If you got it wrong it did not always matter as everybody for miles picked up anyway. Some people even stuck the telephone wire into their radio as an aerial so they could listen to the BBC News and their neighbours gossiping at the same time.

Les Lee sings the country blues in the kitchen at Many Branch.

Stone Runs

"We were aſtoniſhed at the infinite number of ſtones of all ſizes thrown one upon another" wrote the naturalist priest Antoine Joseph Pernetty in 1764. He was describing, for the first time, the enormous river of rocks, now called Princes Street, a couple of hours' walk from the early French settlement at Port Louis. Then, in an historic ecclesiastical bid to become the Island's earliest grafitti artist, Pernetty "attempted in vain to engrave a name upon one of theſe ſtones, which formed a table a foot and a half thick, ten feet long and ſix broad. It was ſo hard that neither my knife nor a punch could make any impreſſion upon it."

45 years later, in the faraway, leafy county of Shropshire, a doctor's wife gave birth to a son who was also destined to stumble down Princes Street on his way to becoming the most famous naturalist of them all. At first, like Pernetty, the youngster appeared pre-ordained for a life of the cloth but, at the age of 21, Charles Darwin rejected the exciting prospects of becoming a village parson. Instead he went to sea.

He made just one voyage, but what a voyage. It lasted almost five years and took him around the world, via the three great Capes, as scientist on board the research ship *HMS Beagle*. During the trip he visited the then remote islands of Galapagos, Tahiti, Mauritius and St Helena. After it he compiled his theory of evolution which so infuriated contemporary clergymen but became the basis of all modern biology.

Accompanied by his manservant, Covington, Darwin twice visited Berkeley Sound for a month in the successive autumns of 1833 and 1834. On board ship he had suffered the misery of prolonged chronic seasickness. Once on land he didn't like it here much either, soon becoming bored and moaning about the weather. On the third day he wrote: "the whole landscape has an air of desolation". To cheer him up, the following day, the ship's clerk drowned while duck hunting.

Nonetheless surrounded by depressing circumstances ashore, which at various times included shipwreck, drunkenness and mass murder, Darwin got on with his work; exploring, making notes and collecting fossils and specimens which were each assiduously

Native strawberry often grows along the verges of stone runs (right).

The snake plant *Nassauvia serpens* is endemic to the stone runs of East and West Falkland.

Princes Street, Darwin's "valley of fragments", runs for four miles and is the largest of all stone runs.

Yellow-flowered *Senecio littoralis* and fern *Polystichum mohrioides* amongst the rocks of Mount Challenger.

preserved and labelled in his cabin on the poop deck. During his ramblings he observed many of the singular geographical features, unique to the Islands, which are now known as 'stone runs'.

"In very many parts of the Island," he noted "the bottoms of the valleys are filled up with an astonishing number of large angular fragments of quartz. The blocks vary in size from a man's chest to ten or twenty times that size… occasionally much larger. In the great "valley of fragments", as he called Princes Street, "it is necessary to cross by jumping from stone to stone… almost half a mile. The scene is like a ruined castle. It is as if from every point in the mountains great streams of white lava had burst forth and subsequently been torn into a myriad of fragments."

Darwin, like Pernetty before him, considered that these streams of stones, which occur along many of the Islands' geologically folded uplands, must have been caused by earthquakes. More recent investigators point the finger of explanation towards the permafrost conditions of the last Ice Age. Tundraic freezing and thawing caused blocks of quartzite to become dislodged along joints and beds, then undermined until they broke off or slid away. The boulders then rolled or slid down into valleys over a carpet of mud.

Stone runs occur in upland areas of Devonian Quartzite throughout the Islands but most spectacularly along the Wickham Heights which form the backbone of East Falkland. From above they look like great, grey glaciers. They are impassable by horse or vehicle. Little grows amongst the tumbled jumble of rock, except lichens other than in places where there are isolated pockets of soil, yet strangely, the weird snake plant *Nassauvia serpens* is found nowhere else in the world.

Winter

Looking south from East Bay towards Lake Sullivan and Fox Bay beyond (left).

The settlement at New Island (above).

Snowbound sheep at South Harbour (right). (Photo Lucy Ellis)

The settlement at Bleaker Island (far right).

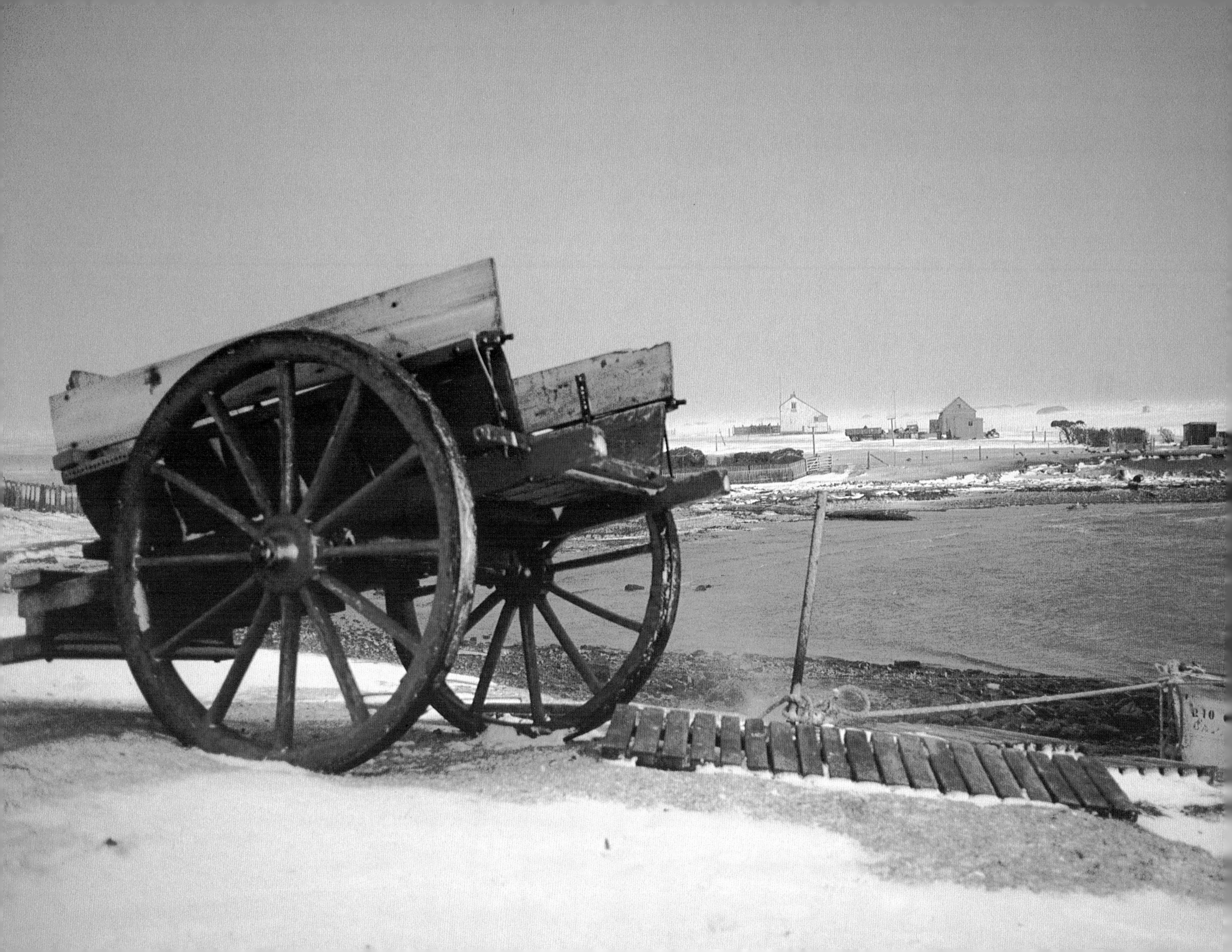

Keppel and the Indians

Robert Whaits, a skilled carpenter, wheelwright and blacksmith, was the last Superintendent of the Keppel Mission which closed in 1898. He later returned to run the farm until the island was sold thirteen years later. Cyril, the Yahgan, lived for years on Keppel with his wife Kate. (Photo by courtesy of Roddy Napier)

Long, long ago in Fireland, the moon fell into the sea and caused a great flood. Everything, even the highest mountain, was submerged, except a small island in the Beagle Channel, which broke away from the sea bed and floated to the surface. When the survivors, Indian, guanaco and fox, gazed around they could see nothing but ocean on all sides. Eventually, when the moon rose up again, the waters receded and life returned to normal. The island settled back into its original place and from it the world was peopled by the Yahgan Indians to whom this legend belongs.

Man first appeared in Patagonia 11,000 years ago and later spread throughout the archipelagic tip of Tierra del Fuego. The Yahgans, a tribe of Mongoloid Canoe Indians calling themselves Yámana (people), eventually settled along the coast and amongst the intricate web of waterways and islands which fringe the Beagle Channel, becoming the southernmost people on earth. They ranged from Desolation Bay on the Pacific coast eastwards to Spaniard Harbour in the Atlantic and down to Cape Horn.

Yahgans were squat, copper-coloured and, in spite of the raw climate, virtually naked nomads, who wore little more than a triangular loin cloth of otterskin. They lived in simple wigwams, bent over branches covered with fern fronds or skins, and paddled the briny arteries of Fuegia in leaky birch-bark canoes, constantly on the move from one traditional encampment to the next. Their one great luxury was fire, kindled by using firestone sparks to ignite the filmy web of a puffball kept dry in a guanaco's bladder. The precious embers travelled with them, smouldering on a pile of turfs in every canoe and Indian eyes were constantly rimmed red and smarting from woodsmoke. Women paddled the vessels and moored them out in the kelp, swimming ashore afterwards, like dogs, through the icy water. Men used slings, stones and arrows to kill birds and spears to stab fish. Wives dived for mussels, and centuries-old mounds of discarded shells, up to four metres high, accumulated in rings around more popular tippee sites.

The Mission Farm Manager's house.

Although a quarrelsome race, frequently settling disputes with a club, the Yahgans were intelligent and communicative people who spoke a language in many ways more expressive and richer than English or Spanish.

There was a scattered community of around 3,000 of these sharp-eyed hunters and fungi gatherers in the sixteenth century when square-rigged European sailing ships began probing for a passage around the Horn. Rumours of these towering white sea monsters on the horizon soon filtered along the Fuegian waterways and the Yahgans gradually came into contact with the seaborne flagbearers of a new civilisation – pirates, explorers and sealers. As two further centuries passed, they came to hate these bearded, pink-faced men with their muskets, syphilis and rum. Then the missionaries arrived bearing gifts of knives, fine white linen and even chamber pots, as the Indians tended to let fly anywhere and at any time. In return the natives only had to smile and mimic strange rhythmic chants. Once the handouts ran dry, God's messengers, like many a ship-wrecked sailor before, were often scorned, beaten up or slaughtered.

The much-publicised deaths in September 1851, of a fanatical 57-year-old lay-preacher from Berkshire, Allen Gardiner, and his companions, who starved to death on a wintery Fuegian beach after fleeing from hostile Yahgans, caused an uproar which shook the Motherland to the keel.

While *The Times* deplored such a senseless waste of lives and money over a few savages, Victorian England passed the hat and funded a mission in the Falklands from which white preachers could cleanse the black hearts of Fireland. Keppel Island was leased for a song by the Patagonian Missionary Society in 1855 and soon became the first established farm on the West Falklands. The station, called Cranmer, was to be "a centre of operations, a place of rendevous for the Missionaries, a safe depot for stores, a model community for the natives and it was hoped that the island might produce considerable revenue". Despite strong local opposition, the Bristol-based catechists began persuading savages to come to Keppel and find 'The Way'. 'The Way' was to work without pay from dawn till dusk and teach the missionaries Yahgan. The first targets for recruitment were Jemmy Button and his family who duly arrived in June 1858 and remained for five moons. Button had been kidnapped from a canoe as a boy by Captain Fitzroy RN and taken to England a quarter century earlier. He learnt English in a Walthamstow boarding school, had an audience with the Queen and developed a taste for white kid gloves and shiny shoes. But Button, now in his forties, was no soft touch and proved it within a year by instigating the murder of eight Englishmen during a Sunday morning service in Fuegia in 1859. Governor Moore temporarily banned further imports of Indians and Reverend Despard, the disillusioned Superintendent of Cranmer, resigned, leaving the mission temporarily under charge of his stepson, an eighteen-year-old orphan, Thomas Bridges. For the rest of his days the sympathetic and laudable Bridges made his home amongst the Indians, at first on Keppel, later in Fireland. He died in 1898 leaving their language in a dictionary and their soon-to-be extinct lives in his diary.

Once established, the Cranmer station was to continue importing Indians and acting as a base for missionary activities in Tierra del Fuego and Patagonia for 40 years, during which over 150 Yahgans were offered salvation as a wage for humping rock, cutting peat and digging potatoes. The farm prospered and by 1877 its 2800 sheep, 500 cattle and five acre vegetable gardens, under the able management of William Bartlett, were coining in £1000 a year. Governor D'Arcy was so impressed by its success that he was prompted to consider bringing over more Indians as cheap labour for other farms.

Meanwhile, in Fuegia, America's southernmost Indian tribes were suffering a tragically similar fate to that experienced by their more famous cousins in the forests and plains of the North. Some were given bibles and told to look up while pink men stole the land beneath them. Others fell prey to firewater. Guanaco were usurped by sheep and tribes decimated by measles. When hungry Indians stole a new rancher's livestock they were shot, their ears bringing a bounty of a pound apiece.

By 1898, with scarcely any Yahgans left to convert, protect or exploit, the Keppel Mission ceased operations marking the end of a curious chapter in the history of Stone Age Man in the New World.

NOTE
Eight years later the remaining 130 Yahgan Indians were placed on Navarino Island, Chile, where gradually they dwindled away. As a tribe they are now extinct.

The sheltered valley site of the five acre gardens with the hills of Pebble Island beyond.

The stone Chapel was converted to a shearing shed using materials from the mission house, by John Dean, who bought the 9,600 acre island in 1911. It was used as such until 1992, when Keppel was de-stocked by new owner Lionel Fell to become a nature reserve.

The headstone of Charles Henry, baby son of William Bartlett who arrived in 1856 and for many years was farm bailiff. Although several Yahgans died at Keppel, their modest graves are unmarked.

Three Old Farms

The neat, spacious settlement at Salvador.

Gibraltar Station

Gibraltar Station has been home to five generations of the Pitaluga family since starting as a sheep ranch in the early 1860's.

Andrez Pitaluga first arrived from Gibraltar, aged 17, in 1838 and three years later returned on contract from Montevideo to become the gaucho boss at Port Louis. He was illiterate and signed his agreement with a cross. For years Andrez rode the range of East and West Falkland, slaughtering thousands of the wild cattle which roamed freely across the unfenced moorland. It was a tough life. Gaucho gangs sought out the feral herds then chased, lassoed and hamstrung individual beasts, returning later to butcher them. By night they hobbled their mounts and slept in shacks or in the open, warmed only by a woollen poncho and a sweaty horserug. In his spare time Pitaluga castrated colts for two shillings a head and constructed various corrals and houses island-wide out of stone, including that now known as 'The Pink Shop', where we live in Stanley.

As land became available for farming in the middle of last century, Andrez managed to acquire 300,000 acres, amounting to most of the north of East Falkland. But various deals whittled his leaseholding down by three-quarters to the area which now comprises the two estates of Gibraltar Station and Rincon Grande.

Gibraltar Station today comprises 52,000 acres, grazes 15,000 sheep and is run by Andrez's great grandson Robin Pitaluga, highly-respected chairman of the Falklands' Sheepowners Association.

Port Stephens

Port Stephens is the home of Ann and Peter Robertson who run 10,000 corriedale sheep over the surrounding 50,000 acres. The farm was begun by Dean and Son in the late 1860's as the centre of a 350 square mile holding which soon became the most important wool producing estate on West Falkland. Although the farm was sold to the Falkland Islands Company in 1945, it remained in essence unchanged until being divided into five smaller farms in 1987. Today the settlement buildings are gradually being dismantled and moved out to their respective owner's new farms.

The Robertsons have lived at Stephens for over twenty years and, as farm manager for much of that time, Peter witnessed many strange things but few as bizarre as the singular events of 14th August 1991. It was Ann who noticed the earliest forebodings of the creeping darkness while they were out fencing that morning:

"It was gradually getting thicker and thicker until at about half past eleven we decided to pack it in. We all had a film of dust on our clothes and faces. As we were coming down off the hills we noticed the visibility deteriorating and by the time we got in here to the house there was this sort of eerie, yellowish light about everything. It got worse and worse. By half past one in the afternoon it was that dark that we had a candle in the kitchen and decided to put the generator on. It was just like a very dark night. You couldn't see anything at all. Most incredible. Then at about 4 o'clock it started to lighten up again."

Elsewhere, too, most of the south and west of the Islands had been temporarily plunged into a total and frightening darkness as volcanic ash rained down for the first time in living memory. Satellite pictures revealed a wind-borne plume, emanating from erupting Mount Hudson, 700 miles away in southern Chile, stretching out over the Atlantic and obliterating the Falklands from view. Fortunately, when the wind changed, the ashy cloud moved away from the Islands, although two years later airborne dust was still to accompany each north-westerly blow.

Meanwhile parts of Patagonia were placed under a state of emergency as dust accumulated, in places, to a depth of several feet, covering grazings and causing thousands of cattle to be destroyed.

The following spring brought forth a fertilized and enriched carpet of wild flowers but found many sheep flocks bare-gummed, with teeth worn to stubs by the abrasive powder. In addition the ash contaminated fleeces, wore the skin off sheep-shearers' fingertips and blunted their cutting gear. At the end of the 1991-92 season it was estimated that, along with the normally snow-white woolclip, Falkland farmers had exported over 200 tonnes of Chile to Bradford at a cost of around £50,000 in freight!

New Island

The farming settlement at New Island is one of the longest established in the Falkland Islands (author's house is that nearest with the bright blue roof). It was begun by the Montevidean firm of Smith Brothers, who acquired the leasehold for £64 down plus £10 a year, in 1860. But it was not the incredibly fertile, rich green pastures which had attracted the new owners' interest, more the smell of dung. For the Island's vast seabird rookeries had, over the centuries, produced impressive deposits of guano, which at that time was fetching high prices in the markets of Europe.

Although the New Island guano turned out to be valueless due to rain leach, by 1861 there were already 500 sheep, 46 cattle and an orderly population of seven men, one woman and a child present on the Island. Ranching for wool has continued ever since although today, with only 300 grazing animals nibbling across our paddocks, compared with 3300 twenty years ago, it is by far the smallest sheep farm in the Falklands. Much of our property, which comprises the northern half of New Island, is now run as a private nature reserve.

Port Stephens (above, right).

New Island (right).

Radio Telephone

"My great, great grandfather and his family came out with Governor Moody", said Eileen Vidal, recalling the arrival from Portsmouth of Private James Biggs at Port Louis in 1842. "There were quite a lot of them and they brought the Falklands' population up to 60".

There are now over 200 Biggses of all shapes and sizes scattered about the Islands. Eileen is one of the best known, for her friendly voice was heard every weekday in every Camper's kitchen for a decade while she was the main Government radio telephone operator.

"This is Stanley. If anyone wants the Doctor, he is here now". It was 8.30am – breakfast time in the Camp – and the doctor had just walked into Eileen's radio shack to take his daily, half hour long clinic. While shepherds scraped their last spoonfuls of porridge and shearers each tore into half a dozen mutton chops, the Doc swiftly dealt with a bad back at Goose Green and a dose of diarrhoea at Dunnose Head. Nothing was private. Savlon was prescribed for the nasty rash on Maria's bottom.

"Rub it in twice a day", said the Doc.

"Some blokes have all the luck", muttered Albert, reaching for another fried egg.

Eileen and her team of four part time operators, Maureen Peck, Nellie Hewitt, Siggie Barnes and Wallace Hirtle, using HF and VHF transceivers and two wind-up telephones, were the hub of communications for all the scattered and outlying farms comprising the camp community. If your wife had given birth or you had just sold your annual wool crop, it was Eileen who broke the news. If you wanted to know whether "that parcel has turned up in this lot of Surface Mail?" Eileen tracked it down. If you had the misfortune to die, it was her job to broadcast the sad news.

The day after the Argentines landed, in 1982, Eileen was back in the radio shack putting a bunch of boarding school children in touch with their worried parents in the Camp. As the children were leaving, and with the streets crawling with enemy troops, a voice came over the airwaves.

"Stanley, this is *Endurance*. Can you tell me the situation, please?"

"I told them what I could, about the troops, Pucaras, helicopters and ships", said Eileen. She was then asked to wait and, incredibly, to repeat it all to a senior officer who came on the air "sounding as though he had a hot potato in his mouth. Once was asking for trouble", she recalled, "twice was plain bloody stupid". But she got away with it and continued to operate for a while during the occupation until closed down by the Argentines.

After the war things settled down again. The R/T came alive each morning at 7.45am with outstations passing weather to the Air Service. The daily operator arrived at 8.15am and began by announcing the estimated arrival times for the aircraft at various settlements. Thereafter followed the traffic of everyday life; people ordering stores, requesting records for 'Friday Hour', asking the vet to castrate a horse and, occasionally, having

4.15pm on a Friday and the end of another week for Eileen Vidal (sitting) as Maureen Peck arrives to take over for the evening shift.

rows, which everyone enjoyed listening in to, of course.

One morning in May 1986 there was a dramatic call from an unarmed Taiwanese squid jigger, 150 miles north of Pebble Island. Everyone in Camp heard it and few will forget.

"Stanley Radio, this is Taiwanese fishing boat *Chian Der 3*. I am under attack and request protection of the British Navy", said a heavily-accented voice, giving his position, which was clearly in international waters.

"Get the Argy to go on 4.5 megahertz", suggested Eileen immediately, while dialling the British military forces for help. "Then the whole world can hear". Suddenly the Argentine gunboat *Perfecto Derbes* came on the air, giving the Taiwanese five minutes to stop engines or "I will shoot until you dip".

There was silence for an hour until we heard, "Mayday. Mayday. This is *Chian Der 3*. The ship is on fire, we are in the lifeboats, this is my last call as my battery is very weak".

Survivors bobbed about in the ocean for several hours while the Argentines stood off, refusing to permit either another jigger or a Lynx helicopter from nearby *H.M.S. Broadsword* to assist. Eventually, with one man dead and three others injured, the Taiwanese were picked up and taken to Argentina. The *Chian Der 3* eventually sank, but thanks to Eileen's quick wittedness, it was not without trace.

Government originally installed the Camp R/T system in 1950 following the arrival of the air service. Sets were provided at each farm, powered by 12 volt batteries charged up with a wind generator. There were two frequencies: 4.5 megahertz was for medicals and business and 2 megahertz, which became known as the 'farmyard', for gossip. The system provided communications and a life line to the camp for 41 years until it was closed down on 31st July 1991, to be replaced by a cheerless network of 'real' telephones. Eileen no longer does daily battle with the ionospherics on our behalf. Instead she retired and sits at home playing with her grandchildren.

Dunbar, West Falkland, home of Marshall and Diedre Barnes. The R/T was on all day in most camper's kitchens so that even the remotest farms kept up with the news and gossip.

Golding Island. On small and isolated island farms like this one the Radio Telephone was a life line.

8 MARINE MAMMALS

Sea Elephant

Bull Sea Elephants (below and far right).

Sea elephants are the largest animals found on the Islands. Hauling out in spring and fully-fattened for the breeding season, the biggest beachmaster bulls weigh four tons, as heavy as a hippopotamus, and reach a length of over five metres; females attain roughly half the length but less than a quarter of the weight.

At sea, elephants spend most of their time submerged. Some females are able to remain underwater for up to two hours and dive to fourteen hundred metres in pursuit of their primary prey – squid. Ashore, the formerly large herds caught the entrepreneurial eyes of the earliest Falkland fur sealers in the 1760's. However, while fur seals were sought for their pelts, the elephant's attraction was its oil, which was found to be similar to whale oil and extractable by the same means of 'trying out' the blubber. 'Elephanting' and whaling became closely tied and were often conducted from the same vessels.

Elephants were sitting ducks, lethargically lying about in bunches on beaches to breed. Cows and calves were clubbed with a seven foot wooden bludgeon called a manduc. Bulls, rearing up to roar at their attackers, were

Females arrive on the beaches in Spring and form up in harems around those bulls already hauled out and established as dominant beachmasters. Each cow usually produces a single, black, woolly-coated pup, four feet long and weighing around 46 kilos, which she feeds on large quantities of exceedingly rich milk. By the end of three weeks the youngsters have quadrupled their weight and are weaned. Their mothers are then mated and return to the sea after barely 30 days onshore. Pups take to the water after moulting at five weeks old, although some are crushed under careless bulls and others are taken by individual marauding sea lions.

shot up through the mouth with a musket. Victims were then lanced through the main arteries, releasing copious quantities of blood. After skinning, the seals' thick, thermal underwear of oil-bearing blubber was scythed off with a curved knife in flaps called 'blanket pieces', up to eight inches thick. These were soaked in water for forty-eight hours to wash out any remaining blood, then minced and boiled in cast iron trypots. A good bull in early Spring could yield over ninety gallons of oil which was stored in oaken casks, to be sold later as lamp fuel or for tanning. The rest of the carcase went to waste, although tasty tongues were a welcome addition to a windjammer's boring cuisine. If seal were plentiful, crews set up tryworks ashore and lived in skin or sail-covered shelters or under upturned boats. Otherwise the blubber 'blankets' were towed out to the ship for rendering down.

Within a century, the sealers had virtually eliminated elephants from the Islands, but fortunately sufficient stocks survived the oilers' onslaught here and elsewhere in the southern oceans and gradually numbers recovered. Some 'elephanting' was again carried out after World War II to supplement disappointing oil returns at Albemarle from dwindling sea lion stocks.

Recently there has been an alarming decline in their numbers, possibly due to competition from the vast south west Atlantic fishing fleet which, while bringing prosperity to the people of the region, is causing paucity and pollution on Falkland beaches. The magnificent sea elephants are rapidly being replaced along the shore by rusty oil drums, lengths of bright green fishing net and plastic detergent bottles.

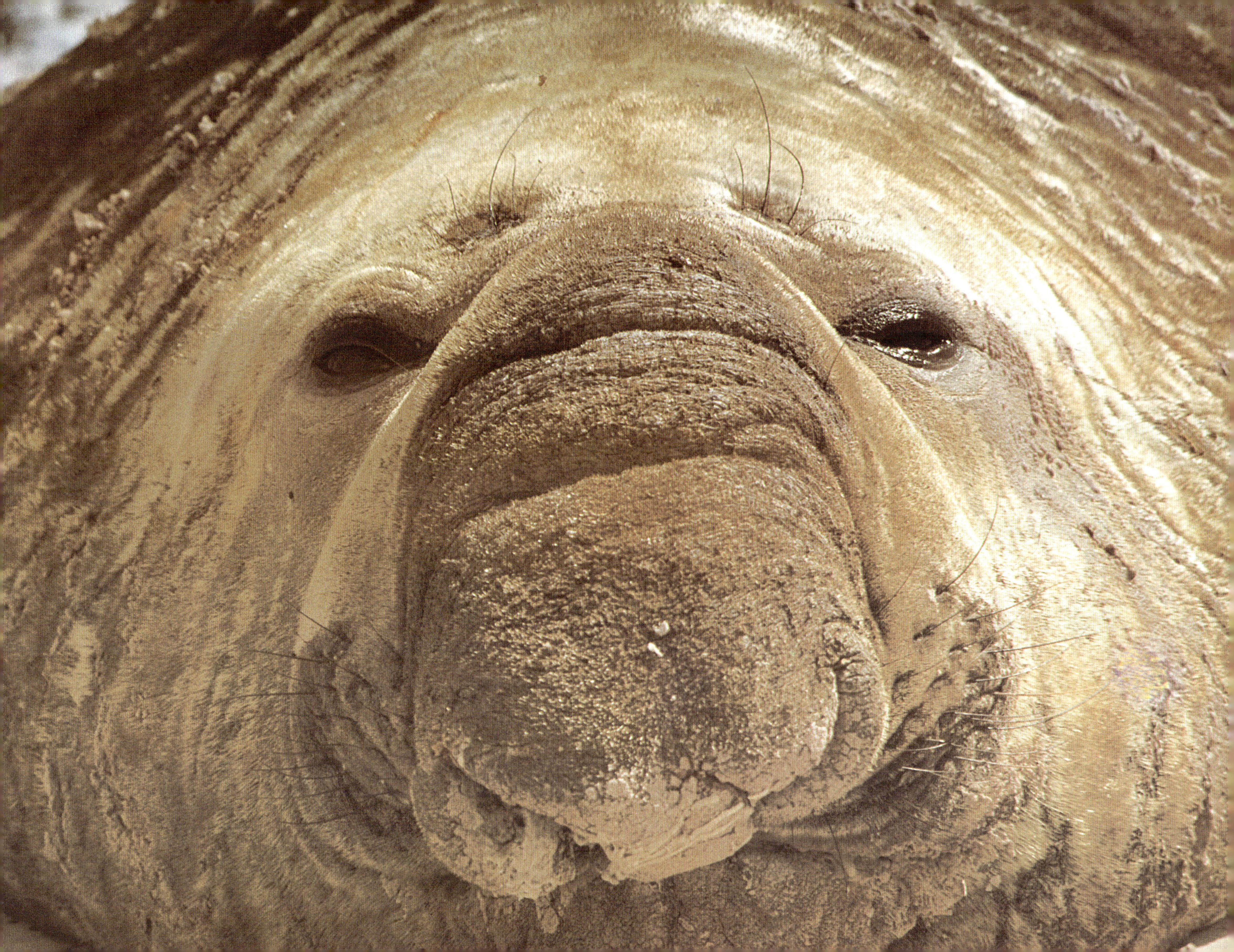

Sealion

Bull sealion in tussac grass, Kidney Island.

In 1764, the poet's grandad, 'Foulweather Jack' Byron, an English naval captain, sailed an experimentally copper-sheathed sloop *Dolphin* to the South Atlantic in search of the mythical Pepys Island. He returned two years later with a clean bottom and a pickled hair seal head which boffins labelled *Otaria byronia*, the Southern Sealion.

This species of hair seal (a sealers' term differentiating the coarser pelted sealions from the more luxuriantly clad fur seal) is found along the South American coastline from Cape Horn north to northern Peru on the west and Southern Brazil on the east. Although widespread and not uncommon in the Falklands, the population has suffered an unexplained decline since the 1930's, when large herds often gathered in areas of strong tides and currents.

The hair seal is a gregarious inshore feeder, living mainly on crustaceans, cephalopods and fish, though some individuals may become partial to penguins and even elephant seal pups. At sea their only enemy is the killer whale; on land, man.

In the water they are playful and inquisitive and in the still water of a Kidney Island dawn we watched six curiously nosing our boat's anchor chain in the shallow, sandy-bottomed bay.

Onshore they are shy and when people come, they fly into the water, except during the rut, when bulls become brave and bombastic. Once, when sealing, Cecil Bertrand watched a Norwegian shipmate tossed through the air with a chunk taken out of his leg by an irate lion, and in 1896 one W. McDaid had a finger nipped off as he plucked a pipe-cleaning whisker from a snoozing bull.

Hair seal like to lie up and breed in thick tussac, flattening the grass bog pedestals and exuding a strong smell. This is just as well because if you wander unknowingly through seal-infested tussac, it can be slightly unnerving to tread on a quarter-ton monster with the roar of a lion and a buffalo's bloodshot eye. Our son Bill, then eight, did so once and both he and the 'jasper' stared at each other, momentarily scared rigid, before running and crashing off in different directions.

Clapmatch and pup, Ship Island. Most pups are born shortly after Christmas.

Adult males can weigh over 700lbs, twice the weight of females. This old bull has several gashes on his face, probably from fighting a rival (right).

A similar thing had happened on 1st February 1764 when, as the wind died away at about 6.0pm, Monsieurs Douat and Le Roy were put ashore from their French expeditionary ship *Aigle* to gather fodder for some hungry cattle onboard. Above the beach they came upon

"an animal of terrible appearance and aftoniſhing ſize lying upon the graff; his head and mane reſembling a lion's; and his whole body covered with hair of a duſty red as long as a goat's. This animal ſeemed to be as large as two oxen, and twelve to fourteen feet in length with hanging ears, as long in proportion as thoſe of a ſpaniel."

So frightened were they of this sealion that they could not even find the courage to shoot it.

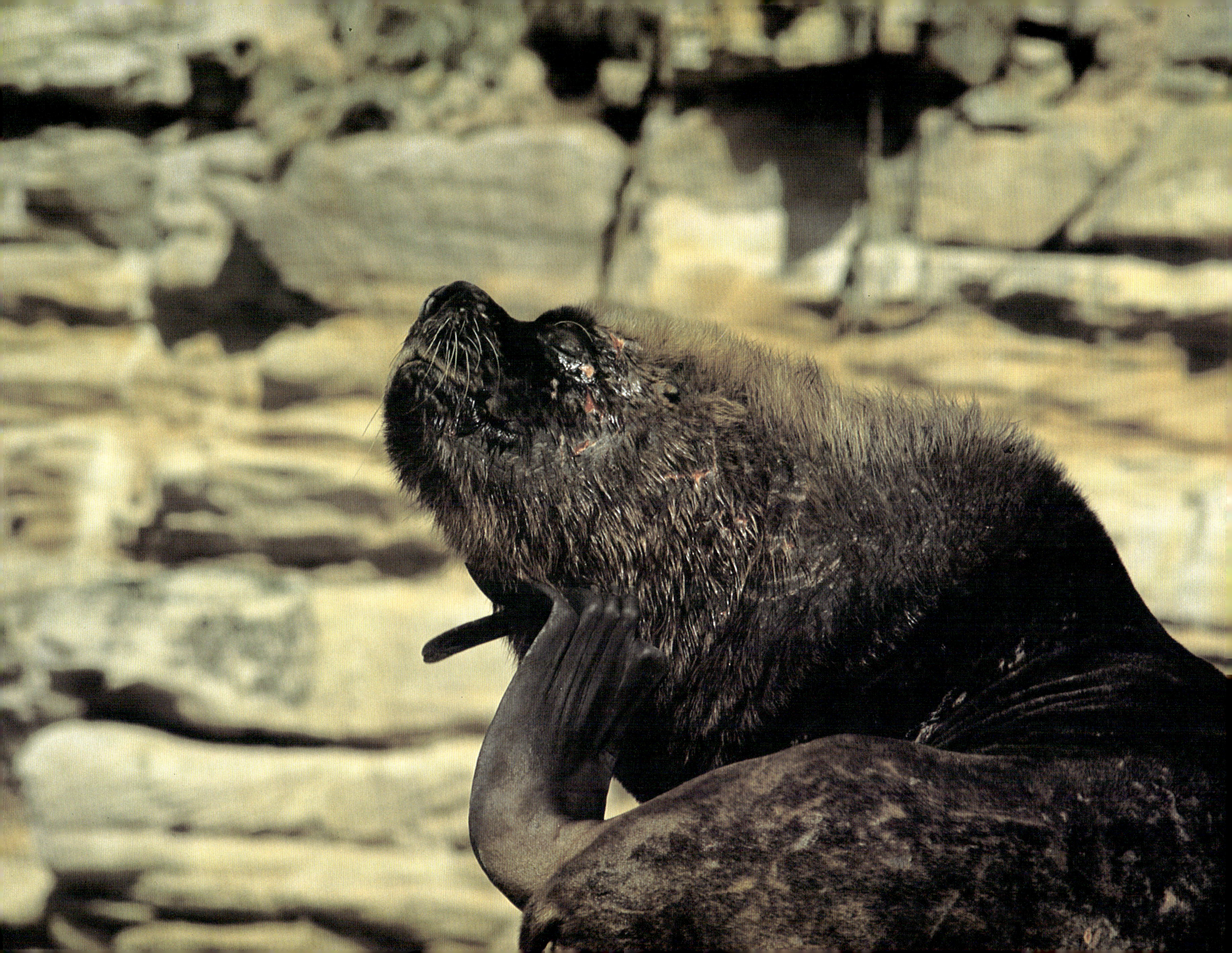

Albemarle

"These islands used to be crawling with hair seal", said former sealer Bob Ferguson, as the *Penelope* motored between the Arch Islands, off Albemarle. "Now they've all gone".

When Bob was born in 1926, an estimated 400,000 Southern Sealion lived around Falkland coasts, a hundred times more than today's total herd. To many sheep farmers they were simply a grass-spoiling and stock-frightening pest. So in 1927, with Government backing, a group of the Islands' landed gentry, together with some South Georgia-based Norwegians, formed the Falkland Islands and Dependencies Sealing Co. Ltd. to exploit the seals by extracting and exporting their oil.

Based in the North West Arm at Albemarle, operations commenced in 1928, using the rusting hulk of the *Bellville* as both accommodation for the thirty hands and as a factory until the shore station was complete.

On a good day 300 seal were gathered using rawhide stockwhips, and cuts of twenty at a time driven into a corral. They were shot with .303 rifles, dragged out on the beach and gutted. 40 carcases were toggled by the neck, two by two, onto strops attached every six feet to a long line and hove on board the *Port Richards*. When the hold was filled they were piled on deck. At the station the bodies were winched up to the digester to be chopped up, dropped in and rendered down. The *Port Richards*, a 75 ft Lowestoft drifter, having arrived in February 1921 as the armed seal rookeries' protection vessel *Afterglow*, was crewed mainly by Norwegians under the command of 'Cracker' Jack Davies.

It was a smelly and brutal business and sometimes things went wrong. On one occasion, several hundred sealion were driven accidentally over a cliff, bursting open on the rocks below. On Barren Island, a shortage of bullets caused 300 elephant seal to be killed by choppers and pickaxes. Most gruesome of all was when 800 lions were driven overland fifteen miles from Cape Lagoon to Albemarle. The journey took a week. Many seal died or escaped, trailing their entrails over the diddle dee, to be found years later as bleached bones in the camp. Only 100 animals made it to the sealing station where they were corralled for the night. By morning just one lion remained, the others having clambered out and escaped. Ted Robson felt sorry for him, opened the gate and let him go down the bank to the sea.

The company operated spasmodically through a depressed decade, taking 40,000 seal, and closed in 1938, a dead loss.

Postwar, the Colonial Development Corporation invested in a second operation, this time based at Jack's Harbour in the West Arm at Albemarle and, with a sealing officer ever present, operations were more strictly controlled. Only male lions over six feet long and large bull elephants were to be taken and the whole carcases utilised. Using the *Golden Chance*, hairseal were hunted in much the same way and at the same places as before – Cape Meredith, Ten Shillings Bay and the Arch Islands, where wooden corrals were erected.

At the station, bodies were hauled up on the plan, skinned and cut into four. Meat and bones were dried, powdered and bagged as guano. Skins were flensed, salted and folded like bullock hides and the blubber tried out for oil, one lion yielding 10-15 gallons. The *Protector* went further afield, hunting elephant seal which hauled up on Carcass, George and Barren Islands, Elephant Cays and Sea Lion Easterly. Once loaded it was necessary to return to Albemarle quickly before the carcases began to decay. *Protector* cruised at nine knots, purred like a sewing machine at twelve and shook at sixteen.

After only two-and-a-half years, due largely to lack of seals (only 3000 were killed), the project ground to a halt and the station closed. "We didn't make much money, but we seen a lot of life", twinkled our neighbour Billy Poole, once cook on the *Protector*.

Daffodils flowering below the ruins of the second Albemarle Sealing Station, 1991.

The original Albemarle sealing, circa 1930 (above). (Photo *Falkland Pictorial*)

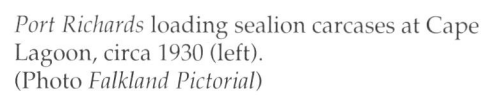

Port Richards loading sealion carcases at Cape Lagoon, circa 1930 (left).
(Photo *Falkland Pictorial*)

Driving sealions to Albemarle using stockwhips, circa 1930.
(Photo *Falkland Pictorial*)

Old Sealers

mv Protector III, a 163 ton minesweeper, was built in Nova Scotia in 1943. Postwar she was purchased by the Colonial Development Corporation for the revitalized "South Atlantic Sealing Company". From working shellfish in Kings Lynn, she was taken for refit in Wivenhoe dock. In August 1949, under command of Adrian Monk and with Chris Bundes as mate, she steamed southward, towing the CDC's other fine investment, the *Golden Chance*, for much of the way.

The latter, a 35-year-old Lowestoft drifter, had been a wartime barrage balloon boat and failed to achieve the Board of Trade standards. She was eventually to make it down only after steel reinforcing in Montevideo prevented her possibly breaking up on the high seas.

The two vessels worked as sealers at Albemarle for three seasons, until the operation was abandoned in 1952.

The *Golden Chance* was pensioned off and now lies in Stanley's Canâche. For a further two years *Protector* ran cargo, especially sheep, around the islands, including carcasses from Ajax Bay (another short-lived CDC project) to freezer ships in San Carlos Water. She eventually became the property of J.J. Davis, who was going to 'do her up, che'. In February 1969, 'Cracker' Jack, borrowing Freddie Jones' *Philomel*, towed *Protector* to New Island via Sparrow Cove 'for wood', Speedwell 'for meat' and Albemarle 'for a boat', stopping the night in Ten Shillings Bay. Approaching the anchorage, Jack's deep voice boomed out to nineteen-year-old Nobby Clarke, 'Get on the windlass, boy. We're towing a ship, so let out 45 fathoms". As Nobby released the windlass brake, the anchor dropped and chain rattled out, supposedly marked white every fifteen fathoms. Painted links passed once, then twice. "Pay her out, son. Pay her out", roared Jack. Then suddenly, as the youngster watched, the unfastened end of the chain whizzed past, down the hawse pipe and disappeared, 'plop', into the sea. Jack, a lover of good chain, was not amused.

Once at New Island, the two vessels were tied stern for stern with the bow of the unmanned and longer *Protector* forward of the *Philomel's*. At four knots on a high spring tide they ran towards the beach in order to put *Protector* up on the shore. But it was the *Philomel* which struck first, hitting a sand bank which sent her crew flying forward on the deck while the bigger boat still floated alongside. Eventually, *Protector* was nosed into the position she still occupies today. 'Cracker' never had time to 'do her up' as before the year was out, he was called from aloft to make his final Great Voyage.

In March 1986, after the ebbing afternoon tide had allowed us up a ladder and on board, Mike and Sandy Goodwin were married on the afterdeck and champagned on the bridge. The bride was given away by Bob Ferguson who, nearly 40 years earlier, had sailed as an able seaman on *mv Protector III*.

'Cracker' Jack Davis, an old time sailor of considerable repute, who captained the sealing vessel Port Richards at Albemarle for many years between the wars.

HMS Afterglow. Built as a drifter in Lowestoft in 1918, the Afterglow arrived in the Islands in 1921 as a seal rookeries' protection vessel. As a sealer, from 1927-38, she became the Port Richards but reverted back to her maiden name when requisitioned by the Royal Navy, as an armed patrol vessel, in World War II.

Protector III lies beached at New Island.

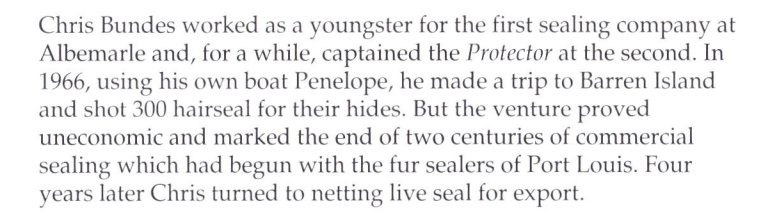

Two old foes, a leopard seal and *Golden Chance*, aground in Stanley's Canâche.

Chris Bundes worked as a youngster for the first sealing company at Albemarle and, for a while, captained the *Protector* at the second. In 1966, using his own boat Penelope, he made a trip to Barren Island and shot 300 hairseal for their hides. But the venture proved uneconomic and marked the end of two centuries of commercial sealing which had begun with the fur sealers of Port Louis. Four years later Chris turned to netting live seal for export.

Sea Leopard

At first glance I mistook him for a gnarled and curiously-shaped tree trunk. Many drift across from Tierra del Fuego to be cast up on these shores. Something made me look again and the log became a leopard, the first I had seen.

Sea Leopards are generally solitary animals of the Antarctic pack ice but during winter they migrate, many occurring on sub-antarctic islands. Although rare in the Falklands today, over 40 years ago they frequently hauled out on favoured beaches between June and November. On one occasion 30 came up at West Point and on another 80 appeared on Leopard Beach, Carcass, behaving not as herds but each as an individual. Most were male.

To man they appear sinister and untrustworthy. One seaman described the eerie sensation as, peeing over the stern of his anchored yacht, he became aware of a large, menacing, snake-like face leering straight up at him from just under the surface. Others have had similar experiences in small pulling boats.

Years ago, many leopards were shot or killed by the blow of a well-aimed fence post, their hides prized by makers of horse gear because of the even thickness and water resistance. They were ideal for cinches.

Hydrurga leptonyx is armed with a mouthful of formidable teeth and can swim at eleven knots yet feeds mainly on krill. Its diet includes fish, squid, carrion, and pups of other species, notably the crabeater seal. Penguins are chased and caught underwater or on ice floes and skinned by violent thrashing on the surface. Hunting leopards can leap a clean two metres out of the water onto the ice. In the Falklands they will prey on gulls sitting on the surface amongst the kelp and one attacked a calf, tearing flesh from its face as it swam ashore from a boat. Their only natural enemy is the Killer Whale.

Females are larger than males, reaching twelve feet, nose to tail, and although little is known about their breeding behaviour, it is thought that they return south to the pack ice to give birth between November and January. No one had seen a female leopard in the Islands since the early 1950's until Roddy Napier found one on West Point in 1991.

Sea Leopard (right and far right).

Shooting a leopard in the 1950's.
(Photo courtesy Bob Ferguson)

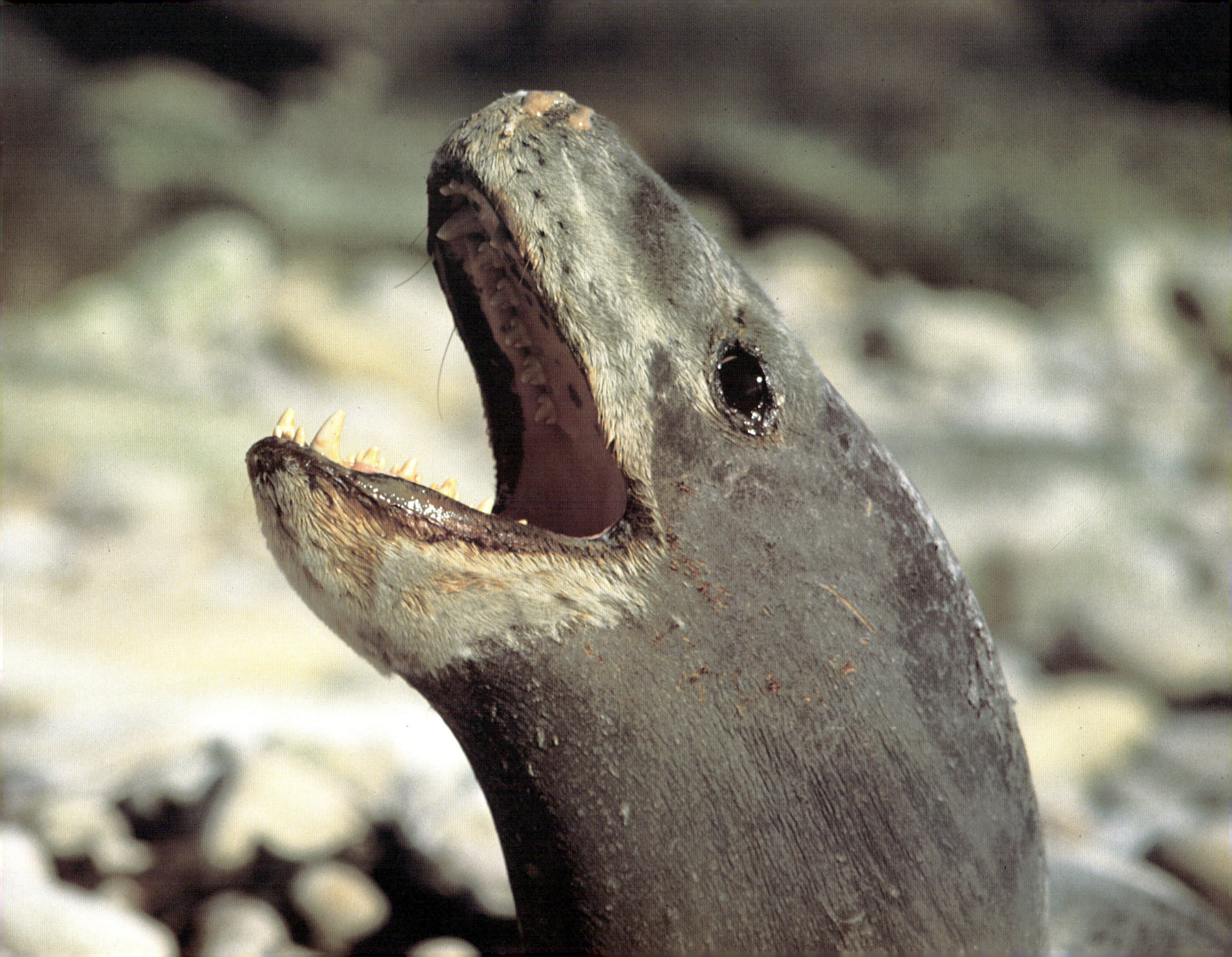

Fur Seal

I lay on an overhanging rock, quietly parted the last green blades of tussac and peered down a few feet to a dank, sheltered gulch, well back from the beach. There was a familiar, sweet stench – a damp, musky blend of rotting bodies, sweat and seal shit.

A wet, whimpering pup eagerly nuzzled his mother for milk, vainly probing under her tail and behind a flipper. Nearby two vultures waged tug o'war with the after-birth while tired mum snapped at the whiskers of a randy 'wig'. Finally the baby seal found an erect, juicy nipple and loud sucklings joined the rookery din of growling and wailing, sniffs and snorts.

Five hundred 'furries' annually come up to breed on the spray-wetted slabs of Landsend Bluff, an hour's walk from our home on New Island. Bulls return from the sea to stake out territories in November. Cows haul up a week or two later and gather five to nine strong around each mature male. Soon after giving birth, 'clapmatches' are mated, although embryo implantation is delayed for several months to ensure that pupping occurs at the same time each year. The rookery is a place of great activity. Rutting bulls, ashore and fasting for up to two months, incessantly fight, flirt and mate. Pods of black pups play in backstreet puddles and under boulders, while troupes of wandering juveniles roam around restlessly or chase and porpoise in the clear and kelp-fringed water. Harem-less males float on their backs, scratching or sleeping, with upturned flippers waving aloft like fronds of seaweed.

Fur seal and their ancestors have been around for over ten million years, gathering to breed on oceanic islands and fearing only killer whale and shark. Although the Uruguayan fur sealing industry, which still exists today, had begun in the sixteenth century, other races of Captain Cook's 'sea bear' remained virtually undisturbed and untouched by man, apart from local natives, until Yankee whaling fleets began scouring the southern oceans in the late eighteenth century. Thereafter, within the span of a single human lifetime, every known fur seal population was decimated by the sealer's club and some species were thought to have been exterminated.

It was a holocaust fired by the demands of the fashion trade for a luxuriant pelt, finer fleeced than any modern merino. Only the Chinese knew the secrets of removing the outer layers of guard hair while leaving undamaged the valuable under-fur from which they manufactured felt. They paid five bucks for a good hide. Sealers swarmed southward, filled their ships with seal skins and became rich in the markets of Canton, whence they could return home, laden with fancy Chinese goods.

The *States,* a 1000-tonner from Boston, was the first vessel known to have been fitted out especially for sealing. In 1784 she took away 13,000 Falkland skins and left her name in a cove on Weddell Island. Other vessels soon followed, dropping parties of men ashore at the rookeries where they lived in rough stone huts roofed with skin or sailcloth.

Seal were stunned with a five foot hickory club, then stabbed or lanced if necessary, but with care to avoid damage to the pelt. A good man could flay 50 in a day, washing each skin in salt water to remove any blood. For the China market, hides were cleaned of blubber, had flipper holes stitched up with twine and were stretched to dry on a sunny bank using ten wooden pegs. European, American and London buyers demanded salted skins for leather and furs. Once pickled, using two quarts of salt to an average skin, the hides were folded as 'books' or piled up to form 'kenches' for shipment.

By 1800 local rookeries had been well hammered and, although some small scale sealing continued sporadically, most sealers' attentions shifted to the vast 'seal cities' of South Georgia and Masafuera. From 1881 the Falkland Islands Government declared a summer closed season to protect remaining stocks, which had all but disappeared.

The early years of this century saw a number of Nova Scotian schooners transhipping skins in Stanley. These seal were mostly procured legally at sea, but not always. In 1907 the *Edna May,* curiously renamed *Baden Powell,* was wrecked on Elephant Jason while poaching and 22 survivors rowed in seven two-man whaleboats to

Clapmatch with her suckling pup.

Carcass Island and thence to Pebble Island. The schooners ceased to operate after 1908, but Patagonian poachers continued to make occasional forays to the Jasons and Bird Island. Fur seal were finally protected in 1921, both by law and the armed patrol vessel *Afterglow*.

The Falkland population has since recovered to 20,000 animals, which now spend their summers scampering about a dozen rookeries, bothered only by old age, low-flying Tornadoes or the occasional seal-watchers from Seattle.

NOTE
'Wig' and 'clapmatch' are sealer's terms for bull and cow seals.

Bull lazing in the water.

Fur Seal Colony, West Falkland. The earliest known shipment of Falkland pelts and oil was transported onboard the *Aigle* to St Malo by the French colonists at Port Louis, in 1766.

Peale's Porpoise

It was oily calm and sunny on the November day we cruised from New Island to West Point. Diminutive diving petrels, so often missed against the seal's confusion, dotted the surface, diving with a 'plop' at the approach of the *Foam*. Others whirred slowly and lowly past like big, piebald bumble bees. At lunch-time we idled away an hour sitting unanchored at the uninhabited Third Passage Island.

A pod of Peale's Porpoise came to play in the bay. Attracted initially by the noise of our engine or propeller, and clearly visible against the shallow, sandy seabed, they lolled around and under the drifting *Foam*. My companion, Alan White, counted seventeen. As we departed they rode the bow wave, sometimes leaping out and whacking their tails on the water.

Long-Finned Pilot Whale

Still yawning and pyjama'd and squinting through the window on an autumn morning, I was astonished to see a group of over 50 'blackfish' in the harbour 150 yards away. By the time I had downed some tea and donned my trousers they had driven in on the *Protector* beach, just a short distance upwind of our house. It took a couple of minutes to walk up to them, during which time I fleetingly considered whale steak for lunch and the longer term prospect of having a heap of rotting carcases for a neighbour. The entire herd was beached and the sound of their blowings mixed with poignant squeakings of obvious distress. The tide had an hour left to rise and I sat on the bank and watched, not wanting to interfere. Three other people waded in and, pushing and shoving in the armpit-high water, managed to get a few afloat. As if by a signal, they all then struggled and wriggled back off the sand into the water. For several hours they milled around in a bunch. Some were upright with their heads in the air as if looking for an exit before they eventually disappeared towards the Grey Channel and the open sea.

9 WAR Sovereignty Dispute

Argentine terrorists from the hijacked Aerolineas Argentinas DC4 which landed on Stanley Racecourse in 1966. The man with the camera was Hector Garcia, editor of the Argentine newspaper *Cronica*. His films were later confiscated. Local hostages huddle under the cockpit. It had been planned that a plane load of reinforcements would follow and then another, loaded with press. However, the Argentine President Ongania, got wind of their plans and, wishing to avoid further embarrassment at a time when he was entertaining HRH the Duke of Edinburgh, temporarily grounded all civilian aircaft. Amongst those passengers unfortunate enough to be onboard the hijacked aircraft, was one Rear Admiral Jose Maria Guzman, Governor of Tierra del Fuego, Antarctica and also, according to Argentina, the Malvinas.
(Photo John Leonard)

To distant observers, an Argentine invasion of the Falklands must have seemed unlikely, but to Kelpers it had always been a very real fear. In the early 1960's, following a resurgence of interest in the dispute, the Argentine government aroused a dormant national passion to take the 'Malvinas'.

Using the United Nations, diplomatic pressure was increased on Britain and the Islanders for a change of sovereignty. A number of incidents took place, often little noticed by the rest of the world, which exposed the Falklands' vulnerability to military action.

On 8th September 1964 Stanley residents were surprised to hear a strange light aircraft, a Cessna 172, which circled the town and landed on the racecourse. The pilot, Miguel Fitzgerald, popped out, planted an Argentine flag, handed a letter declaring Argentine sovereignty to a bemused bystander, Jim Shirtcliffe, and flew away again.

Two years later, just before 10.0am on Wednesday 28th September, an equally unexpected Aerolineas Argentinas DC4 flew up the harbour, landing again on the racecourse, where it narrowly missed the grandstand, walloped two telephone poles and sank up to the axles in a bog hole. The entire force of six Royal Marines tore up towards the aircraft. Anxious mothers rushed to school to retrieve children and every Land Rover in town roared up the front road as curious Islanders went for a look. Some even broke the speed limit of 20mph.

The plane had been hijacked, while on an internal flight, by twenty nationalists calling themselves the 'Condors', led by 'La Palomina', a striking 27-year-old journalist Maria Verrier, who became known locally as the Blonde Bombshell.

Armed with mausers they walked out of the door and into world headlines, taking the nearest four Islanders hostage, and declaring 'The Malvinas are Argentine'. Their DC4 was promptly surrounded by the local Defence Force who laid siege with ·303 rifles in the rain and vied with each other as to who would later strip search the five foot one inch blonde.

"We will die rather than surrender", declared the pirates but after one cold night on board they'd had enough and surrendered to a priest. 32 hours after landing, they were warmly imprisoned in St Mary's Church Annexe, causing indignation amongst local card players forced to cancel their weekly whist drive in the hall.

On Saturday morning, Islanders lined the quayside as the 'invaders' were ferried, in the hold of the *Philomel*, out towards the Argentine naval ship, *Bahia Buen Suceso*, anchored off Mengeary Point to collect them. "We will be back", screeched the Bombshell as they departed with a patriotic rendering of their national anthem and, by lunchtime, they were. Unable to get alongside the transport ship in a heavy swell, the 'Condors' returned, spirits doused by seasickness and having lost both their singing voices and breakfasts. They eventually made it home to receive nominal prison sentences, having pulled off a successful and bloodless stunt which made the columns of the *New York Times*, the Jamaican *Daily Gleaner* and the *Meat Trades Journal*.

Lord Chalfont, Minister of State at the Foreign and Commonwealth Office, made a "hurricane" visit to the Islands in November 1968 to allay Islanders' fears after news leaked out that Britain was secretly negotiating sovereignty with Argentina. During his public meeting in the Town Hall a light aircraft containing three Argentine publicity seekers suddenly appeared over Stanley and crash-landed on the Eliza Cove road. Everybody; people, policemen, press and dignitaries, whizzed off, except one. John Leonard was stringing for Associated Press at the time and, sensing a scoop, was attaching a telephoto lens to his camera. The operation took a little while and by the time he came out of the main doors there was not a soul or a vehicle in sight. How could he get to the scene? Just then an old jeep came trundling along. John flagged it down. Inside, with an army rifle on his knee, sat none other than the minister, and next to him, at the wheel, the acting Governor. They drove directly to the airplane, past a hastily-erected barricade, holding back both crowd and press, and John shot this picture of Sergeant Walter Felton and some Royal Marines guarding the plane. He didn't need his telephoto after all. (Photo John Leonard)

Other incidents took place. Another small press-sponsored plane crash-landed in 1968. In 1976 the unarmed British research ship *Shackleton* was fired on near Stanley by an Argentine gunboat and, in the same year, an illegal military base was set up on Southern Thule, a remote Falklands' Dependency.

But by far the most sinister incursion, which was to remain secret for many years, occurred just before Christmas 1966. About fifteen Argentine marines were dropped off for a few hours on successive nights by the submarine *Santiago del Estero*, to reconnoitre a potential landing beach north of Stanley. Second officer on board was Juan Jose Lombardo. Fifteen years later, as Chief of Naval Operations, Lombardo was tasked, on 15th December 1981, to plan and execute the 1982 invasion.

Maria Cristina Verrier, the 'Blonde Bombshell', described by one seasoned onlooker as being "really quite fetching".

135

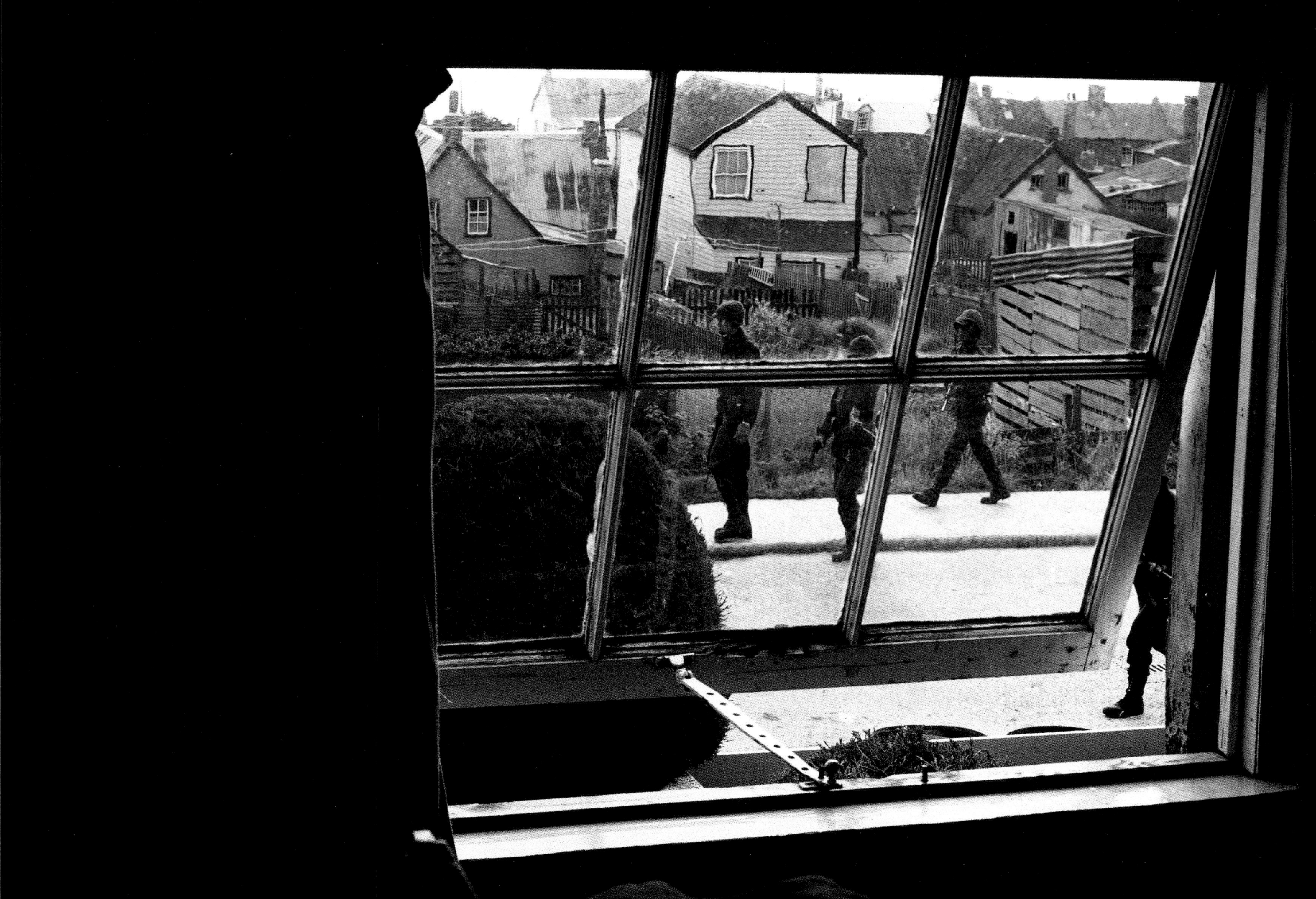

Invasion

It was on the second of April
Nineteen hundred and eighty two
That the Argies invaded the Falklands
And took down the red, white and blue.

Their navy, army and airforce
Was off the light by dawn
And as our defences were very weak
They were soon on the Governor's lawn.

Oh Galtieri, you've blundered,
So you'd better make out your will.
Remember what happened to Hitler
And also to Kaiser Bill.

Des Peck

Kelpers and Argentinians are separated by temperament, culture and a turbulent stretch of South Atlantic Ocean ten times the width of the English Channel. 'Across the water' tangos, gestapos and inflation flow like wine, while we live in the land of the mutton chop, Patsy Cline and a quiet game of darts after supper.

One clear autumn morning, on a tide of national emotion, a massive Argentinian naval task force sailed into Port William, without warning, and attacked Stanley to enforce their spurious sovereignty claim.

It was the day after April Fool's, 1982.

Eleven bloody weeks later, as a result of the hard-drinking President Galtieri's folly, 910 were dead and thousands more left with injuries and scars to carry with them into the next century...

Invading Argentine Marines advancing westward along Fitzroy Road at about 8.0am on 2nd April, 1982 (left).

Argentine soldier on guard outside the Ionospheric Station, Stanley.

Radio Station – The Falkland Islands Broadcasting Station (FIBS)

Patrick Watts cleverly relayed descriptive telephone calls live over the airwaves as the invasion was actually taking place. He was later ordered by the Gestapo to cease playing the recordings of *Dad's Army*, in case they inspired a local resistance movement. The Radio Station continued broadcasting for a month until it was closed down. The last programme, on 29th April, was *Round the Horn*.

By the time Governor Rex Hunt made his radio announcement at 8.15pm on 1st April most people had already guessed or heard what was coming – it's a small community.

"Good evening. I have an important announcement to make", he spoke gravely. "…There is mounting evidence that the Argentine Armed Forces are preparing to attack the Falkland Islands".

The Radio Station was to remain on the air until further notice and throughout the Islands everyone listened. Few slept that night.

To disrupt any plans the Argentines may have had of flying in troops, a group of volunteers went down to block the runway at Stanley Airport. Amongst us was Billy Poole. "We took about six or eight tractors and I don't know how many trailers to barricade it and some heavy plant", he said. "There was no way anything could have landed, really. Well, a helicopter might have come down in between, but that's about all".

We finished on the runway at 10.0pm and anxiously crowded round a Rover to hear the BBC news relayed by FIBS from London. A dozen dark figures craned towards the radio, grim faces lit only by the glow of a cigarette, then gazed into the silent, starry night. The news had only confirmed our deepest fears and each one of us briefly and privately pondered the impending end of our way of life.

"Well, I think I'll have a piss on this airstrip while it's still ours", said a voice in the darkness, and then we all went home.

With the imminent arrival of the Argentine fleet, some other unwelcome visitors had found their way through the air vents and into our 130-year-old house. Unable to rest, we set a mousetrap and lay down to await further developments over the radio.

Just after midnight the music stopped and the Governor spoke.

"Good morning… there is no indication that the Argentine Navy task force heading this way has changed course. Unless it does so we can expect it off Cape Pembroke by dawn".

Outside there was neither wind nor street lights. It was 'High Noon' at midnight as we waited for our sleepy little sheep town to be stormed.

A Whiter Shade of Pale drifted around the bedroom, suddenly punctuated by a snap from the kitchen below.

"No more invasions for you, mate".

I re-sprung the trap and cremated the dead mouse in the stove while Ray Conniff performed *We May Never Meet Again*. Three rodents later, His Excellency nervously declared a State of Emergency, putting down the microphone with a clatter. The ether prickled tension and Burt Bacharach's piano played *Close to You*.

Shooting broke out just before dawn, echoing around the darkened town. Mortars crumped, machine guns rattled and the mousetrap clacked.

"They must have two hun, two hundred odd around us now", telephoned a breathless and stunned Hunt from under his desk at Government House. "They, they've been throwing grenades at us, er, rifle grenades …'I think maybe mortars… I don't know… we can't move without being shot at …I'm afraid it's just a matter of time".

There was a lull while Billy Vaughan played *I'm Sorry*. As daylight came in, Broadcasting Officer Patrick Watts spasmodically interrupted the music to relay 'phone calls from townsfolk glimpsing the renewed action through net curtains.

"The whole place is shaking… I can see smoke… I'm lying on the floor, boy", said Alistair Grieve.

"Keep your head down, Ali", replied Patrick. "If you can see them passing, perhaps you'd give us a call."

"There's a gaping hole about six feet wide in the roof", lilted Welshman Tom Davies, whose house had been hit by a mortar. "We're paddling around in water hy'ere".

Other callers reported our Marines withdrawing through gardens and hen-runs as a line of huge amphibious personnel carriers rumbled into town. From our window I saw a Chaplinesque scene as three bemused invaders, 'guarding' Fitzroy Road with a monstrous machine gun, were confronted by a finger-wagging septuagenarian, Henry Halliday, armed with a plastic bag and pointing back towards Argentina. When he had finished with them, Henry waddled off, unperturbed, to 'turn to' at the dockyard and next encountered our own authorities as he passed the Constabulary in Ross Road.

"Good morning, ladies and gentlemen", announced Police Chief Lamb in his finest radio tones. "Only a few minutes ago a somewhat bewildered elderly gentleman was expressing indignation that my men had dragged him off the streets. He was sublimely on his way to work".

Then, the besieged Governor returned to the telephone. "They've got us well and truly pinned down", he said, conscious that the Argentine commanders might be tuned in. "I'm hopeful that they'll send somebody in to talk… but I'm not walking out… I'm not surrendering to the bloody Argies, Patrick, certainly not!"

Strangers in the Night was interrupted by a weird Hispanic voice transmitting on a neighbouring frequency. "Eet was a corl to the Breeteesh colonial ortoritees", said the stranger. "Our concern ees for thee safety of thee people of thee Malvinas".

Using FIBS, Patrick established contact over the air with the invaders. Firing ceased and, as we listened, talks were arranged by Hector Gilobert, a bi-lingual Argentine Airforce Officer, well-known in Stanley. Delegations from both sides met in the empty street outside the Town Hall. With our people carrying a rolled-up brolly with a lace curtain stuck on top as a white flag and the Argentines waving a white, waste disposal bag, they then made their way, together, towards the surrounded Seat of Government, for peace talks with Rex Hunt.

At 9.30am, just as Patrick announced "A truce has been agreed…" the Radio Station door opened and several heavily-armed Argentines burst in. "Just a minute", he said calmly, "Take the gun out of my back… You're not pointing that at me, are you? Please don't, it puts me off when I'm on the air". A very tired Watts eventually went home at mid-day and was later awarded the MBE for a memorable and courageous, sixteen hour, solo broadcasting marathon.

A jubilant Amtrac crewman waves to Argentine pressmen outside the 'West Store'.

Ex bomber pilot Dave Emsley, broadcast for many hours on the day of the invasion, mentioning casually (after a beer or two) "I'd give anything to see the Sutherland Highlanders marching down John Street right now, but it's not very likely, so instead I'll give you a little bit of Scottish music". After British Forces recaptured South Georgia on 20th April 1982, Dave got into trouble with the nasty Major Dowling, of the secret police, when he played *Georgia on my Mind* and he was subsequently banned from broadcasting.

Cape Pembroke Lighthouse

Aerial view of Cape Pembroke showing the lighthouse, and waves breaking over the infamous Billy Rock.

Basil Biggs with Captain Nick Barker, RN, of *HMS Endurance* on the lighthouse balcony in early 1982. (Photo courtesy Betty Biggs)

Basil Biggs was the head Lighthouse Keeper in 1982. It was his job to maintain the Cape Pembroke light as a warning to shipping but at 8.0pm on 1st April he was ordered by the Governor to turn it out.

"Me and old Charlie McKenzie was on duty that night". Basil spoke softly and thoughtfully, with a voice like thick brown gravy.

"It would have been about 2.0am when they finally turned up I s'pose. We saw blue lights coming in and the silhouettes of two ships and reported through right away…. Early the following morning they walked up covering the whole of the Cape in a line, came fairly close to the lighthouse and got down behind grass bogs, clicking back their old bolts, you know, ready to fire. 'You come here', they said, so we had to go. They searched the building but found nobody. There was only two of us, Charlie and me.

"The night after, they laid siege for six hours in the rain hoping to catch (our) Marines, but eventually gave up, soaking wet and freezing. So I gave them all black coffee… even if they were bloody Argies.

"'Are you angry at us for taking the Malvinas?' asked the head one.

"'Yes I am', I said. 'We're all very angry, but it's only temporary.'

"'Oh no, no', he insisted. 'No, no, no, it's forever.'

"'Only temporary', I said, but I thought it probably was bloody forever."

Cape Pembroke Point is the easternmost land in the Falklands. Inside it lies Port William and thence Stanley

Cape Pembroke Lighthouse 1991.

The lighthouse has remained unlit and unoccupied ever since the Argentine invasion. It was vandalised after the war, the equipment ruined and the glazing diamonds smashed by bullets. Although the building has since been renovated, by the Alistair Cameron Memorial Trust, its vital duties are now performed by an automatic solar-powered lantern and radar beacon situated nearby.

Harbour. Outside runs a nasty tide race and a perilous chain of islets, reefs and rocks including the notorious and semi-submerged Billy Rock just half a mile offshore.

The earliest navigation beacon, a 38 foot high balk of wood surmounted by a red and white triangular box was erected at the time of the establishment of Stanley in the 1840's. By 1849 this was replaced by a more conspicuous affair capped with a flagstaff and, in 1855, a 60 foot cast iron lighthouse from London was completed, to be kept by William Creed, who was also imported that year. When he lit up the rape seed oil lamps on 1st December, the constant light shone out a welcome warning to mariners up to fourteen miles away. The Creeds lived, all found, in a cottage near the foot of the white tower and kept goats, a garden and horses to ride to town seven miles away. He was paid £12 10s a month, with his daughter earning a further £2 as assistant keeper. While maintaining a watch they kept records, trimmed wicks, polished reflectors, and refuelled the lamps which burned, in total, over 1000 gallons of oil annually. Sea lion oil was unsuccessfully tried to reduce costs and later a new set of Argand lamps with silver reflectors were installed.

As Stanley became a busy port, many ships sailed under the eye of the light. Often 'lame ducks' limped into port on fire or with broken spars and torn sails. A few vessels came to grief within sight of safety. By day shipping movements were relayed to the capital via signal flags; by night by mounted messenger.

In the early hours of 14th May 1896, assistant keeper Hardy galloped into town.

"There's a ship on the Billy Rock!"

The ketch *Result* and launch *Sissie* immediately went to assist but with a big sea running they could only stand by as the stranded crew of the *City of Philadelphia* cried out in the darkness from the stricken ship's rigging. By dawn, together with all 31 on board, she had gone to the bottom.

In 1906 the lighthouse was rebuilt on new foundations. In the turret was a modern dioptic paraffin light mounted on a revolving base, which could be seen up to sixteen miles away, flashing once every ten seconds. By the hour subsequent keepers wound up the clockwork mechanism which turned the platform nightly for over 75 years, until the Argentine landings three miles away at Yorke Bay.

The last of six known wrecks on the Billy Rock was on the rainy night of 12th November 1912 when *RMS Oravia*, with 261 passengers, stuck fast at 10.22pm. Assistant Keeper Paice had been unable to warn the ship's Master as he watched her straying too close in towards the light. Fortunately all the passengers were saved after Stanley was alerted via the newly-opened wireless station and *Samson*, *Plym*, *Penguin* and several visiting Norwegian whale catchers steamed out to the rescue.

In earlier years, the lighthouse supplies of coal, oil and food were replenished by boat and landed in a gulch eighty metres away. In 1922, as a fifteen-year-old 'boy of the gang', Des Peck accompanied fifteen men on board the steam launch *Penguin* and wrote a poem about his 'Lucky Escape':

The Landing Stage, Cape Pembroke, circa 1920's.

LUCKY ESCAPE

We set out on the *Penguin*
Towing a loaded scow
Bound for Cape Pembroke Lighthouse
The swell nearly broke to the bow.

The Gulch is always dangerous
That's why there is a long spar
Which was laid out to put a rope over
To check the scow going too far.

The next thing we know, Bert shouted
Don't move! Sit tight where you are",
The dreadful thing had happened
Bert had missed the spar.

The swell was really nerve racking.
Lighthouse Keepers stood aghast.
Would the scow get safely in
Or would this be her last?

Lucky for us the swell had a heart
And tossed us back, right to the start.
This time Bert, with rope in hand
Had it over the spar and we could all safely land.

My mates have now all passed on
But when I think of the Lighthouse tower
How near to death we all were
And all for a shilling an hour.

Des Peck

Telephone Exchange

Hilda Perry, who worked as an operator in the Telephone Exchange from 1963-89.

Although some limited scale telephones were in operation in the town by 1890, the first single wire line was put up in 1897, and joined the lighthouse to Stanley Police Station seven miles away. An Exchange was opened in the jail in 1906 and within a few years the town was bristling with telephone poles. By the early '20's there was a 60-line board in Stanley Town Hall. In 1931, the Exchange was relocated in the Police Station, where it continued to grow until moving in 1957 to a purpose-built building across the road, fitted with a 400-line capacity. This had swelled to 600 by the time the ageing Government telephone system closed down in 1989. Hilda and her team were then replaced by an efficient but impersonal, computerised system which neither knows nor cares where the doctor is dancing or who is buying Corn Flakes in the West Store.

"Number please?"

"262, four rings, please".

"If it's Peter or Rosemary you're wanting, they've just gone past, down towards the West Store", commented the helpful operator.

"O.K. Thanks. I'll try again later".

Hilda Perry watched the comings and goings on Stanley's main street, Ross Road, through the window of the Telephone Exchange, where she worked, for 26 years. If someone had moved house, Hilda or one of the others would know the new address. When a doctor was needed on Friday night, the operator had a good idea whose party he might be at. For those who had lost their 12-page directory, it didn't matter, the Exchange ladies knew everybody's numbers by heart anyway.

To ring someone you just turned the handle on the side of the box and picked up the handpiece. Down in the Exchange there was a buzz and a little flap next to your number dropped open to alert the operator, who connected up to the required number, and gave a ring.

At night, lines were open for emergencies only and between midnight and 6.0am a watchman slept by the line board on a camp bed. Late night 'phone calls automatically switched on an alarm bell and a light in the Exchange, causing the snoozing incumbent to spring out of a sleeping bag, grab the headset and answer.

People talked for hours about nothing and at no charge. At the end of a call, they gave the handle a sharp turn to "ring off".

For this service, which was amusing, homely, and now departed, the total subscription charge was less than 10p a day.

Throughout the night of the invasion Hilda and Camilla Clarke were on duty from 8.0pm until 6.0am in the morning. As the first shots rang out they were relieved by Alana Morris and Shelley McKay. Without them, sitting in their exposed building on the seafront, connecting up lines between Government House, the Radio Station and thence to the attacking forces, no one would have known what was happening.

From the first day of the occupation the Exchange was taken over, operated and lived in by the Argentines. "Call the studio on 90 and pass your messages", urged the disc jockey, Dave Emsley over the air on the first evening, "and keep that bloke down there at the Exchange working his bony fingers". Phoned requests poured in for two hours.

However, the soldiers managed quite a good job and eleven weeks later at the surrender, they alerted Bill Etheridge, the Postmaster, being worried that nobody would be on at the Exchange when they had gone. Bill rang Hilda.

"When can you start?"

"Right away", she replied from her house across the road. As she walked back into work she met one of the departing young Argentines in the doorway and asked him:

"Are you looking forward to going home?"

"Yes, of course", he said warmly in English. "Goodbye señora."

Radar Watch

Captain Jack Sollis had been at sea as long as anyone could remember and knew the Falkland coastlines intimately. On the night of the invasion, just one month before he was due to retire as master of the 85 ft Government coaster, *mv Forrest*, he was sent out to monitor the incoming Argentine fleet. His dapper little ship was unarmed, blacked out and maintaining radio silence. Ranged against him were three enemy warships and a submarine. Jack was ill at ease.

"We left Stanley at seven o'clock in the evening and anchored in Rabbit Cove and was doing a radar watch, of course. At ten past two in the morning we saw two ships on the radar, five miles east of Mengeary and returned to Stanley to report it. We arrived back at the jetty about 3.0am.

"Major Gareth Noott, the officer commanding the outgoing Royal Marine Detachment, rang from Government House. 'What are you doing?' he demanded. 'Go back out and see where they're landing.'

"I went out slowly and got as far as Ordinance Point. They was coming up Port William about then at roughly ten knots, so I came back. The ships were less than a mile and a half astern of us, roughly about half a mile west of Arrow Point when we turned off Navy Point and came in through the Narrows. There was three of them and two was a bit further back but they was all on the radar."

After their successful invasion, the Argentines commandeered *Forrest*, painted her black and used her to freight military supplies to their camp bases. But the subsequent British victory returned Jack to his now bullet-holed ship. His last job as skipper was to ferry thousands of prisoners of war, 500 at a time, from the Public Jetty out to the *Canberra*, anchored in Port William. The dejected and defeated troops left the decks of *Forrest* plastered with excreta before boarding the luxury liner for onward shipment home to a cheerless welcome in Puerto Madryn.

The late Captain Jack Sollis and *mv Forrest*.

Mike Butcher

Metalworker, Mike Butcher, outside his workshop (right).

Peter, probably the oldest sheep in the Falklands, was fourteen in 1993. He watched the comings and goings of the Argentine troops from behind bars while chewing the cud in Mike Butcher's garden in 1982 and now shares the lawn with the impressive skulls of killer whale (pictured) and sperm whale.

Michael Butcher, the metalworker, leads the 'Falklands Against Whaling Nations' (FAWN). He lives in an unpretentious steel-framed house which he built himself and welds in an iron-clad workshop at the bottom of the garden.

"I prefer metal", he told me as we had smoko in the kitchen. "Don't like wood."

A large, white sheep peered in expectantly through the open door. "Peter's come for his sweets", said the whaleman, defrocking a boiled fruit. "He always sits on that hump over there afterwards", and sure enough, once satisfied, Peter reclined on cue.

During the occupation Mike was reported to Argentine Intelligence for photographing anti-aircraft gunners and earned a visit from the sinister Major Dowling.

"His sidekick had half a nose and part of his temple shot away", said Mike's wife Trudy. "They sat him in here with me while interrogating Mike in the bedroom, every word of which I could hear. Afterwards, Dowling came in here and clonked his helmet on the table. He told me my husband was a very stupid man. He asked me questions and thumped the table. They had found some flippers and a photograph of Mike in Defence Force uniform and decided he must be a frogman as well. I looked towards the stove. The bread was ready to go in. 'Am I permitted to put my bread in the oven?' I asked. 'Certainly, certainly', said Dowling. Then they took Mike and left me wondering if I would ever see him again but in the end he was only away for about an hour."

Across the road another sheep was tethered and chomping the grass, a black one this time.

"That's Baa", said Mike. "She and Peter don't get on."

Billy Poole

"You can have my ducks, you can have my chickens, and you can have my pig. I'm off", growled Billy next door as half a dozen victorious Argentine Marines trooped past his kitchen window. But it took more than a mere 10,000 invaders to get 'Pooley' down for long.

"So I went to the butchery to work, to help keep the town supplied with meat", he recalled later. "50-odd Argies lived in there, navy blokes. They was quite friendly and gave us fruit. They wouldn't give it to their army lot outside. Sooner chuck it on the beach."

Bill and Evelyn Poole live in an old stone house with walls two feet thick and throughout the occupation had a crowd of relatives and friends lodging with them.

"In the house here", said Pooley, "we had thirteen living, four kids and the rest grown-ups. When the curfew was on, we battened down from 4.30pm each evening to half-past-eight in the morning. But we used to go out in the underpants and have a look at the flashes when our ships were blasting over the town. The only one who didn't hear so much was the wife 'cos she's a bit deaf, you see".

Like the Argentines, Bill's grandfather, Charles, also arrived in the Islands by sea, although he had turned up 101 years earlier on a wintery August dawn, in heavy surf, hanging onto a pig box, after being shipwrecked near Limpet Creek, East Falkland. 17-year-old Charles Poole, a steward on board, made it ashore with a line which saved five of the crew, though the captain and two mates perished. A fortnight later the survivors reached Stanley with the news. Their ship, the 130 foot German schooner, *Concordia*, had been en route for Guayaquil from Marseille via the Horn with a hold full of wines and spirits. Later, while the cargo was being salvaged, a policeman was sent out from Stanley to guard the wreck and lived in a tent on the beach nearby. People rode for miles to help him, towing a carguero or two. The story goes that one old shepherd is said to have taken a fortnight off work from North Arm to go. He rode over 80 miles, spliced the good officer's mainbrace, and made off with a case of finest German table wine in his molitos. But, by the time he got to San Carlos he'd sold it and had to go back for more.

Five years later Poole was again shipwrecked, this time aboard the *Hadassah*, a 37 ton local schooner which ran aground on Weddel Island with a cargo of 5000 mollymauk eggs from New Island bound for Stanley.

In about 1899 he bought the schooner *Allen Gardiner*, taught himself navigation, and became well-known, sealing and trading around the Islands. But one calm and foggy night in March 1902, she too was lost, running into the cliffs at Cape Bougainville. All ten on board escaped in a rowing boat and three dogs swam ashore but down to the bottom went a Hill Cove horse, the entire West Point wool-clip and Rupert Valentin's prized zoological collection from West Falkland.

Nothing was heard of Charles for some time afterwards until one day a mysterious but familiar-looking black sealing schooner, the *Rapida*, dropped anchor in West Point Harbour under his command. On board and free of charge was a full load of timber and fencing from South America to replace the drowned wool-clip.

In 1908, after a relatively unsuccessful sealing trip around the Jasons, he left the few skins he had obtained salted down in barrels in a shed at West Point and sailed off to Patagonia. He never returned.

Life on those schooners was tough and attracted hardened men. Crews often consisted of criminals, drunks and deserters from other sealing ships and Poole always slept with a revolver under his pillow. Following a row with a one-eared man called Amelia, he was thrown overboard and shot dead in the water by three bullets from a sealing rifle. Charles Poole was just 34.

The *Rapida* returned a few months later and, under her original name of *Hattie LM*, ran mails, passengers and freight around the Islands. She ended her days, piled up on a Bleaker Island reef, in July 1910.

NOTE
Carguero and molitos are gaucho terms for pack horse and saddle bags respectively.

Billy Poole at the Stanley Raft Race, New Year's Day 1983.

The *Rapida*, under Charles Poole, in West Point Harbour, probably in 1908. (Photo courtesy of Roddy Napier)

Cecil and Kitty

The Occupation was a fortnight old. Seventy-three-year-old Cecil Bertrand sat quiet and still on a chair in his front porch as wife Kitty trimmed his silver hair. Peering through the pot plants, he contemplated a large anti-aircraft gun glinting in the afternoon sun, across the road. It sat on a grassy bank just above the sea, barrel pointing towards the tiny entrance of Stanley Harbour a mile away. Near the cannon, Bertrand's new neighbours, three young Argentine gunners, had just dug a large hole. Over it they built a cosy house from two oil drums and some wriggly tin, garnished with a lump of wood. Once finished, and satisfied with a job well done, they disappeared inside.

Kitty swept up Cecil's shorn locks with a goose wing and burnt them in the peat stove, rejoining him on watch at the window. After a while, up through a disused nail-hole in the rusty iron, poked a long antenna which bent over like a grass blade, and the Bertrands grinned as the whole structure swayed gently in the breeze.

"I suppose," said the old sea dog, his deep, resonant voice suppressing a chuckle, "they think HMS Invincible is about to sail in through The Narrows."

Cecil Bertrand, whose grandfather pioneered Roy Cove in 1869, worked on or around boats for half a century as a sealer, a whaler and captain of the Islands' last trading schooner, *Porvenir*. In 1953 he and Kitty bought Carcass Island and later had the auxiliary ketch *Foam* (which I now own) built in Denmark.

In his sixties Cecil, after a lifetime's labour, had the urge to become an author and took out a correspondence course on short story writing. His best effort was sent off in 1978 to a boating magazine whose name Kitty has since forgotten. They turned it down, later going out of business.

Seven years later, Cecil passed away, the returned manuscript remaining unpublished in a brown manilla envelope.

This is his story. The events related took place in May 1945 on board the *Porvenir*, in which Cecil later owned a share. The captain's name was Billy Miller and his mate was Peter Anderson. All the places exist.

Cecil Bertrand, 1955.

Kitty Bertrand in her 'Tortoise', 1992.

Alongside the Public Jetty, Stanley.

Porvenir at sea.

Porvenir at West Point.

Overboard on the Kelper Coast was written by Cecil Bertrand and is reproduced by kind permission of Kitty Bertrand, who also allowed me to use photographs from the family albums.

'OVERBOARD ON THE KELPER COAST'
By 'A.B. Jones'

"I don't like the look of that," said the skipper.

"What?" I asked. He pointed to a black undulating line to the south'ard.

"Oh, that, only shags."

"Only shags!" the Old Man fairly bristled, eyes on the mass of birds now passing us, "when shags make for the land before midday, keep a weather eye lifted, there's dirty weather about."

A shoal of penguins cut through our wake. We were outward bound from Port Stanley to West Falkland ports. The heavily loaded schooner made the most of a fresh wind on the quarter, and late afternoon saw us running through the Jump. On deck we made all secure, tightening wedges and double lashing the eighteen-foot boat. The bung was taken out and a life-line rigged along the port side.

In the twilight Bleaker Island and Lafonia ground looked cold and desolate under snow. Close abeam the wreck of an iron ship showed through the surf. Outside a southerly ground swell made itself felt; stew slopped out of the pot and we made haste to sup while there was time. The low glass and southerly swell had the Old Man worried and Bull Point was decided as the night's anchorage.

An hour later the wind shifted to west with snow, and our chance of a night's sleep had gone, a course was laid to clear Bull Point, and we pressed on.

When the snow cleared Bull Point light showed momentarily abeam, only to be blotted out with more snow. The stiff breeze stepped up to 40 knots or more, with a nasty sea. The cold was intense, in spite of oilskins we were soaked and half frozen, spray swept across the schooner in solid sheet. An hour at the wheel was enough.

Below, in the cabin, all was confusion, but it was comfort de luxe after a spell on deck. The big stove glowed cheerfully, well stoked with tussac peat. A mug of steaming coffee and a smoke made things bearable.

The Skipper showed in the open scuttle, standing with his head just clear of the coaming. He leaned over the half doors and shouted:

"How's it going?"

"O.K.," was the answer.

"Well, keep an eye to the south-west. The glass has started to rise."

Later my mate pointed to the south-west.

"Yes," I said, "the overcast is breaking up and another squall is coming." With blinding hail the sou'-wester arrived. In half an hour the sea was so big it was useless trying to stay the schooner. Built for Cape Horn fur-sealing, the sturdy 46 footer made for the lee of Sea Lion Islands where we hoped for flatter water, clear of tide rips, to come about.

At 11 p.m., with the Skipper at the wheel, we ran into the islands' lee, to the bellow of, "Lay-o."

We sheeted home on the port tack. With wind and tide against us progress was slow, two brief bearings on the light showed we were making considerable leeway, and likely to make land round Porpoise Islands.

Around midnight, glancing at the cabin clock I saw it was time for my trick, and relieved the Skipper at the wheel. He stepped to one side and took a firm grip of the cabin lee hand rail. Taking his place, I stared at the compass, struggling to feel the right amount of helm. The schooner was labouring heavily and solid water coming aboard.

Perhaps minutes went by before I noticed he was no longer there, but did not worry, thinking he had moved for'ard in the hope of seeing land to loo'ard.

Next time I glanced aside I noticed the handy-billy tackle had unhooked from the rail and was two blocks under the boom. The fall led astern like a bear. As the schooner lifted to a sea something black showed in the phosphorescent wake, fast to the fall.

Even as the incredible possibility of somebody holding there at our speed struck me, I yelled, "Quick!", and let the schooner come into the wind. As the stern-board came, my hand found the rope, and kneeling on the sheet grating I brought it in hand over hand. With barely a foot of bulwark for my knees to hold to, I leaned over and gripped the Skipper. Down swept a savage squall, the schooner gathered way, then my mate landed kneeling alongside me. One hand gripped my back and the other fastened onto the Skipper. A lurch, and the rail was under water; off balance we were kept aboard only by our knees. With no-one at the wheel, the schooner tore through the night.

Try as we might, the smooth surface of oilskins a size too small offered little hold to our desperately clutching hands. Each sea that swept the schooner tried to include us with the other moveables that had gone before.

After what seemed hours, with a thunder of canvas we were up in the wind again. With that chance we got our balance, and moved the Skipper along the lee rail, there, by brute force trying to pull him in, but so strong was the suck of our drift it proved impossible.

Realising we were driving rapidly on a lee ashore and just about exhausted, we redoubled our efforts.

"It's no good!" shouted my mate, "we'll never do it."

"Can you hold him?" I gasped. There was a strangled "Yes," and I let go. I gripped a cleat, and astride the rail ducked under water and tried to get my right arm through the Skipper's legs. The fourth try was successful. As we hove, the schooner came into the wind again and all three landed inboard. The long fall had taken several turns round my mate and the Skipper. As the boom whipped back and forth they were jerked up and down across from lee to weather. Juggling the wheel to keep the stern-board, I tried desperately to get at my knife but oilskins and body lashings defeated me, so I hove the main sheet tight and made fast. Having reduced the boom play to a minimum, I found it was possible after a short struggle to clear the tangle. Prising his hands from the knotted end, we bundled the Skipper below.

Frantically we slacked the sheet. As the schooner paid off, my mate fought his way for'ard ready to come about. With no way on the ship came the shout – "Breakers to loo'ard!"

With our only chance more speed, I held her a good full. A patch of smoother water, and we took our chance. Round the vessel staggered. As she did do, out of the dark a huge backwash boarded across the starboard quarter drowning the shouts of – "Hang on!"

Over went the schooner on her beam ends. Our luck seemed to be out. Gradually she righted. The next ones were not so bad and the reef spouted well astern. It was a relief when my mate showed up, I thought he had gone. His first words were: "Is the rudder all right?"

"Yes, it seems all right, but the compass lamp has gone."

Soon the damaged foresail started to go. After a hurried consultation we decided to hang onto it till further off the land. During the next half hour its usefulness decreased rapidly, so in the end it had to be stowed.

Everything being snug for the time being, my mate went below, undressed the Skipper, gave him a good towelling to restore circulation, then mixed a hot rum. After the patient had managed to swallow most of it he was chocked off in his bunk and all spare blankets heaped on top of him. There was now time to stoke the fire, enjoy a smoke and sip a coffee. Glancing through the half-inch open cabin scuttle, I envied the meagre comfort my mate enjoyed below.

Before long he was on deck and with a cheerful, "Let's sell the ship and buy a farm!" took the wheel, and I was free to stumble below and thaw out.

All too soon we were into smoother water and I made haste to stand by the headsails. The island showed close ahead, and skirting the kelp we were soon on the port tack heading west again.

Dawn came slowly with little let up in wind or squalls, as visibility improved, to loo'ard a long line of mountainous surf showed, and indistinctly, the low-lying land behind.

My mate shivered at the wheel as by the wind he nursed the ship through the steep seas. Clinging to the cabin hand-rail I kept him company and watched for Barren Island hidden in the gloom to windward.

Suddenly the scuttle shot back and to our amazement the Old Man came on deck. After a few terse inquiries concerning our whereabouts, he made his way to the weather rigging. Despite his 60 odd years and the absence of rat lines, he seemed to work his light weight aloft with little effort. There he remained, ignoring the lashing hail, until, a quarter of an hour later, he sighted Barren Reef. Satisfied, he was soon on deck. Pausing before going below, he said: "Bloody annoying trip. Nothing for it but to stop at Speedwell and repair sails. Well, I'll just have a mug of coffee before taking the wheel."

THE END

Under Occupation

Royal Navy Sea Harriers often flew, clearly visible, over Stanley. They were comparatively safe while remaining over 21,000ft which was above the ceiling for any Argentine surface to air missiles. Sometimes pilots encouragingly drew vapour victory signs in the sky (above).

Pucara over Stanley 25th May 1982 (top right).

Oerlikon 40mm twin-barrelled anti-aircraft gun. At least nine of these were positioned in or around the town and burst into life every time a plane from either side flew over.

The Islands remained under occupation for 74 days. Our new masters had commanded that life was to remain normal "in an atmosphere of peace and harmony". But their resolve was as fickle as our weather and their fine words washed away with the tide.

"We are doing all sorts of things to conquer the hearts and minds of the Islanders," their Ambassador in London had boasted, twelve months earlier. "We are doing our best to show what we really are."

But a week after the invasion, ex President Videla came clean in Stanley's Town Hall. "The people of the Islands are of no consequence," he said. "We regard them as enemies."

On day one, Stanley became Puerto Rivero, re-named after a noted Argentinian mass murderer. We were ordered to remain indoors and issued with a series of edicts.

Within a month the "whole of the Malvinas Islands" were subjected to a dusk to dawn curfew and blackout, the radio station had been shut down, and people were being taken from their homes and either deported, put under house arrest, or sent to a secret location.

We were under the jackboot of a military régime well-practiced in authorised terrorism, the instigators of a six-year 'Dirty War' in which thousands of their own innocent countrymen had been liquidated. Were some of us about to join the 'Disappeared'? Would political pressure force the advancing Task Force to turn back without a shot being fired? It was an eerie feeling; waiting and wondering.

Then, one morning, the earth moved. Just before dawn, on May Day, ten tons of high explosive were dropped out of the darkness and onto nearby Stanley airfield from an ageing British bomber.

"They're here," cried a neighbour and relief flooded through the community. The Empire was striking back. War had begun.

Since the invasion the BBC World Service had been broadcasting a nightly half hour *Calling the Falklands* by order of the Prime Minister. That evening a new presenter introduced the programme.

"Hello, I'm Peter King," said a familiar, old-fashioned BBC voice. "I read the news for over 30 years before I retired. They've de-mothballed me and it's good to be back with you."

Peter was an inspired choice, who touched hearts in every kitchen and finished each programme by saying, "Remember Kelpers, keep your heads down, and your hearts high". He linked us all up when the invaders tried to cut us off and break us down. *Calling the Falklands* was full of personal messages and amongst the first voices

Hermes – Throughout the occupation, as the schools were closed, Annie taught a collection of children every day in our sitting room. After lessons they scoured the garden for junk to make guns, planes and aircraft. This was the carrier *HMS Hermes,* a great favourite, and from it they shot down every Argie plane that dared pass by. Every time one of ours went over, the youngsters chanted, "Harrier, Harrier," while real anti-aircraft batteries spat lead at the tiny specks above.

Monsignor Daniel Spraggon was the son of a Newcastle butcher. Throughout the occupation he was magnificent, striding forth in his robes, beaming encouragement to Islanders while influencing and, where necessary, bullying the Catholic Argentines. One night a flurry of bullets smashed through his new house. Two went whistling through the loo, but fortunately the old boy was otherwise engaged at the time.

He narrowly missed death again in 1984 when, as a patient, he was carried unconscious, with face blackened and ribs broken, from the fire-raged Stanley Hospital. "The Good Lord obviously doesn't want me yet," he said, but the Almighty must have heard for the unforgettable Monsignor passed on the following year.

which came bouncing down off the ionosphere, along the aerial, and out of our radio, was that of my mother. It was a very moving moment.

Throughout the occupation I kept a diary. This is what happened on 25th May: Argentina's Independence Day…

Early in the afternoon two Pucaras came over, very low, and flew round and round Stanley. There was a Harrier circling directly above, leaving a sweeping vapour trail. A bunch of neighbours gathered in our garden, at the front of the Pink Shop, watching and enjoying the spectacle, joined by Heather Pettersson who happened by, taking her dog for a walk. The Harrier pilot was unable to attack in case he hit the town. The Pucara pilots were waiting for the British fighter to run out of fuel. Eventually he flew off and the Argentines landed on the northern grass verge of the strip at Stanley Airport.

A group of Argy conscripts were also watching the events from the back of the house opposite, known as the 'Pig and Whistle'. One of them spotted my camera and reported back inside. A fat, balding sergeant emerged, and half ran up the yard towards us, mistakenly accusing Billy Morrison of spying and threatening to shoot him. Billy treated him with disdain. The young soldiers found all this very funny. Fatso got mad. He tried to pull his pistol out but it was stuck in its canvas holster. The more he struggled, the more his countrymen sniggered and the redder he went. Finally, having issued Billy with a further stern warning, he stomped off.

Later, when they had all gone, I retrieved my camera from out of the bush where it had been hastily concealed.

The following day, on the BBC World Service, we learned that at the precise time we had been cheering on our Harrier pilot, three well-aimed 1000lb bombs from Primer Teniente Mariano Velasco's Skyhawk had driven deep into the guts of *HMS Coventry* and exploded. Nineteen sailors were killed and many more wounded. The destroyer was disabled with gaping holes in her port side. Within an hour she rolled over and later sank.

The West Store is the biggest store in town. By day it was a meeting place where people could exchange news and information as they purchased groceries. At night it became a dormitory with up to 126 people scattered about the floor in sleeping bags between the oxo cubes, the 'Y' fronts and the china horses. The lucky ones slept under the liquor shelf, the faint-hearted were upstairs away from the mice. DAP was painted on many stone buildings designating them as 'safe houses', but nobody really knew what it meant.

The Argentine hospital ship *Bahia Paraiso* anchored in Stanley on 1st June, having been checked by the Royal Navy, and remained in port for 24 hours. During that time she offloaded "stores" non-stop from both sides. The "stores" included land-based Exocet missiles and special forces. At night she was lit up like a Christmas tree while we were all in darkness, so it was easy for us to see what they were doing. Ten days later *HMS Glamorgan* was hit by an Exocet fired from the Eliza Cove Road in Stanley.

Concentrations in Camp

A bird's eye view of these isolated Camp stations reveals little of those few traumatic weeks of occupation. The farms are peaceful places, worked up by a succession of stockmen for well over a century. Each settlement consists of a clutch of gaily-coloured buildings surrounded by a patchwork of bright green, sheep-holding paddocks, sited usually in a sheltered bay. They look well nestling amongst the buffs, greys and olives of the moorland; a pleasing touch of order amid the random patterns of nature.

Although the main body of Argentine forces were based in or around Stanley, some 3000 were scattered strategically in the Camp. The settlements at Goose Green, Fox Bay and Port Howard each played unwilling host to large numbers of enemy troops, while smaller

GOOSE GREEN, easily the largest camp settlement, where 119 residents with ages ranging from three months to over 80 years old, were locked up in the community hall with barely any sanitation for nearly a month while their homes were abused. The settlement had begun life in the early 1880's as a tallow works annually turning 10,000 old sheep into dripping. A century later it was to fleetingly become the most famous hamlet in the world. The action to regain the settlement on 28th May 1982 was one of Britain's biggest battles since Hitler. After fourteen bloody hours, 267 bodies reddened Goose Green's whitegrass as 1400 Argentines surrendered to a single battalion of Paratroopers whose charismatic commander Col. 'H' Jones lay dead on Darwin Hill.

The farm manager's house at FOX BAY EAST acted as a prison for fourteen people considered undesirables and expelled by the Gestapo from Stanley, on 27th April. The two neighbouring Fox Bay settlements (see pages 7 and 102), containing around 50 civilians, were garrisoned by 1000 invaders.

PORT HOWARD, a settlement of two dozen people, was occupied by about 1000 Argentine troops. By the time of the surrender, army rations were so low that soldiers were seen scooping up food put out for the chickens and competing for bones with the sheepdogs. It was here at Howard, watched by farm workers standing in the stable yard and the dairywoman, Pauline McCormick, who was carrying a bucket of milk up the green, that Flt. Lt. Jeff Glover's Harrier was shot down, by a Blowpipe missile, at breakfast time on 21st May. At the end of the war Glover was the only British POW held in Argentina. He returned to England three weeks after the surrender.

PEBBLE ISLAND. The 25 inhabitants were outnumbered about six to one by Argentines, and spent 31 days imprisoned by them in the 'Big House' after a spectacular night raid on the airstrip by the SAS on 15th May.

groups were stationed at Pebble Island, Port San Carlos and elsewhere.

Most of these soldiers played little part in the war but in many places they left a deadly legacy of scattered minefields. These are mostly peppered with virtually undetectable plastic anti-personnel mines capable of killing a man or blowing the legs off a stray cow.

Although the danger areas are all securely fenced off with barbed wire and very clearly marked, they remain a problem requiring constant vigilance for, as the years pass by and memories fade, the mines are gradually becoming completely overgrown and the lethal explosive within them increasingly unstable.

Ironically the minefields have now become both miniature nature reserves and a somewhat macabre tourist attraction.

Surrender
14th June 1982

Joe's Golf Course. On 13th June, in the middle of Sunday lunch, twenty terrified soldiers abandoned their 105mm howitzers on the outskirts of Stanley, after coming under prolonged and accurate British artillery fire. They ran into town, jumped over a couple of garden fences, and sat down on Joe King's back garden lawn which for years he had lovingly tended as a putting green. The men, mostly teenagers, immediately offered to surrender, but following negotiations, decided instead to go away again after five minutes.

Heavily-armed Argentine soldier passing our house.

Argentine troops lounging around outside Fred Whitney's Paint Shop.

When we awoke that morning, the barrage had ceased. For what seemed like the first time in 60 hours there were no incoming British shells whistling overhead, pounding Argentine positions barely a quarter of a mile behind our house. The enemy artillery too was silent including, thankfully, the enormous howitzer which had been firing day and night from various positions along Callaghan Road, two blocks away. Each of its 155mm shells had been despatched with an earth-shuddering bang, rattling teacups and straining our nerves, followed by a weird, gurgling whoosh, rather like the sound of wind in a drainpipe, only infinitely more sinister. We could hear them landing a few seconds later, several miles away amongst our advancing troops, with clearly audible crumps.

It was bitterly cold so I stayed in bed watching the snowflakes accumulating along the window frame, my mind still numbed by the bombardment. There was an eerie hush. A cock crowed in a neighbour's hen run. A machine gun crackled uneasily at the west end of town.

After a while the smell of burning fuel seeped into our room. We heard muffled voices and footsteps outside and the sounds of wood being smashed and splintered. I got up and looked out at a scene we had dreamed of for weeks.

A dusting of snow had fallen overnight. What wind there was hardly rippled the harbour or bent the vertical plumes of peat smoke rising from the town's chimney pots and up into a dark and wintery sky. The murkiness was enhanced by ominous clouds of black smoke, oozing from various, scattered fires, which had spread out to form a bluish pall over our tiny city.

On the pavement opposite, smoking a cigarette, a disconsolate Argentine officer stood gazing into space while a conscript with a pickaxe wrecked radio equipment in front of Doug Hansen's peatshed. A bunch of soldiers sat, eating their breakfast out of mess tins, by

Fred Whitney's paint shop; others fouled the grass behind. Two friends shook hands, laughed and embraced. Many others simply stood in silence. In an overgrown yard below us, in John Street, 20 or 30 squaddies were burning piles of documents in a rusty oil drum, chattering and enjoying the warmth of the blaze.

The kerbside and verges were littered with unspent bullets, rifles, helmets and bed rolls. A discarded pistol lay, cradled by frost-bitten godetias, in one of our flower beds. Three live mortar bombs had been thrown on the lawn. A long belt of ammunition hung on the garden gate next door.

Down the whole length of the street, limping and shuffling, a stream of several hundred tired, dirty and dejected men drifted eastwards away from the battlefields. Inspired by a small man with a loud, squeaky voice, a spirited group of them defiantly chanted "Viva Argentina" and "Viva la Patria", their misty breaths exhaling in unison, their din echoing around the houses and abandoned military vehicles.

The army of occupation was in full retreat and the siege of Stanley had, apparently, ended. For several hours, together with what were soon to be thousands of armed men, we waited anxiously.

After lunch, a friend tried to get hold of the Argentine Vicecomodoro, Bloomer-Reeve:

"…to find out what the hell was happening. I rang his home in Racecourse Road. Someone picked up but did not speak.

"'Comodoro Bloomer-Reeve por favour' I said.

"'Wrong number, old fruit' came the reply in a clipped, Sandhurst accent. 'This is the British Army.'"

The war, it seemed, was over.

NOTE
There was to be no more fighting. Brigadier Mario Benjamin Menéndez, the Argentine Commanding Officer, signed a document agreeing to the surrender of all Argentine forces on the Falkland Islands, at 9.30pm that evening in the presence of Major-General Jeremy Moore.

Demoralised troops retreating eastward along Fitzroy Road.

As the inevitability of defeat became inescapable the Argentines parked all twelve of their scarcely used Panhard AML 90 armoured cars in a line on Philomel Hill. They immobilised the vehicles and threw away the keys.

Prisoners of War
16th June 1982

Throughout the morning a bedraggled line of beaten, kit-bagged troops, traipsed eastwards along the narrow road towards Stanley airfield. Some still carried their rifles, many wore plastic ponchos to keep out the cold. There was a man sporting a knitted pink bobble hat. I wondered where he'd got it from. They were largely silent but for the occasional muffled conversation and the tramping of army boots, like a file of green ants carrying bits of leaf and twig along a well-worn path back to their nest.

Half way down the road, by a cattle grid a mile outside town, at a checkpoint manned by a small party of Royal Marines, the insect trickle briefly halted while each Argentine was stripped of arms and booty before moving on. Helmets labelled 'Carlos' and 'Hernando' were cast aside to join the discarded jumble of bayonets, choppers and folding shovels. There was a huge pile of pistols and automatic rifles, some with butts bearing taped-on images of the Virgin Mary, the Pope or Maradona. The growing heaps glittered briefly during a break in the cloud cover; cold steel reflecting wintery sun.

The raw southerly wind slowly increased, quietly piping across gun barrels, hissing over the whitegrass and murmuring through and around roadside peatstacks. A Wessex helicopter whined and clattered overhead before beating its way over Stanley Harbour. The confiscated pink hat blew unwanted into a ditch.

By afternoon most of the soldiers had crossed the narrow and heavily-mined isthmus of Surf Bay and reached Cape Pembroke Peninsula where their main invasion force had come ashore eleven weeks earlier. The scene was desolate. Although the temperature was hovering around zero, it felt much colder, particularly during the hail squalls which were lashing down with increased frequency as the day moved on. Stanley airfield which, as 'Base Aerea Militar Malvinas', had for six weeks been a primary target for British bombs, was now a prisoner-of-war camp, with 4000 hungry men milling around, making shelters and trying to keep warm.

mv Forrest ferrying Argentine POW's from the Public Jetty to the P&O liner *Canberra*, anchored in Port William, for onward transport to Puerto Madryn, 17th June 1982. (Photo PO Peter Holdgate. From the collection of the Royal Marines Museum)

Hungry POW's queuing for food at Stanley Airport (top right).

Naval party 8901, Royal Marines, search and disarm Argentine servicemen half way along the Airport Road.

154

I hitched a lift there from a couple of British Naval officers and remained alone amongst the internees for several hours, wandering slowly around puddles, under broken aircraft wings and through ranks of dejected men who were trying to fend off the icy blast with only thin clothes and sodden blankets. Everywhere was mud, the piercing smell of spilt gasoline and that now all too familiar stench of Argies who permanently reeked of cheap tobacco and maté.

A shanty town of bivouacs and hastily propped up sheets of tin stretched from the Canopus Gun for several hundred yards across the runway to the sand dunes.

Behind the shelter of a Nissen hut, burnt out and peppered by cluster bombs, an NCO ladled out steaming soup to a long and orderly queue of haggard-faced conscripts.

A naval captain, well-known in Stanley, was screaming at two Red Cross officials, complaining about inhuman treatment by the British. A few months previously the same man had quietly strolled along the Yorke Bay sand beach, only a few hundred yards away, taking intelligence photographs in preparation for the invasion.

A group of smiling squaddies posed for a snapshot, obviously proud of their neat shack made of alloy runway sections, while above them, on a long piece of bent piping, fluttered a tiny blue and white flag.

A man shattered the cockpit canopy of a jet fighter and pulled out a white silk parachute to wrap around himself. Four others slept shivering in the buckled body of the FIGAS Islander. Those less fortunate and less clever huddled under the lip of a water-filled bomb crater.

"Excuse me," said a heavily-accented voice behind me, "do you live here?"

I turned to find an open-faced, intelligent-looking commando backed by a number of curious onlookers.

"My name is George. I am a doctor." he said, then added with concern, "Do you know what is going to happen to us?"

The BBC had broadcast news at midday that the passenger ships *Canberra* and *Norland* were imminently to ferry the POW's home. I passed it on and word filtered quickly around the bleak airfield.

An hour later George and I watched *Canberra*'s famous twin yellow funnels come into view through a gap in the sand dunes as the huge liner anchored in nearby Port William. At the same time a British Hercules transport plane, the first we had seen, flew over the runway, leaving in its wake a cluster of descending parachutes, each carrying a crate of emergency supplies. There was a loud and deeply-felt chorus of cheers and whistles as relief rolled like a wave across the airfield. For the first time in ten weeks the Argentines had something to celebrate. At last they were going home.

The POW camp kitchen.

Part of the defeated army marching towards Stanley Airport (bottom, left).

Argentine soldier taking the parachute from a vandalised Aermacchi MB 339-A light attack jet aircraft.

Aftermath

The hulks of two of the nine UH-1H Iroquois helicopters, used by the Argentine Army Air Corps in the Falklands, lying near Stanley racecourse in June 1982.

The 'Pig and Whistle' in John Street, Stanley, was clandestinely used by a small group of Argentines for about ten days after the surrender as a communications centre. It is believed they may have been under command of the maverick Major Aldo Rico who later organised two unsuccessful *coups d'etat* in Buenos Aires during the 1980's. Transmissions were only discovered when they began interfering with those of the local radio station.

Two Argentine soldiers lie dead and covered by corrugated iron in Ross Road West, Stanley, 15th June. Beyond is the monument commemorating the Battle of the Falkland Islands in 1914. Four days earlier, three women (Doreen Bonner, Mary Goodwin and Susan Whitley) had been killed in a house just a few metres away during a night-time naval bombardment. They were the only islanders to loose their lives during the fighting (Photo Paul Haley, *Soldier Magazine*).

One of a battery of Italian built 105mm howitzers positioned on the outskirts of Stanley. I had watched from inside a friend's hen house, merely 100 yards away, as this gun was repeatedly fired but had to clear out when the British return fire got too close. Minutes later the house next door to where I had been standing, belonging to Wilfred 'Pop' Newman, was accidentally destroyed by a direct hit from a British artillery shell.

Many of the Argentines had to live in squalid shelters and dugouts like this one behind the old Beaver Hangar. Similar constructions littered the peatbogs and hillsides around Stanley.

Five of the devastating Exocet anti-ship missiles arrived in Stanley during the last three weeks of fighting. Two were fired from an improvised mobile launcher on the Airport Road, one of which hit and damaged *HMS Glamorgan* at 3.36am on Saturday 12th June, killing thirteen. The other three and two empty cannisters were left abandoned by the roadside.

The Ro-ro ferry *St Edmund* sailed into Stanley harbour a couple of days after the surrender. There was something reassuring yet incongruous about the sight of that British Rail insignia on her funnel.

Stanley residents help themselves to Argentine stores in the FIC transit warehouse. Although many of the occupying troops had not been very well fed, several of the town's warehouses were piled high with an incredible assortment of food and supplies. Stanley residents needed little encouragement to help clear the area. A fleet of landrovers, unserviceable a month before when the Argies had tried to commandeer them, took on a remarkable new lease of life and joined an armada of wheelbarrows, as people scurried hither and thither with sacks of flour and sugar, crates of tinned tomatoes and cases of cooking oil. Almost before you could say "Up your Junta" several tons of stores had simply vanished.

Meanwhile on the front road crowds of people, like swarming bumble bees, were milling around a row of opened containers loaded with other goodies. The first one was stacked with case upon case of Wellington boots. From within came sounds of rummaging and tearing of cardboard.

"Any size tens in there?" I inquired at the door.

"Over in the corner old boy" replied a disembodied voice from deep within, "but watch it they're all in bloody Continental sizes."

The 'shop' next door was brimful with officer's ration packs. These were rumoured to be different from those of mere mortals and someone had wasted no time investigating such a scurrilous allegation. As a result each carton now had a small hole in the side, as if drilled by an alcoholic woodpecker, through which the tot bottle of whiskey had been removed.

In another container I came across a familiar figure struggling with a large cardboard box marked 'Telefunken Color Television'. "Here give us a hand with this mate," said Don gleefully and we carried it up the road, into his porch and opened it. To his dismay it was full of cigarettes. He muttered something rather rude concerning General Galtieri's legitimacy from which I concluded that Don didn't smoke. Then we went back to do a bit more 'tidying up' until an indignant Sergeant Major came along and, rather unsportingly, threw everybody out.

The Globe Store

Argentine soldiers clean up the mess by the Globe Store on Philomel Hill on the morning after the fire, supervised by British Paratroopers.

Charlie Blackley serving Mike Murphy in the mid 70's. (Photo Pete Gilding)

The Globe Store, with shutters closed, in 1980.

In many ways the most frightening night of all occurred not during the fighting but two nights after the surrender when over 4000 prisoners of war suddenly appeared in Stanley in the early hours of 17th June. They roamed around the unlit and drizzle-dampened streets virtually uncontrolled until dawn, waiting to be ferried out to the liner *Canberra* for repatriation. Some of the prisoners had regained their weapons from heaps by the road where they had previously been disarmed. The men were hungry, thirsty and wet and, as the night progressed, a few went on the rampage, looting shops for food and liquor. Their ugly mood was further soured by the news that the national soccer team had just lost to Belgium in the opening game of the World Cup in Spain. As the booze took effect and tension grew to near riot proportions, several buildings, including the Globe Store (right) were deliberately set on fire and destroyed. Local firemen, wearing boiler suits over their pyjamas, fought desperately and successfully to control the blazes which threatened to engulf the wooden town, as a handful of Royal Marines with heavy machine-guns herded the angry mob into the FIC wool and cement storage sheds on the East Jetty. The following morning a stunned capital awoke to find the air thick with smoke and the streets littered with debris and excrement.

From the time of Queen Victoria, the Globe Store supplied and amused the public with every essential from teats to tombstones (finest Italian white marble, specially imported of course). In the early days, many goods came from a large American sailing ship, *J.R. Kelly*, wrecked in Port William in May 1899 and acquired for £200 by Louis Williams, son of the store's founder. Later, the business was run with equal panache by a cantankerous Anglo-Argentine, Ernesto Rowe, although it never seemed quite clear whether he was the owner or not. Rowe's wardrobe was as rich and varied as the goods he stocked. He wore homburgs, herringbones and hacking jackets and always sported a cane. He imported finest cut French wines, vast yellow blocks of Uruguayan butter, and cheeses deftly cut by Frank Howett or Charlie Blackley to a customer's requirement. It was a store from a bygone age; of polished counters, swept floorboards, hand-written accounts and unhurried shopkeepers in overalls of brown linen. There was a silence broken only by conversation, the tinkling door bell, or the settling of a peat sod in the open grate.

The death of the enigmatic Rowe through old age in 1975 ended an era, and three years later the store was locked up and closed down for business.

During the early hours of 17th June 1982 barely two days after the surrender, hundreds of defeated and rain-drenched Argentine prisoners-of-war were roaming freely around the sleeping town. My wife woke me in alarm as light from a towering blaze, 150 yards away, gilded our bedroom ceiling. In disbelief she said, "They've burned down the Globe".

Advertisements from the Globe Store featured regularly in the *Falkland Islands Church Magazine* in the early part of the century.

THE GLOBE STORE

Once upon a Time,

Many years ago,
Truth and Falsehood went bathing together.
Falsehood left the water before Truth and stole Truth's clothes.
Ever since then it has been called the "NAKED TRUTH."
When I tell you that "SINGER'S SEWING MACHINES" are the best in the market and that you can get
a first class hand machine for only £4. 0. 0. complete, net price with cover and accessories, I am telling you the "NAKED TRUTH."

Mysto Automatic Mouse Traps.
Caustic Soda, Soft Soap, Owbridges Lung Tonic, Dr. Hairs Cough Cure, Phosferine, Haymans Balsam of Horehound, Browns Bronchial Trouches, Peps, Kays Compound, Venos Cough Cure, Terebene Balsam, Doans Backache and Dinner Pills, Beechams Pills.

Madame Vigor's Magnetic Electric Corset- Health is Happiness-

A Boon to Women of all Ages.
Madame Vigor's Magnetic Electric Corset will cure
Weak Back, Indigestion, Lassitude, Headache.
RESTORES
Nerve Power, Energy, &c. &c.

Kount on Kiltie Kippers Keeping you Keen. 1/3 per pair.

Ganary Guano.
Promotes the growth of Roses and other flowers to a great extent.

GENTLEMEN'S DANCING SHOES, MOLESKIN PANTS, a large assortment of underclothing, Tweed Suits. Diagonal Suits. PIGSKIN PUTTIE LEGGINGS, Graphophone and Records,

Our Troops In Town

Expelled as Governor on 2nd April, a tired but triumphant Rex Hunt returned with the new title of Civil Commissioner on 25th June 1982. He was officially welcomed by Maj. Gen. Jeremy Moore, Admiral Sandy Woodward and a guard of honour on Stanley Football Field. Despite continuous rain a considerable proportion of Stanley residents turned up to witness events and listen to the brass band, some of whom had to drain their instruments of water before playing.

At the end of the war thousands of battleworn British troops streamed in from the mountains to be welcomed and billeted, in twos and threes, all around a tired little town partly bereft of water and power. The capital's population quadrupled overnight. The accommodation problem was eased by using the ships *Scottish Eagle, Tor Caledonia* and most notably, *Rangatiri,* a 9387 ton ferry, locally dubbed 'Rangatraz', which for 14½ months anchored off Stanley's East Jetty and crammed in 800 men a day. On evenings prior to the arrival of the fortnightly ferry from Ascension, her inmates' spirited football chants of "Going home, going home, going home," echoed around the port and during a northerly blow an indelicate odour from the ship's stern bathed the city's streets. We genuinely missed her when she had gone.

Until the opening of the airfield at Mount Pleasant in April 1985 the main body of servicemen remained near Stanley. Most of the infantrymen, engineers, navy and airforce personnel spent their three months housed either in one of the three specially-imported 'coastels' a mile to the east, or at the Ghurka-built 'portakabinopolis' across the harbour, called Navy Point.

Seldom can civil/military relations have been better anywhere than in Stanley during this claustrophobic yet exhilarating period of rehabilitation.

The airfield was temporarily extended with aluminium plates and shared by FIGAS Islanders, Hercules transports, Phantoms and Harriers. The world's first floating port and storage system, FIPASS, was installed and remains today as the capital's premier wharf. Vast quantities of rock were quarried and crushed to form roads, jetties and hardstandings. Medical, sports and fuel facilities were shared. Shops, pubs and restaurants flourished and a lively Folk Club sprang up.

The local rock group, 'The Fighting Pig Band' received frequent requests for evening entertainment although one night they 'died' at an officers' candlelit dinner when 'Jailhouse Rock' curdled the prawn cocktail. But everybody danced at the Sergeants' Mess where they somehow always had the prettiest girls and barrelled bitter. While playing at the Junior Ranks' Club, known as 'The Shed', the Pigs nearly brought the house down. By midnight, rival London soccer supporters had begun debagging and facing up across the dance floor. During Gerard Robson's frenetic rendering of *Johnny B Goode,* the first volley of opened beer cans shot across the band's bows and they upped their drumsticks, grabbed their instruments and scarpered into the night.

The five little piggies don't rock or roll quite so much any more. In recent years two members have been elected as councillors and represented the Islands at the United Nations and the Commonwealth Parliamentry Association, two more hold key posts in local government and the other is now a detective in the Royal Falkland Islands Police Force.

Dawn in Stanley Harbour, March 1983. Bomb damaged *Sir Tristram,* Falklands' supply vessel *mv AES, RRS Bransfield* and the ocean-going tug *Yorkshireman* lie side-by-side tied up to the East Jetty. Beyond and in centre harbour the *Rangatiri* swings on her mooring.

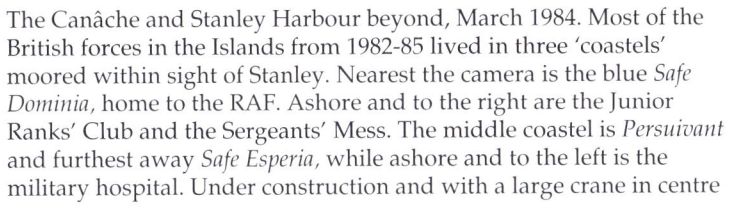

The Canâche and Stanley Harbour beyond, March 1984. Most of the British forces in the Islands from 1982-85 lived in three 'coastels' moored within sight of Stanley. Nearest the camera is the blue *Safe Dominia*, home to the RAF. Ashore and to the right are the Junior Ranks' Club and the Sergeants' Mess. The middle coastel is *Persuivant* and furthest away *Safe Esperia*, while ashore and to the left is the military hospital. Under construction and with a large crane in centre picture is FIPASS. Top right is Navy Point. Following the departure of the military to Mount Pleasant in 1985 the 'coastels' returned northward and all three took up service in the United States. *Persuivant* became a construction barge and *Safe Dominia* a holding centre for immigrants. *Safe Esperia*, where so many of our children learned to swim, and which hosted a night heron rookery on the roof, is now a floating penitentiary in New York.

Gerard 'Fred' Robson – lead guitarist of the 'Fighting Pig Band'.

An RAF Chinook flying over the Canâche in July 1982, showing the *Rangatiri* and other ships beyond in Stanley Harbour.

The Premier and the 'Commodore'

Islanders wave as the Prime Minister, on her arrival (8th January 1983), is driven along Fitzroy Road, Stanley by the Governor's chauffeur, Don Bonner, in the famous London taxi. Her hectic, three days in the Islands included numerous receptions, dinners, speeches and interviews. She visited a memorial, a battlefield, a warship, half a dozen camp settlements and, at 6.0am before she departed, went 'jollying' to a penguin rookery.

'Commodore' Frank Rowlands at the wheel of the *Fortuna* circa 1906.
(Photo courtesy Roddy Napier)

Out of the blue Margaret Thatcher visited the Islands in January 1983, the first and only British Premier to do so.

It was Saturday and I was cutting peat on the common, radio perched on a grass bog. A brass band marched around my head, continuing to play out BBC *Sports Report* two hours after the programme had finished. I remembered the theme from my childhood. Some things never change. Palace had lost again.

"Good afternoon", said the radio. "I have a very special announcement to make. The Prime Minister will be arriving at Stanley Airport in five minutes."

On the third kick, my geriatric Suzuki exploded into life with a backfire and roared along the two mile track into town as an incoming Hercules and two flanking fighters flew overhead. Stanley's twelve hundred normally undemonstrative residents appeared as if by magic from behind curtains, under lines of washing and out of cabbage patches, to line roads and crowd street corners with waving, cheers and even tears.

Two days later, 600 people packed the Town Hall as a jubilant Mrs T. was presented with a kiss and the Freedom of Stanley by an emotional Harold Rowlands. As Financial Secretary, he had led the Falklands Government during the occupation. Harold is fiercely patriotic, with remarkable 'legs' and stories to charm every dinner table. His grandfather, Frank, was a shipwrecked Swede.

At four bells of the first watch on 13th August 1860, Frank Rowlands, aged 25, was relieved after a spell on the wheel. He was able seaman on board *Colonsay*, a 598-ton barque bound for London with a cargo of Peruvian guano, supposedly on course to pass close by the Beauchênes. But Rowlands had been at sea since he was eleven and by the smoothening swells he sensed they were nearing land. Three times his warnings to the mate were ignored. Three quarters of an hour after midnight, making 9 knots, the ship struck hard on Speedwell Island. As she broke up, all eighteen on board crowded into the Captain's pinnace and made shore. They survived on beef, biscuits and the bodies of two sheep and a pig which washed up on the beach. Using some salvaged canvas they rigged a lugsail and sailed 25 miles to Bull Cove, meeting by chance the anchored schooner *Malvinas* by which they were rescued.

Frank Rowlands settled in the Falklands, at first sealing with the legendary Captain Smylie and later becoming the esteemed captain of several FIC schooners.

In his 70th year he was in command of the 165-ton *Fortuna*, described by many as the finest schooner that ever came to the Islands. En route from San Carlos to Fox Bay, on Saturday 19th May 1906, she grounded on a reef on West Island, bumping hard all night. At first light the passengers landed on the small tussac island, made a tent from oars and sailcloth, and lit a fire to confront the freezing easterly wind. They were picked up by another schooner, *Lafonia,* the following day. *Fortuna* was the only ship lost by 'Commodore' Rowlands in 36 years of command under sail around the Falkland coasts.

Ignoring continuous drizzle and accompanied by Admiral Sir John Fieldhouse, overall Commander of the British Forces during the conflict, Margaret Thatcher salutes the dead of previous wars, at Stanley's Cross of Sacrifice. Sunday 9th January 1983 (right).

"Our Margaret" Thatcher receives the Freedom of Stanley from Harold Rowlands on 10th January 1983. 600 people packed the Town Hall, the largest number ever assembled there, to listen to her passionate 20-minute speech, delivered without notes or preparation, for which she justly received a tumultuous ovation.

The Thatchers are led towards Government House, through a crowd of well-wishers, by Governor Rex Hunt while, unnoticed, Sir John Fieldhouse (top right of picture) quietly walks around the scene, accompanied by the then Commander of British Forces, General David Thorne.

In Memoriam

24th June 1982.
A simple iron cross stands on Darwin Hill. On a wintery afternoon Major Chris Keeble, of the 2nd Battalion, the Parachute Regiment, reads the lesson during the service of dedication, remembering those who had died in battle a month earlier, freeing the twin settlements of Goose Green and Darwin. Men representing all the units involved had flown out from Stanley by Chinook, Gazelle and Wessex helicopter, to join the resident islanders who had chosen the site and built the basement plinth of stone. After a minute's silence a Ghurka bugler sounded 'Reveille', followed by the 'Last Post'. Then, from a nearby fold in the hill, at the exact spot where Lt. Col. 'H' Jones and three comrades had fallen, another Ghurka piped a lament. His plaintive notes hung in the chill air, then slowly drifted away over the whitegrass.

The Falklands War ended eleven years ago.

252 British members of the Task Force and three Islanders died in the fighting; many more were wounded.

In addition to those who were lost or buried at sea, sixteen men, killed in action, remain here in the Falklands, in accordance with family wishes. Their resting places are caringly tended by Islanders and planted with daffodils, shrubs and young trees.

Each year, on the appropriate dates, people return to these gravesides and all the other memorials to hold services, or simply to stand quietly and remember.

The Argentine losses were enormous although the full extent of their casualties will probably never come to light. At the time of writing their leaders have still not sought repatriation for the 233 men buried, under the

The 1982 War Memorial in Stanley was officially unveiled on 14th June 1984, the second anniversary of the Argentine surrender, by the Civil Commissioner, Sir Rex Hunt, and the Military Commissioner, Major-General Keith Spacie. Beyond are the hills of Tumbledown, Two Sisters and Mount Kent.

Mount Pleasant Airport, the central base for British Forces serving in the Falklands, under construction in March 1985. A remarkable feat of engineering and hard work, the airport was officially opened by HRH Prince Andrew, Duke of York, on 12th May 1985, barely sixteen months after the work began on a virgin shore. For the first time long-range, wide-bodied jets were able to land in the Islands.

"As the first aircraft touches down let us all remember the British sacrifice that restored the Islands to freedom; the British endeavour that made the airport a reality; and let us hope that Falkland Islanders will now prosper in peace and security." Major-General Sir Peter de la Billière, CBE, DSO, MC, Commander of the British Forces, Falkland Islands, 1985.

The military cemetery at San Carlos, where fourteen British Servicemen of the Task Force were laid to rest. Beyond is Blue Beach Two. It was here, at 4.30am on 21st May 1982, that men of the 2nd Battalion, the Parachute Regiment became the first wave of troops to wade ashore during the British landings which led to their famous victory.

Watched by the entire population of Stanley and many other visiting dignitaries, Lady Thatcher lays a wreath at the 1982 War Memorial in Stanley on 14th June 1992. The date marked the tenth anniversary of the surrender of Argentine forces at the end of the Falklands War.

auspices of the Commonwealth War Graves Commission, in a neat, secluded cemetery near Darwin. Nor yet, have they declared a formal cessation of hostilities.

But, as seismic surveys progress and the possibility of vast and tappable reserves of oil and gas being discovered within our continental shelf appears ever more likely, the Argentine Government have begun once more to vigorously pursue their antiquated and frail claim to sovereignty over the Falklands.

2000 British servicemen and women are today serving in the Islands to prevent the unthinkable happening again.

10 NAMES, SOURCES and CREDITS

The following Fauna and Flora are mentioned in text. The local common names are in brackets.

BIRDS
King Penguin *Aptenodytes p. patagonia*
Gentoo Penguin *Pygoscelis papua*
Rockhopper Penguin *Eudyptes crestatus*
Magellanic Penguin *Spheniscus magellanicus*
(Mollymauk) Black-browed Albatross *Diomedea melanophris*
(Stinker) Northern Giant Petrel *Macronectes halli*
(Stinker) Southern Giant Petrel *Macronectes giganteus*
(Firebird) Slender-billed Prion *Pachyptila belcheri*
Fairy Prion *Pachyptila turtur*
(Cobbler) White-chinned Petrel *Procellaria aequinoctialis*
Sooty Shearwater *Puffinus griseus*
Wilson's Storm Petrel *Oceanites oceanicus*
Grey-backed Storm Petrel *Garrodia nereis*
Falkland Diving Petrel *Pelecanoides urinatrix berard*
Rock Shag *Phalacrocorax magellanicus*
King Cormorant *Phalacrocorax atriceps albiventer*
(Quark) Black-crowned Night Heron *Nycticorax n. cyanocephalus*
Upland Goose *Chloephaga picta leucoptera*
Kelp Goose *Chloephaga hybrida malvinarum*
(Grey Duck) Patagonian Crested Duck *Lophonetta s. specularoides*
(Logger Duck) Falkland Flightless Steamer Duck
 Tachyeres brachypterus
(Pampa Teal) Silver Teal *Anas versicolor fretensis*
Turkey Vulture *Carthartes aura falklandica*
Red-backed Buzzard *Buteo polyosoma*
(Johnny Rook) Striated Caracara *Phalcoboenus australis*
(Carancho) Crested Caracara *Polyborus p. plancus*
Cassin's Peregrine Falcon *Falco peregrinus cassini*
(Black and White Curloo) Magellanic Oystercatcher
 Haematopus leucopodus
(Black Curloo) Black Oystercatcher *Haematopus ater*
Two-banded Plover *Charadrius falklandicus*
Rufous-chested Dotterel *Charadrius modestus*
Magellan Snipe *Gallinago paraguaiae*
(Sea Hen) Antarctic Skua *Catharacta skua antarctica*
Grass Wren *Cistothorus platensis falklandicus*
(Rock Wren) Cobb's Wren *Troglodytes aedon cobbi*
Falkland Thrush *Turdus falcklandii falcklandii*
(Skylark) Falkland Pipit *Anthus correndera grayi*
(Robin) Long-tailed Meadow Lark *Sturnella loyca falklandica*
Black-chinned Siskin *Carduelis barbata*

MAMMALS
Fuegian Fox *Dusicyon culpaeus lycoides*
Patagonian Fox *Dusicyon griseus griseus*
Warrah (extinct) *Dusicyon australis*
Cottontail Rabbit *Sylviagus sp.*
House Mouse *Mus musculus*
Norway Rat *Rattus norvegicus*
Black Rat *Rattus rattus*
Blue Whale *Balaenoptera musculus*
Sei Whale *Balaenoptera borealis*
Minke Whale *Balaenoptera acutorostrata*
Fin Whale *Balaenoptera physalus*
Humpback Whale *Megaptera novae-angliae*
Sperm Whale *Physeter macrocephalus*
Killer Whale *Orcinus orca*
(Blackfish) Long-finned Pilot Whale *Globicephala melaena*
Peale's Porpoise *Lagenorhynchus australis*
(Puffin' Pig) Commerson's Dolphin *Celhorhynchus commersonii*
Fuegian Sea Otter *Lutra felina*
(Hair Seal) Southern Sea Lion *Otaria byronia*
South American Fur Seal *Arctocephalus australis australis*
(Sea Elephant) Southern Elephant Seal *Mirounga leonina*
(Sea Leopard) Leopard Seal *Hydrurga leptonyx*
Guanaco *Lama guanicoe*

FISH
Falkland Trout *Apolchiton zebra*
Mullet *Eleginops maclovinus*
(Loligo) Patagonian Squid *Loligo gahi*
(Illex) Argentinian Short-finned squid *Illex argentinus*

FLORA
Tussac Grass *Poa flabellata*
Native Strawberry *Rubus geoides*
Yellow Daisy *Senecio littoralis*
Native Boxwood *Hebe elliptica*
Fachine *Chiliotrichum diffusum*
Diddle Dee *Empetrum rubrum*
Scurvy Grass *Oxalis euneaphylla*
Native Pansy *Viola maculata*
Pale Maiden *Sisyrinchium filifolium*
Lady's Slipper *Calceolaria fothergillii*
White Grass *Cordateria pilosa*
Balsam Bog *Bolax gummifera*

The Lady's Slipper is one of the most striking of Falkland flowers. It grows only very locally in dry areas and blooms in mid-November.

SOME SOURCES

BERNHARDSON, W. *Land and life in the Falkland Islands* (1989)

BOYSON, V.F. *The Falkland Islands* (Oxford 1924)

BRIDGES, E.L. *Uttermost Part of the Earth* (Readers Union. Hodder & Stoughton 1951)

BURDEN, R.A., DRAPER, M.I., ROUGH, D.A. and SMITH, C.R. *Falklands – The Air War* (Arms and Armour Press 1986)

BUTCHER, M. *A Falkland Family at War*

CAWKELL, M.B.R., MALING, D.H. and CAWKELL, E.M. *The Falkland Islands* (Macmillan and Company Limited 1960)

COBB, A.F. *Birds of the Falkland Islands* (H.F. & G. Witherby 1933)

DAVIES, T.H. and McADAM, J.H. (Falkland Islands Trust) *Wild Flowers of the Falkland Islands* (Bluntisham Books 1989)

DODGE, B.S. *Marooned* (Wesleyan University Press 1979)

FANNING, E. *Voyages Round the World* (The Gregg Press 1970)

FORDHAM, A. *Maps of the Falkland Islands* (The Map Collectors' Circle 1964)

FOX, R. *Eyewitness Falklands* (Methuen 1982)

HARRISON, P. *Seabirds* (Croom Helm 1983)

HEADLAND, R. *The Island of South Georgia* (Cambridge University Press 1984)

HUNT, R. *My Falkland Days* (David & Charles 1992)

LEWIS SMITH, R.I. and PRINCE, P.A. *The Natural History of Beauchêne Island* (Biological Journal of the Linnean Society 1985)

MIDDLEBROOK, M. *Operation Corporate* (Viking 1985)

MIDDLEBROOK, M. *The Fight for the 'Malvinas'* (Viking 1989)

MILLER, S. *The Life of Our Choice*

PERNETTY, D. *Histoire d'un Voyage aux Isles Malouines fait en 1763 et 1764* (1770)

RIESENBERG, F. *Cape Horn* (Robert Hale)

SMITH, J. *74 Days* (Century Publishing Co Ltd 1984)

SMITH, J. (Falkland Islands Trust) *Those Were The Days* (Bluntisham Books 1989)

The Falkland Islands Journal 1967-1993

The Falkland Islands Magazine 1889-1933

The Falkland Islands Monthly Review

The Falkland Islands Times 1978-1982

The Penguin News 1979-1993

Falkland Island Government Archives

TREHEARN, M. *Falkland Heritage* (Arthur H. Stockwell Ltd 1978)

WOODS, R. *The Birds of the Falkland Islands* (Anthony Nelson, 1975, 1982, 1988)

North and Saddle Islands.

CREDITS

Many people have become involved with the preparation of this book. Some have allowed me to rummage through scrapbooks, family albums and memories, others provided statistics and dates. Many have donated their time and skills in various ways. To all of the following I owe my gratitude:

Andy Alsop, Paul and Christine Ambrose, Millie Anderson, Dick Baker, Kitty Bertrand, Bernard Betts, George Betts, Betty Biggs, Madge Biggs, Don Bonner, Myriam Booth, Chris Bundes, Mike and Trudy Butcher, Jane Cameron, Derek Clarke, Marvin Clarke, Nobby Clarke, Ronnie Clarke, Stephen Clifton, Lucy Ellis, Bob and John Ferguson, Peter Gilding, Philip and Gillian Gillmor, Fred Gooch, Nut Goodwin, Bill Goss, Eric Goss, David Healey, Grace Hiscocks, Sir Rex Hunt, Klaus-Peter Kiedel, Joe King, Robert King, Les Lee, Robin Lee, John Leonard, Willie and Heather May, Elaine McCallum, Roy McGill, Mandy McRae, Martin Middlebrooke, Betty Miller, Alana Morris, Roddy and Lilly Napier, Gordon Peck, Pat Peck, Hilda Perry, Jerôme Poncet, Geoff Porter, Billy and Evelyn Poole, Bill Roberts, Janet Robertson, Peter and Ann Robertson, Nigel Shorrock, Teen and Joe Short, John Smith, Maud Sollis, Vic Spencer, Joan and Terry Spruce, Vernon Steen, Wendy Teggart, Dr Kate Thompson, Eileen Vidal, Leona Vidal, Maud Watson, Patrick Watts, Clive and Rosemary Wilkinson, Gen Williams, Kristin Wohlers and, for their special co-operation, The Penna Press, Mac Graphics, Photolit Repro Ltd, Photolit Scanning Ltd and White Crescent Press Ltd.

Photograph of handshearer on page 92 reproduced by courtesy of the Falkland Islands Company Ltd.

Aerial photography made possible by the co-operation of both the Falkland Islands Government Air Service and the Royal Navy.

The late Des Peck's 'pomes' reproduced by kind permission of his son Burned.

I am also grateful to Hector Anderson, Basil Biggs, Sydney Miller and Jack Sollis, all sadly no longer with us.

Finally, and most of all, I thank my wife, Annie, and our two sons, Tom and Bill, for their wonderful support. Each has helped enormously in their own individual way to bring this book to fruition.

10 THE FUTURE

"The future begins here with our own school and our own people."
John Cheek,
17th August 1992.

At the time I began researching for this book, the Falkland Islands Community School was nothing more than a rather large hole in the ground. Now, as I reach the last page, the building has already been completed and in use for a year and is proving to be a great success.

During the same period, extensive investigations have taken place into the nature of the surrounding continental shelf with a view to the possible future exploitation of oil.

If hydrocarbons are discovered nearby in sufficient quantities to make commercial drilling worthwhile, and the indications to date are positive, the effect on the Islands, their people and wildlife will doubtless be considerable.

This tiny community is now 160 years old and the students pictured here represent the entire age group of between twelve and seventeen years. These are the people who will lead the Islands into the next century. It will be their responsibility to handle the problems of pollution, inflation, immigration and the ever-changing kaleidoscope of international relations. It will be up to them to continue and develop the industries, traditions and way of life that make up the Falklands.

Pupils and staff assemble outside the £13.7 million Falkland Islands Community School in Stanley for the first day of the Spring term on 17th September 1992. The building was officially opened a month earlier, in the absence of Lord Shackleton, by his daughter, The Hon. Mrs Zaz Bergel. In addition to providing secondary education for all the Islanders' children, this superb new complex provides the public with a swimming pool, a library and extensive sporting, educational and leisure facilities. It was funded entirely by the Falkland Islands Government using monies accrued from the offshore fisheries licensing scheme.

The new school symbolises this community's commitment to and belief in a secure future, a future made possible by the efforts and sacrifices of so many British people on our behalf in 1982.